WHEN I WAS

also by Desmond Hawkins

Hardy's Wessex
Hardy, Novelist and Poet
Cranborne Chase
Avalon and Sedgemoor

WHEN I WAS

a memoir of the years between the wars

Desmond Hawkins

MACMILLAN
LONDON

First published 1989 by
MACMILLAN LONDON LIMITED
4 Little Essex Street London WC2R 3LF
and Basingstoke

Associated companies in Auckland, Delhi, Dublin, Gaborone,
Hamburg, Harare, Hong Kong, Johannesburg, Kuala Lumpur,
Lagos, Manzini, Melbourne, Mexico City, Nairobi, New York,
Singapore and Tokyo

British Library Cataloguing in Publication Data
Hawkins, Desmond
When I was: a memoir of the years between the wars.
1. London, 1918–1940 – Biographies
I. Title
942.1083'092'4

ISBN 0-333-48968-3

Typeset by Wyvern Typesetting Ltd, Bristol
Printed in China

To the living presence of Bruce Hunter
and the green memory of David Higham

Contents

Contents

Acknowledgments

I am grateful to the following for permission to publish material in their care: the trustees for the copyrights of Dylan Thomas; Mrs Valerie Eliot and Faber & Faber Ltd, © Set copyrights 1989 (for T.S. Eliot); Laurence Pollinger Ltd and the estate of Frieda Lawrence-Rabagli (for Frieda Lawrence); the Ezra Pound Literary Property Trust and Faber & Faber Ltd, © Ezra Pound Literary Property Trust 1989 (for Ezra Pound); the estate of the late Sonia Brownwell Orwell and Secker & Warburg Ltd (for George Orwell); and to those of my friends and contemporaries who have allowed me to quote their letters, etc. – George Barker, the late Sir John Betjeman, Sir V.S. Pritchett, Sir Stephen Spender, Julian Symons and Geoffrey Trease (for an excerpt from his autobiography *A Whiff of Burnt Boats*).

I acknowledge with gratitude the assistance of my cousin, Kenneth Hawkins, and James Marsh of Alexander Hawkins & Sons Ltd; the local studies librarians in Guildford, Richmond and East Sheen; Mrs Mary Symons for biographical information about Travers Symons; Jeremy Goring for similar information about the publisher C.W. Daniel; the Humanities Research Center, University of Texas, for giving me photocopies of my letters to George Barker; and especially my sympathetic and encouraging editor, Brenda Thomson.

Foreword

WHEN my children were young they made their own division of Time into three parts. There was the present when we were all alive. There was the past when people like Jesus and Shakespeare were alive but none of us was. And then there was a rather troublesome and imprecise interlude between the two when I was alive but they weren't. Their explorations of this historical border-country usually led to the question: 'Was that when you were alive?'

The answer 'Yes' fits well enough the period between the wars. I was six years old in 1914; my first child was born in 1936. This book is the story of 'when I was alive', as my children would have understood the words.

To attempt an autobiography of any kind is to invite a charge of egotism. I am compelled perforce to interpret the period in terms of my own preoccupations and experience, though I am well aware that they will appear insignificant against the background of national events. The testimony I offer needs nevertheless to be personal to have any value at all. I write as a witness simply – one accurately described in a poem by a friend who will be mentioned frequently in the following pages:

> No! I am not Prince Hamlet, nor was meant to be;
> Am an attendant lord, one that will do
> To swell a progress, start a scene or two.

In brief, I was among those present: and it was a great company to be in.

Desmond Hawkins, 1988

In literature young men usually begin their careers by being judges, and as wisdom and old experience arrive they reach the dignity of standing as culprits at the bar before new young bloods who have in their turn sprung up in the judgment-seat.

Thomas Hardy (*The Life of Thomas Hardy*)

Chapter One

'The Armistice' we called it. At first it was a sudden jubilation; and then it became a reverent annual silence, deepening with the years and punctiliously observed as we grew from children to young men of military age; until by stages it was ritualised, swallowed up in a second war and eventually moved to a Sunday because it was interfering with the serious purposes of life – disrupting traffic and halting machinery.

For us, in 1918, it was simply a moment of rejoicing, before it began to reverberate down our years; and by 'us' I mean the four schoolboys who on that November evening leaned out of a bedroom window at a boarding-school in Bognor, eager to catch every sight and sound of the cheering and clapping, the fireworks, the band playing and the procession. Our school stood on a road which ran inland from the sea-front, at right angles to the promenade, so we craned out of the open window and looked to the top of the road where the crowds were passing.

One of the maidservants came in and reminded us that we were supposed to be in bed and going to sleep – we knew what the headmaster would do if he caught us. Indeed we did know. He would take one of our slippers, tell us to bend over, and beat us. The headmaster was very handy with the slipper. Not tonight, though – not on 'the Armistice'. We felt quite safe. Children are quick to recognise, and exploit, those rare freakish moments when normal grown-up conventions are in abeyance. This was one such moment.

I had just passed my tenth birthday so I had only the vaguest idea of what 'peace' was like. Soldiers and guns were what I was used to. I had one treasured memory of a soldier in pre-war uniform, a mounted drummer I had seen in Richmond Park, with a large drum on either side of his horse, and himself resplendent in a gold-coloured uniform with a sort of peaked jockey's cap. He was exceptional, however; the soldiers I knew all wore khaki, like Corporal Fennel and Sergeant Lewis, who were billeted on us at home, at East Sheen on the Surrey outskirts of London.

I name them because they stayed longer with us than the others, and I made friends with them. Some stayed only a short time and then a fresh troop marched up the Avenue and halted outside our house. The officer came to the front-door and spoke to my mother: 'I see you are listed here for two men.' He gave her the men's ration-books, summoned them in with their kitbags, and moved his dwindling troop on until the last man was settled. When the time came for them to leave us for the Front we all went down to Mortlake railway station to see the troop-train depart, with much weeping and kissing and waving.

By 1918 some of the soldiers were scarcely older than my brother Stanley. He was my senior by seven years, and already the names of some of his older schoolfriends were beginning to appear in the lists of casualties. There had been anxiety at home that his call-up was coming perilously closer. I know what my mother's first thought must have been at the Armistice.

Life after the Armistice soon became disappointingly similar to what it had been before, from a schoolboy's point of view. Thursdays still brought the ordeal of boiled mutton and caper sauce, all of which had somehow to be swallowed or otherwise disposed of, on pain of punishment. The only escape was to drop the unchewable gristly lumps surreptitiously into an envelope, to be pocketed until an opportunity came to fling the packet into the sea. This would be when our daily walk, two by two in a school crocodile, took us along the promenade.

I was properly grateful that my brother would not now have to go and be killed, but peace had its disadvantages also. In the holidays I missed the companionship of the soldiers. My father worked long days during the week, so my home-life was dominated by women – my mother, her sister Jessie and our maid-of-all-work. Corporal Fennel, Sergeant Lewis and their fellow soldiers had brought a rough sort of maleness into the home. The khaki they wore was rough to the touch, their breath had unfamiliar but acceptable aromas compounded of beer and tobacco, their regimental buttons and badges were somehow glamorous and occasionally given to me as keep-sakes. They came from other parts of the country and different walks of life. It was Fennel who took me to see my first professional football match, perched on his shoulders as he stood on the terrace at Craven Cottage. I suppose I was company of a sort for this lonely kindly man. We cheered for Fulham then, and to this day my eye wanders automatically down the league tables in the sports pages to see how Fulham are doing.

Lost also were those disturbingly dramatic occasions when I was lifted out of bed in the depths of night-time and carried downstairs. The first time was wholly inexplicable. By rights grown-ups as well as children should have been in their beds, but here seated in the dining room were the rest of the family behaving as if a midnight tea-party were a normal event. I was to learn that nothing could be less normal. In all previous wars danger had threatened by land or sea, but the sky had always been neutral. That neutrality ended during my childhood.

It was the German Zeppelins which prompted these gatherings downstairs in the small hours. Their bombing raids on the London area in 1916 involved the civilian population in a way that would have been inconceivable to my grandparents and certainly came as an unpleasant surprise to my parents. To a seven-year-old almost everything is new and unpredictable, and therefore not especially surprising. Air-raids, like anything which became repetitious, quicky developed a routine. Our next-door neighbours came in to join us as soon as the alarm was given, which meant that I had a boy of my own age to play games with. The parents chatted and drank tea. Errol and I set out our toy soldiers on the floor.

And then there came the night when we were suddenly picked up and carried out through the front-door, along the path and through the gate into the road. Other neighbours were standing in groups and pointing. 'Look!' they said. 'Look!' There was a flickering light in the sky: not a star but a flickering burning wavering light. It was moving very slowly downwards, but still at a great height and far off. Nothing like it had ever been seen. It was what became known as the Cuffley Zeppelin – 'Cuffley' because that was the name of the place where the burning debris came to earth. The Potters Bar Zeppelin met a similar fate a month later.

These attacking airships were part of a larger innovation. Our Victorian ancestors had seen sail give way to steam in warfare. We were the first witnesses of the horse's replacement by the internal-combustion engine. The working horse still had a recognised place

3

in the early years of my childhood. There were hackney carriages waiting for hire at the railway station: wartime shortage of petrol, no doubt, added to their usefulness. There were horse-drawn omnibuses in my earliest memories. The petrol-driven *char-à-banc* did not translate itself into our familiar vocabulary as 'the sharra' until after the war. Before that it had been quite normal for my mother to hire a horse-and-carriage and take me for an afternoon drive through Richmond Park to Coombe Warren. As I write these words I can recall the distinctive smell of leather and horse-sweat, the rhythmical thud of the animal's hooves and the steady rumble of the wheels.

That rumbling of steel-rimmed wheels on carriage, wagon and dray was a loud and unwelcome sound in houses where an invalid lay. When one of our neighbours was ill a deep litter of straw was laid in the road to deaden the sound of passing vehicles, which seemed to tiptoe past as they came to the broad golden bed of straw. This was not an unusual sight. Bedroom curtains drawn close in daytime and a great heap of straw in the road were the signal of somebody seriously ill and probably dying.

Our road – East Sheen Avenue was its name – had its regular visitors who linger still in the remembered scenes of childhood. There was the muffin-man, a tall striding figure carrying a tray of muffins on his head and swinging a large hand-bell. He strode along so briskly that I doubted if he could stop, but I suppose he intended to reach his recognised customers while his muffins were still warm. There was another man who sold cockles and winkles. My mother had a secret fondness for winkles, which were scorned socially as a low-class taste; she bought some occasionally and taught me to extract them from their shells with a pin. A knife-grinder and a barrel-organ added their colour and sound to the Avenue but the two principal figures, who haunt me still, were of a different kind. One was a grim-faced woman, her features partly concealed by a black shawl, who sold lavender. She moved very slowly and she intoned her traditional cry very slowly. As she came into view she seemed to drift forward with a deliberate tidal surge. And the long-drawn cadences came imperceptibly closer: 'O lavender – my pretty lavender – oh won't you buy my lavender.' The syllables of lav-en-der were drawn out each time in a harsh melancholy cry. Perhaps, on reflection 'melancholy' is not the right word. It should be more deeply tragic than that. She appeared to bear witness to some ancient sorrow.

The other figure was a seafarer of some kind. His trade proclaimed

4

itself in his dark-blue suit, blue sweater and nautical cap. He carried nothing and offered no service. All that could be described as his stock-in-trade was a weird sort of tuneless singing, unrecognisable as a melody. For all practical purposes he was a beggar but this low-pitched chanting noise possibly raised his dignity a touch above that description. What distinguished him – and fascinated me – was his lack of a nose. Where his nose ought to have been there was a neat piece of sticking plaster. His eyes were watery. His voice was confused and indistinct, caught in some turmoil where the roof of his mouth met the gap that had been his nose. His words slurred and whistled, and he was altogether so unprepossessing that any child might have been frightened by him.

Yet that was not the case at all. We even formed a friendship of a kind. I looked forward to his visits. When he appeared I had my penny ready to give him and I went out to meet him. He stooped down to make a relationship with me, smiled, touched my hand, made friendly little gestures and kept muttering something like 'Bless you, bless you,' until at last he stood up, turned away and resumed his tuneless chanting.

These were all figures of the daytime. There was one who belonged to the night. Standing sometimes at my bedroom window I would see the lamp-lighter cycling towards the street-lamp on the opposite corner. He carried a long pole in a rather ceremonial way, or as a marching soldier carried a rifle, sloped against his shoulder. At the lamp he stopped, lifted his pole to turn the key in the base of the lantern and ignited the gas. That done, he cycled away round the corner to the next lamp. An orderly and satisfying life his seemed to be, creating these sudden balls of white light in the darkness and cycling onwards.

The bicycle was a powerful social influence in the transitional period between the horse and the motor-car. Horses drew the carriages of the well-to-do, the plough of the farmer, the carts and wagons of the trader – but it was 'Shanks's pony' for everyone else until, as General Pitt-Rivers pointed out in 1891, 'the enormous distances bicyclists can go by road, especially on a Sunday, has rendered the population of country districts locomotive to an extent that has never been known before.'

It is in that cycling boom of the later Victorian years that I see my father most clearly as a young man. He was a passionate cyclist. He won races galore: his silver cups and trophies formed a special shrine in our home. Six days a week he was at work but on Sundays and the weekly early-closing day, and on summer evenings as well, he was away on his bicycle, racing or touring through Surrey and Sussex and Hampshire with the cycling club. My mother's brothers were members of the same club and introduced my father to their young sister. Marriage had a suitable sort of inevitability.

Having mentioned my father's work I must be more specific about it. The starting-point is 1844, in which year my great-grandfather Alexander Hawkins started an ironmongery business in the London borough of Southwark, in that short and quite unremarkable stretch of road which links St George's Circus with the Elephant and Castle and is named London Road – a rather pretentious name in the circumstances. About this founder of my dynasty I learned very little: a West Country origin probably, a rumour of his elopement with a 'county' lady, a liking for driving his own horses to a country retreat, and this newly founded business in London Road, London.

Of the proprietor in the next generation, Alexander the Second, I know more. There was his large framed photograph, to start with – a bearded patriarchal figure whom I was never to see in the flesh, since he died before I was born. His was a forthright character, plainly defined – a staunch nonconformist, a Gladstonian Liberal, a teetotaller and public-spirited freeman of the City of London. Each year he made up his trading accounts, calculated his personal income and allotted ten per cent to charitable purposes. If ever a man epitomised the solid, obstinate, right-minded Victorian middle class it was grandfather Hawkins: on such men a queen could build an empire, with hardly a qualm.

He had three sons, Alec, Herbert (my father) and Frank. The eldest, Alec, was a rather cantankerous man, made more cantankerous by increasing deafness. He soon discovered that he could not get on with my grandfather so he left the family business and started a garage at Petersfield, where he gradually discovered that he could not get on with anybody. He was a pioneer motorist, a gifted and perfectionist mechanic and a commercial failure. Success must always have eluded any man who was so thorough, so conscientious and so slow. When he came to visit us he spent every possible moment in the inspection-pit under my father's car, emerging with ill-concealed reluctance when my mother called him in to a meal. He never married and had no close friends.

With the worldly eclipse of Alec the leadership of the three sons passed to my father, who was made nearly enough in the same mould as my grandfather, though without the earlier generation's unyielding convictions and intolerant spirit. In the genially melting agnosticism of the twentieth century he began to soften, and even to

7

blur, the hard demarcation lines of Victorian right-and-wrong. As a lover of outdoor games he came to feel that God and golf were not incompatible on the Sabbath. Certain entrenched customs were preserved, however. After our Christmas dinner we always made a collection for the Royal National Lifeboat Institution, and for many years a great Christmas hamper went to the blind man who tuned our piano: as children we had to understand that our blessings carried obligations.

In the business world my father was popular and respected as a dependable and good-natured man of a rather old-fashioned sort, to whom a friend in need could turn for unobtrusive help. In my world he was a sometimes remote and frowning parent, with unexpected, wonderful moments of a shy warmth and fondness.

The youngest of the three brothers, Frank, was an electrical engineer and developed that side of the business when he and my father entered into partnership after the death of Alexander the Second. Uncle Frank was a jolly laughing man whose hobby was woodwork and who played the violin in music-making sessions with two or three neighbours – usually in the classical repertoire of piano trios. He and my father had an unusually close brotherly intimacy and, with a striking physical resemblance, they were frequently thought to be twins. They shared the ownership of a car and they built houses on adjoining plots of land when we moved from East Sheen to Guildford. As Frank had three sons, and my father had two, the succession in the business partnership looked safe enough.

My mother's background was different – less urban and not so clear-cut. Her childhood memories were of uncles and aunts and cousins in rural Berkshire. Her father was an Oxford graduate, but surprisingly so and not from any family tradition. A mysterious benefactor had arranged it. Armed with these academic credentials my grandfather Shepherd set up a school with which to support his increasing obligation to a family of seven children – four boys and three girls. As they grew up the children helped in the school-work and the youngest girl, my Aunt Jessie, subsequently started a kindergarten of her own which she ran creditably until she was persuaded to retire on her eightieth birthday. On the whole, though, the general picture is one of financial anxieties and a dismal lack of success.

My Shepherd grandparents both died before their family had completely grown up. Their eldest daughter, Alice, was settled in marriage but Mary (my mother) and the youngest, Jessie, were cared for by the unmarried brothers – charming but rather ineffectual men who struggled through life's difficulties with a cheerful optimism that was never justified. My mother's inheritance included a deep sense of insecurity, to which my ebullient father was an excellent antidote. She leaned heavily on him for his stability, but at the same time she had a hard-headed shrewdness which gradually took some of the marital initiatives from his easygoing nature.

Being a wife was more agreeable and more important to her than being a mother. This was compensated in our particular circumstances by the permanent presence in our family circle of my mother's sister Jessie. I was in some measure adopted by Jessie, as my surrogate mother. She had a wonderful knack for companionship on level terms with young children, which made her so successful in her kindergarten. Inevitably I became the favourite pupil, until my father decided it was time for me to go to boarding-school. Somewhere on the Sussex coast was ideal for visits at half-term, so to Bognor I was sent.

And there I was, leaning out of the bedroom window on that November evening in 1918, when the fireworks lit the sky and the band played and we knew the war was over.

9

Chapter Two

BOGNOR was not yet Regis during my schooldays. That had to wait for King George's convalescence in the town after his serious illness in 1929. In 1918 it was a moderately prosperous seaside town, with a pier, a promenade, a row of beach-huts, a shopping arcade and several hotels of which one – the Norfolk – was a rather fashionable and prestigious place. It faced the sea with an impressive lawn extending from its frontage to the promenade. Tea at the Norfolk was a social event. I used to wish that my parents would stay there when they came to visit me at half-term but they always mistrusted anything they considered 'too grand' for them, though they might admire it. Their choice was always the decent second-best.

We met at such times in all the falsity of a contrived situation, quite different from our normal family-life at home. An absence of six weeks can beget a mini-estrangement. The vacuum quickly fills with other interests which are not shared. By half-term I was fully absorbed in school-life – the dangerous, cruel, intense, secret life that I shared with other boys, but with nobody else. When my parents asked the usual anxiously considerate questions I gave the normal reassuring but untruthful answers. To some degree they had become bystanders, removed from the heat of the action in which I was involved. The half-term visit was a delightful but irrelevant inter-lude. I was treated to tea-time delicacies and a new book from the arcade – a Rider Haggard or a Percy F. Westerman, my two favourite authors. We went on the pier and I enjoyed once again my favourite slot-machine drama – the burning house, with the gesticulating woman at the reddening window, and the gallant firemen riding in to the rescue. Great stuff for a penny!

And then it was back to school for the rest of the term, back to real life and the mental and emotional struggle for survival. Even now, after so many years, I find it difficult to look back with detachment at the Bognor School: its memories, both good and evil, are still compelling. When I last saw the building it had been converted to flats but the school crest and motto survived incongruously over the main doorway.

In my time there the school had as its speciality the preparation of candidates for the naval colleges at Osborne and Dartmouth. Its strict, competitive, forcing atmosphere was aimed at academic excellence. Its methods would have appealed to Samuel Johnson, who, according to Boswell, 'upon all occasions expressed his approbation of enforcing instruction by means of the rod.' At our lessons we were cuffed, pinched and beaten into proficiency. One of the two partner-headmasters, Mr Healey, would make you stand beside his chair while you construed Latin verse, so that he could take a firm grip of your bottom with his finger and thumb and give you a sharp twist of pain at each mistake.

It was, however, his partner, Mr Black, who was the more fearsome of the two. Mr Black was a big heavy man with a flat sallow face and spectacles. He moved slowly, held his head to one side and looked at you in a sideways fashion. Where Mr Healey was often genial in an eccentric way, Mr Black was chilling and seemingly suspicious of evil-doing on all sides and at all times. Mr Black haunted my sleep for many years, intermittently. I can still in my imagination hear the slow heavy padding of his feet on the linoleum between the cubicles where we slept, the click of a latch and then the sudden repeated smacking and a boy's screams.

The terrors of childhood have no parallel in later years. Adults have the great advantage of comparative instances, rationalisations and acquired techniques; for a child, fear can be boundless and unique.

What makes such terrors endurable is the comradeship that binds the victims together. The pains of boarding-school life were offset by the pleasures that came from the company of friends and the occasions when tension suddenly relaxed. On summer Sunday afternoons we were free to stroll about the grounds, with their great cedars and a goldfish pond with a stone dolphin in the middle. There were balustrades and stone benches where we settled down to write the dutiful weekly letter home. At other times there were cricket matches with the neighbouring schools and village teams culminating in great teas of strawberries and cream, when even Mr Black seemed harmless enough.

Our standard dress was the short Eton jacket – the bum-freezer, as it was known – with a starched collar, a straw-hat for the summer and at other times a cap. It is to the summer that the mind returns most readily. The winters seem in retrospect to have been abominably cold. It was customary at that time to heat only downstairs rooms. Corridors, passages, halls and bedrooms were unheated. I was constantly plagued with chilblains for which the only palliative was a greasy stick of magenta-coloured ointment. We were bathed once a week in an infusion of carbolic by an old crone who set about us with a long-handled scrubbing brush, guaranteed to remove every trace of dirt and several layers of skin as well.

In the summer there was no shortage of ways to occupy any leisure hours that were permitted to us but in the winter some ingenuity was called for. At one stage I started a Sexton Blake library, renting out copies of the intrepid detective's adventures for a modest sum payable in winegums, our only suitable currency. This was frowned on by authority because Sexton Blake was considered to be educationally worthless, like the comics we furtively read. My eventual disenchantment came about through a volume called *The Chink in the Armour*. This suggested to me a tremendous encounter for my hero with a villainous Fu Manchu kind of 'chinky' Chinaman in the impregnable battle-dress of a mediaeval knight, but it proved to be nothing of the sort and I abandoned it in disillusionment.

Another project sprang from my newly adopted interest in astronomy. Recognising the need for a telescope I acquired a cardboard-tube, combined it with the glass from my pocket-torch and began casting around for a magnifying lens. The box Brownie camera belonging to Mr Black's little granddaughter Kate offered the only solution. With Kate's enthusiastic support I cut the lens out of her camera with my penknife and embodied it in our telescope. So engrossed was I that I quite failed at first to realise that the mangled remains of the camera would not please Mr Black. When I did so I knelt by my bed that night and prayed more fervently than ever before that the headmaster's wrath might somehow be turned away from me. Miraculously it was; though more, I fancy, by the intervention of Kate than of the Almighty.

My taste for scientific experiment had more severe and lasting consequences in an event during the holidays at home, when I attempted to construct a simple telephone system from two Oxo tins and a ball of string. The recommended technique was to secure each end of the string with a knot through a hole in the Oxo tin and to pull the string taut enough to vibrate. One tin would then gather the speaker's voice in a crude sort of microphone and transmit it along the string to the other tin, which acted as a receiver. That, at any rate, was the theory.

To get a clear run for the string out of doors it was necessary to rise above obstacles of various kinds. While my friend, Basil, held the other end I climbed on top of the tool-shed. Our first attempt at long-distance conversation was less successful than I had hoped, so I decided that the string needed to be pulled tighter and I stepped backwards. This was a well calculated move apart from one consideration: I had forgotten that I was standing on the edge of the roof.

I landed on a concrete path between the shed and a raised rockery. Luckily my head missed the rockery. The main impact was taken by my right elbow-joint which was broken and splintered. The movement of the joint was reconstituted as well as possible but with a permanent deformity: I could never straighten my arm. I suppose I was about ten years old at the time. For the rest of my schooldays I was morbidly self-conscious about my 'gonky' arm.

Basil was my constant companion in other and happier activities during the school holidays. We produced a newspaper which ran for at least two issues, we shared the higher command of an army into which half a dozen other boys were recruited at lower ranks, and we formed a detective agency which did not allow a lack of clients to discourage sleuthing: we would designate a 'suspect' – perhaps a woman doing her shopping – follow her until she reached her home and then put through her letter-plate a 'dossier' of our observations. We even invented a crime to investigate by cutting the edge of a wooden window-frame in my bedroom to simulate a break-in; a further touch of realism was the bloodstains which I added by deliberately cutting my finger. When the clues were in place we went downstairs, came up again and 'discovered' the unmistakable signs of a forced entry. At a more practical level we studied the notices outside the police station and copied down the details of 'wanted' criminals, but our vigilance went unrewarded: we never got on the trail of a single one of them.

On wet days we played billiards. My father had turned one of the downstairs rooms into a billiard-room. It was his pride and joy: every time the table was used the glistening green cloth was brushed with due piety and frequently warmed and pressed with a special smoothing iron. There was the constant anxiety that a careless jab with a cue might tear the cloth. As time passed, however, confidence was established sufficiently to permit me to play on it unsupervised in the daytime. Great marathons of a thousand-up were undertaken in which I was Melbourne Inman and Basil was either Tom Reece or Willie Smith. I did not really mind who Basil was, so long as I was Melbourne Inman.

Today Inman may be forgotten, but in 1920 his name was a household word and more particularly his nose enjoyed such celebrity that I can describe it only as a national treasure. Not a week passed without the *Daily Mail*'s famous cartoonist, Tom Webster, bringing Inman's nose into one of his cartoons. To mention even Schnozzle Durante as a more recent and comparable example is to do less than justice to Inman.

I saw the great man in action at Thurston's in Leicester Square. Thurston's were the leading manufacturers of billiard-tables and equipment and they promoted match-play by the professional champions. The serious contests were at billiards, not snooker. The relationship of snooker to billiards was rather like that of one-day or limited-over cricket to a Test match. At home my father and his friends played for fun a variation of snooker – 'Volunteer' snooker – but when he took me to Thurston's it was to see billiards. I recall the atmosphere as even more subdued and devout than I was used to during the Reverend Thomas's extempore prayers in our Congregationalist chapel. In the gloom surrounding the brightly lit green cloth shadowy figures tiptoed in and out, freezing to immobility when a stroke was to be played. Equally motionless my hero sat, arms folded, legs crossed, the great prow of his nose lifted and poised with dignity, while his opponent struggled on. A difficult cannon off three cushes failed to connect, the player withdrew to sit down, and Inman walked slowly and thoughtfully to the table, contemplated his 'leave' and decided his tactics – a screwed in–off perhaps, manoeuvring the red and the object-white into a fruitful proximity. If the balls ran well he might hold the table for the rest of the session.

Thanks to my father I had a liberal education in the public events and amusements that provided Londoners with their entertainment in the days before the 'wireless'. He was a man who positively and exuberantly enjoyed an outing – to the Lord Mayor's Show, the Varsity Boat Race, cricket at the Oval or Lords, lawn tennis at Roehampton or Wimbledon, smoking concerts at the Cannon Street Hotel, theatres, music-halls, boxing matches and anything else that caught his fancy. To offset the more grievous of life's disappointments I can, thanks to him, call on the imperishable memory of a double-century by Jack Hobbs, hit off the Yorkshire bowling – which adds a special relish – and including a six which narrowly missed the clock on the top of the main stand at the Oval. No less splendid was the visit to Jack Hobbs's shop in Fleet Street where my father bought me a bat, autographed by the master, to take back to school. Such moments are not to be treated lightly.

The music hall provided the staple of my father's monotonous humming and chanting in the bathroom each morning. I suppose his repertoire included the well-worn favourites of the time but the two songs I associate with him are unfamiliar ones. There was this fragmentary verse:

> Then the band played –
> And up to the moon he bunked:
> All through tickling a bull
> That poor young man's defunct.

Hardly a masterpiece but he never tired of it, usually adding a tremolo effect to accompany the rigorous use of a towel. The other one seems to me now to have the stamp of George Robey on it. It made fun of the new craze for scientific terms and the 'long words' that were coming into use through popular education. Words like 'epizootic' and 'pericardium' were distinct novelties to music-hall audiences: my father savoured them with a comic gusto worthy of Robey himself:

> Ooh – I've got the awful
> Eppy
> zootic
> On the perry
> Cardy
> um!

From my earliest childhood to the end of my schooldays it was the songs and the personalities of the music hall which excited my imagination. An unsympathetic observer would have classed mine as a philistine family, and with some justification. Apart from the obligatory volumes of Dickens our bookshelves carried detective stories for my father and light romances for my mother. The pictures on the walls were mostly photos of the Swiss Alps – honeymoon souvenirs. Of opera and ballet we were ignorant and I did not hear a string quartet or a symphony until the BBC came into being. Previously my outstanding musical experience had been Rossini's 'William Tell' overture played on the great organ at the Crystal Palace.

With all that said, I shall nevertheless claim that we found our true artistic experience in its vernacular form, in the music halls. The greatest of the performers were not just singers or comedians of high accomplishment. Each created a persona, a character, as rich in human reference and as potent in tragi-comic overtones as if they had been wrought by a novelist or a playwright. The point of Marie Lloyd or Little Tich did not lie in what they said or did on the stage so much as on what they were. To hear recordings of them or painstakingly accurate reconstructions of their acts by those who knew them is to realise how little the material mattered and how vital were the essential style of the artiste and the interplay with the audience.

This was in the truest sense a folk-art. Its characters were archetypal – the miner, the mill-girl, the barrow-boy, the genteel clerk, the con-man and the tart, the underprivileged and the handicapped – all of them caught up in that new harsh urban life which changed the face of Victorian Britain. It was from its roots in hardship and privation that music hall drew its wonderfully resilient qualities of satirical merriment and compassion. The two dominant styles were Cockney and North Country – the characteristic underdogs of what a Marxist would define as the industrial proletariat. From their tribulations and their pleasures they made a vernacular art so close to their audience that performance became a community action.

The 1890s and the Edwardian years must have been the golden age of the music hall. Some of the legendary stars of that epoch were past their prime when I saw them but I treasure my recollections nevertheless. There were the 'male' impersonators – Hetty King, Ella Shields and Vesta Tilley – mixing patriotic songs in army or navy uniform with sly send-ups of the 'Burlington Berties' in a class-conscious and male-dominated society. Marie Lloyd I remember for her spectacular tight-fitting dress and a tall ebony stick with a massive jewelled top that she used to emphasise her rhythm. I was perhaps too young and innocent for every nuance of her story-telling but I understood well enough the contrast between her affectation of a simpering coyness and then the sudden down-to-earth comment. When she sang she had the authentic Cockney whine of an earlier generation – that distinctive nasal twang of which Gus Elen, singing 'The Likes of 'Er', is the best example and seems to take us back at once to Sam Weller.

My own prime favourite was Little Tich. As an undersized little runt myself I could easily identify with him: I too had had to learn how to use my wits to compensate for lack of inches and poundage. Accordingly in each school holiday I looked to see where he might be performing. There were many possibilities. In the heart of London's theatreland were the Coliseum, Alhambra, Palladium and Holborn Empire, with an inner ring that included Collins's music hall, the Metropolitan in Edgware Road, the South London Palace, the Shepherd's Bush Empire and an outer ripple of Palaces and Empires to the furthest suburb – all presenting a variety bill in the music-hall manner.

My great hope was to see him wearing his famous long boots. Every drawing of Tich – notably in the weekly comic strip that I read regularly – showed him in boots which were almost as long as he was tall. They were his trade-mark, his personal symbol, but the tap dance he performed in them must have made heavy physical demands and in his later years he dispensed with them. In desperation I wrote a request to him and asked an usherette to take it round to his dressing room. She came back with a charming note of regret that was some consolation to me, but to my sorrow I never did see those boots. Instead I saw the dapper little figure with the Punch-like features and very red complexion moving about the stage with a quick birdlike elegance. His presence was electrifying – so deft and unpredictable in motion and gesture. It is in terms of movement particularly that I think of him: he brought into play the whole of his diminutive body. In a drag act as a débutante preparing to be presented at Court he achieved a remarkable blend of fastidious movement and sudden deliberate vulgarity which pointed up the most hilarious contrasts as his struggle to master a long sweeping train became increasingly desperate. I can quite understand why he had a sensational triumph in Paris and became the darling of the French intelligentsia. Although he used words, he did not need them. He was a master of silent comedy, and of something deeper than this suggests – an imp-like fusion of pathos and defiance.

The ending of the Great War brought my first real prospect of going abroad. To be precise I think the year must have been 1920, when my father was taken with the strange notion of visiting the battlefields of Flanders. Yet it was perhaps not so strange after years concentrated obsessively on Ypres, Cambrai, Arras, Menin and a host of obscure villages and hamlets in the Low Countries. We went first to Ostend and then up the Belgian coast to Blankenberg. How capricious are the impressions of boyhood! I retain a mixed bag of drinking grenadine, seeing a little milk-cart pulled by a large dog harnessed in its shafts, discovering a temple of wickedness bearing the word 'Casino', trying out my schoolboy French and finding in the shattered buildings of Ypres an unbroken WC pan with half its wooden seat in place.

The desolation of some of the battle areas was still untouched. At one place an elaborate system of trenches and dug-outs had apparently been mined by enemy sappers. There was a huge crater and the surface of the earth now partially covered a miscellaneous debris of steel stakes laced with barbed-wire, planks of wood, cartridge cases and spent cartridges, military impedimenta in a variety of forms. To restore it to normal farmland was evidently a task too difficult as yet to undertake. As boys will, I poked about in unfeeling curiosity, looking for some unusual souvenirs to take home. There was nothing suitable but I well remember one item that my fingers pulled out of the mud. It was a piece of cloth, its texture half-rotted and hard to distinguish but evidently some part of a uniform. As I pulled it the material tore. I threw it away.

Chapter Three

THE residential development of East Sheen started probably at the end of Victoria's reign. It was in effect an extension of Mortlake southwards, across the Upper Richmond Road to the boundaries of Palewell Common and Richmond Park. My first home – 103 East Sheen Avenue – was one of a row of Edwardian semi-detached houses with only a narrow passage separating each pair. It had not occurred to the builder that a garage would soon be thought a necessary feature. This did not matter to my parents at first. They had no motor-car. When they wanted to go to a dance or a theatre they made up a large enough party of friends and neighbours to hire an omnibus. I remember pressing against a window to see my mother, looking beautiful in her evening dress, stepping into the brightly lit omnibus with my father. When they drove away I had a sudden pang of sadness and anxiety. I was about five years old and I had not before seen them leave me at night and go off into the darkness.

I have only such fitful scraps of recollection of that first home. It was called Rosewood because of my father's love of roses, which he planted and cultivated with great devotion. Two mop-headed acacias dominated the front garden. The back garden was enclosed by wooden fences, with my friends Basil and Errol on either side: one or two knot-holes at a convenient height in the fence-palings were useful for rudimentary communication.

Our removal from Rosewood when I was about eight took us no

further than a hundred yards up the same Avenue but it represented a slight rise in social status. We now had the corner house, with a larger garden and a longer frontage that made it possible to have a separate garage. We were entering the era of the motor-car.

I had my first experience of motoring at a very early age when Uncle Alec drove up from his Petersfield garage in a three-wheeler that he steered with something like a tiller. The front consisted of a flat panel which was hinged to allow driver and passenger to get into their seats, with the engine behind them. During the war my Uncle Frank had an Overland, which he drove as a volunteer ambulance in the air-raids. He lived not far from us at Putney, and I fancy my father had a share in the Overland. In those early days it was a great challenge to drive to Guildford and climb the Hog's Back. The new breed of motorists, with their caps on backwards and their goggles, would boast of such feats. The steep lower half of Guildford High Street was also a severe test. Once when it defeated us my father turned the car round, put it into reverse and went up backwards, to the accompaniment of much cheering.

The siege conditions of wartime made for a scarcity of many things, including petrol. This in turn prompted an ingenuity in the use of alternative fuels. The steam-car became quite a familiar sight. It was handicapped by the time required to get the coal-furnace going and a sufficient head of steam to operate, but once that tedious business was accomplished the steam-car ran well. Another method made use of gas, and cars began to appear with great gasbags on their roofs.

Our second home in the Avenue is best identified here by its number – 108 – since my father was apt to transfer the name Rosewood to each successive residence. Its position was at a T-junction with Vicarage Road: as you came up the Avenue the roadway to the left ran a short distance to Palewell Common, while the right joined Sheen Lane as it approached the gate into Richmond Park. The Common and the Park were my holiday playgrounds where I went sliding on frozen ponds, birdsnesting or collecting conkers, according to the season.

Adjoining the park were several fine mansions set in their own grounds behind high walls. Admiral Hood, of Jutland fame, lived in one. Another belonged to the Duke of Fife. As a result of the demolition or alteration of one of these we enjoyed one or two touches of salvaged luxury which, in their redundancy, had been incorporated in No. 108. Our main room doors were unusually stout and nobly proportioned: their hinges had an elegance that my father, as an ironmonger, could appreciate with the discrimination of a connoisseur in such things.

What principally appealed to my parents, I believe, was that it was a good house for entertaining. They were sociable people who enjoyed the companionship of club-life with their fellow cyclists or tennis players or golfers. To have a home in which to entertain their friends gave them great pleasure, and No. 108 was excellent for the purpose. The billiard room and the drawing room were connected by a wide archway so that there was an open social interchange between the two when the mobile partition was folded back. While the men played snooker the women sat round the drawing-room fire and chatted; and occasional bursts of conversation passed between the two groups.

The aftermath of the war brought an increasing informality of manners but the old social code gave ground slowly in East Sheen. My parents were 'At Home' on Thursday evenings during the darker months of the year. The guests who could expect to be welcomed were those on whom my mother had at some previous time made a social call. This would have been a strictly formal occasion when she performed what I used to call her three card trick. Visiting in the afternoon and meeting the lady of the house my mother, on her departure, would leave three visiting-cards, one of her own and two of my father's: her own was for the husband whom she had not met, my father's were for both parties.

That was the protocol and it had its benefits. Newcomers could expect to be quietly observed, then 'called on' and gradually brought into the community, until they in turn began to sponsor the next arrivals. The At Home did away with the business of sending and receiving, accepting or declining invitations. If you liked the hosts you sometimes attended; if not, you stayed away. And when you yourself were not 'at home' you could confidently expect to be spared unexpected and possibly inconvenient callers.

At first I was too young to stay up for our At Home nights and I watched the arrivals from the top of the stairs. As year passed year I graduated by degrees until I was permitted to take a cue if an extra player was needed for a game of snooker. As I was so much younger than my brother I was in many ways equivalent to an only child and I enjoyed the company of adults. I liked to listen to their conversation: I was tolerated, or ignored, impartially by the women in the drawing room and the men round the billiard-table. Two such different worlds! The women, in their party mood, were subtle, vivacious, sharp-witted, sharing quick confidences and rather proud of their young motherhood, their pretty dresses and their accomplishments. The men, unlike their womenfolk, had been competitive during the day and were now content to relax in a pervasive bonhomie, with much chaffing and anecdotage and a mutually supportive confidence of manner. Their careers and vocations were modest enough in reality but you could not doubt for a moment that they were extremely successful and almost indispensable at whatever they did. I half believe that Mr Pooter joined us occasionally though I never identified him.

The women drank coffee, whether they would have chosen it or not. The men mostly had whisky: although my father was a teetotaller, he did not seek to impose his convictions on his guests. As an alternative to snooker and conversation there was music. These were the days when entertainment was still in the main a do-it-yourself activity. In any properly furnished home a piano was regarded as a normal item and everyone was expected to cultivate a talent – no matter how exiguous – for playing or singing or making some form of contribution to an evening's entertainment. Forgetting to bring one's music was considered a coward's way out of the general obligation.

In our circle there was a great diversity of styles. My father favoured a rumbustious Peter Dawson-type piece called 'The Sergeant Major', with a lavish sprinkling of 'Pick-'em up, Pick-'em up'. My brother concentrated on a sentimental ballad about a blind ploughman who, in an impassioned climax, assured us that God took away his sight so that his soul might see. This usually produced a somewhat gloomy hush. Uncle Frank, if he listened to my pleadings, would fiddle a *moto perpetuo* of which I never tired because its speed and dexterity dazzled me. Foremost among the ladies was Kathy W, a nobly built woman who played and sang with almost professional skill; but what I admired even more than her playing and singing was her ivory-white acreage of chest and bosom which rose and fell in such a spell-binding way.

Here I must not omit one of my mother's brothers, George Shepherd, who also lived in East Sheen and added greatly to our musical pleasures. So often the English tenor voice is dry and lacking in warmth of tone, but when Uncle George sang he might have been an Italian. His voice had an uncommonly liquid, lyrical quality with beautifully modulated head-notes. If I could call back one singing voice from the past it would be his, singing perhaps 'The Last Rose of Summer' or Handel's 'Where E'er You Walk'. His voice served him excellently also in quite a different capacity, as a raconteur. He was a master of the tall story. He could outrage all common sense and carry absolute conviction simultaneously. I never dared to disbelieve anything he told me because he always left that lingering suspicion that it might after all be the truth – against all the odds, but *possibly* so.

There was for instance the case of the camomile lawn. Uncle George had seen it in a large walled garden on some great estate – a greener, smoother, better lawn than your common everyday grass ones. The only problem with camomile was that lawn-mowers did not suit it. So how was this camomile lawn manicured so exquisitely?

Here Uncle George warmed to his narrative. It was late afternoon when he was shown the lawn. He was instructed to watch closely the door in the garden-wall. For a few minutes nothing happened, but then suddenly the door opened and – can you believe it? – a pack of hungry guinea-pigs raced on to the lawn and began feeding on the camomile. In due course a clapping of hands and a few shouts of command rounded up the guinea-pigs, which disappeared from sight through the doorway in the wall. They were fed for the night and the lawn was trimmed. It was all so simple, and logical too. Uncle George's countenance was inscrutable. To this day that stampeding horde of guinea-pigs troubles me.

Such simple pleasures as our homespun entertainments were soon to face a challenge destined to extinguish the drawing-room ballad and make a million upright pianos redundant. For centuries the choices for an evening's amusement had lain between an outing to a professional place of entertainment and an amateur effort at home. The two fitted well together, even reinforcing each other. The professionals set standards, the amateurs learned from their own endeavours to appreciate the finer points. Nothing could beat an outing to a theatre or a music hall, but there were two disincentives: the price of admission had to be found and the inclemencies of weather had to be braved. I don't think it occurred to any of us when the war ended that such obstacles could ever be overcome.

Yet the clues were there, as is so often the case, if one could have recognised them. Wireless telegraphy existed. With his electrical knowledge Uncle Frank demonstrated a little transmitter to us. It had a buzzer-key and short horizontal aerial-arms extending on either side. When he pressed the buzzer a bell rang in the next room. We then trooped into the next room to stand by the receiver and watch the bell. For no visible reason it began to ring in short and long bursts. Gravely Uncle Frank assured us that there were no hidden wires and that his transmitter could send out a kind of electrical waves that passed through a brick wall and started the bell ringing. We were mightily impressed of course, but who would want to spend an evening listening to the short–long monotony of the Morse code?

The one vocal signal of modern technology that had penetrated our homes was the telephone. To combine it with some form of entertainment became a dawning possibility when a London theatre manager realised that he might increase his audience by installing microphones connected to the telephone exchange. An experimental service of West End theatre relays was offered in the London area and I heard *The Maid of the Mountains* in this way in the home of some friendly neighbours who subscribed to the service. The method, as I recall it, was to book a line beforehand and use special earphones supplied by the Post Office for the purpose: a fixed proportion of the rental would have gone to the theatre management and a modest fraction may even have reached the cast.

This innovation by the Post Office was swiftly overtaken by greater events. The two marvels of the microphone and the electrical signals-without-wires came into conjunction, so far as we were concerned, in the broadcast voices of 'Two Emma Tock' at Writtle in Essex and, shortly afterwards, of London's 2LO. The year was 1922. I may earlier have heard experimental radio transmissions from Chelmsford, which operated for a time in 1920, or from the continental transmitters at The Hague and the Eiffel Tower, but it was not until 1922 that broadcasting began to make a lasting impression on me and my contemporaries. Perhaps nothing else separates us so distinctly from previous generations. If one had to name the two greatest inventions of the present century it would not be easy to disagree with that shrewd observer, Alfred Hitchcock, who chose broadcasting and domestic plumbing because they both make it possible to satisfy a basic human need without going out in the rain.

The boom in radio had some effect on Uncle Frank's side of the family business, which supplied the components from which receivers were made. I had a ready access therefore to the crystals, cat's whiskers, ebonite panels and other bits and pieces from which a simple crystal-set could be made by any schoolboy. Making my own was a pleasant hobby during the weeks at boarding-school. A fine wire had to be wound tightly on to a rigid tube to form a tuning-coil of the right wavelength; the various parts had to be mounted on the ebonite, with the delicately spiralled wire of the cat's whisker adjusted to make contact with the most sensitive spot on the crystal; and a slide along the tuning-coil tried to seek out an incoming signal.

By 1922 I had left the prepschool at Bognor and moved on to a public school at Cranleigh in Surrey. I was by now something of a veteran of boarding-school life and made the change easily enough. At Bognor there had been about seventy boys, at Cranleigh there were perhaps five times that number. The greater size was at first overwhelming but in practice we were divided into 'houses' and had little contact with boys from other houses except in the classroom or the games team to which we were allocated.

The word 'house' in this context had a mystical or tribal significance which fell short of reality. The main building, surrounding a quadrangle, contained the classrooms, dormitories and dining hall, which we all shared, but the individual 'houses' were large wooden huts, such as we were accustomed to see in army camps and which were now surplus to the military requirements of peacetime. Here we did our evening prep and spent our daytime leisure. The huts were furnished with long heavy tables and stout wooden benches to match. Each boy had a locker for his books and papers and personal effects. The names of the houses had no historical or legendary overtones, consisting only of points of the compass and numbers. I was assigned to One North.

There was not much history or legend of any kind at Cranleigh. The school's origins were recent, a late Victorian foundation – one of several which had sprung up in that period to satisfy the ambitions of a middle class ever increasing in numbers and affluence. Prominent among the parents were farmers, solicitors, administrators of the Empire, men who were 'something in the City' and even some who, like my father, bore the stigma of being 'in trade'. I was coming to an age to be conscious of such distinctions. 'Class' was not a subject which appeared in the curriculum at Cranleigh but it was certainly taught and learned there.

I was still physically undeveloped when I arrived to start my first term. To my dismay I was called upon to box for my house for no better reason than that nobody else could qualify for the lightest weight-category, under six stone. Fortunately my opponent was as timid as I was: we put on a lively display of menacing footwork without actually landing a blow that hurt.

Another unsought prominence of a modest kind was in the school choir. Each new boy had to present himself to the music master and undergo a test. As one's leisure was precious there was an understandable desire to fail. I thought I had done badly enough but I was reluctantly conscripted from what was evidently a poor field. The outcome was happier than I anticipated. I learned to read music fluently and I had my first taste of the classical composers in forms that I could comprehend and enjoy. I sang alto and was able to stay in the choir until I left the school as my voice did not break in the usual way but gradually deepened. After the nightmare memories of the Bognor prepschool I must be thankful to Cranleigh for 'Jesu, Joy of Man's Desiring' and 'O for the Wings of a Dove'.

I was less thankful for Cranleigh's speciality, which was rugger. Presumably the headmaster or the governors had decided that the only way to put the school on the map nationally was to make it outstanding in one particular feature of school-life. In an ill-omened hour they chose rugger and hired a coarse-mouthed, semi-literate Welshman to create an invincible team. This, it must be allowed, he proceeded to do. Suddenly Old Cranleighans began to be capped internationally, appear with the leading club sides and produce a formidable club side of their own. It was like being caught up in some wild crusade. We played cricket and hockey like reasonable beings but rugger meant a term of mass-hysteria. How I dreaded those wet and dreary afternoons on the rugger field, spent in trying to avoid notice and keep out of harm's way! The early experience of breaking my arm, with the Oxo telephone, made me extremely reluctant to fracture anything else.

By one of life's little ironies rugger was compulsory, but cricket – the king of all games – was not. It required nearly as much cunning to get into a game of cricket as to be excused from rugger, so we were often left to our own devices in May and June. We could watch the first or second eleven playing a school match, and this was pleasant enough on a sunny afternoon, lying on the grass in the shade of a tree with a friend for company. In a more active mood we went birdsnesting, thanks principally to one of my closest friends, Neville Reeves. He lived in Wales, on the Dovey estuary, where he had the opportunity to get to know wild birds in great variety and abundance. He could boast, for instance, of his buzzards when this species was considered extinct in southern England, apart from a few pairs that lingered on the high moors of the far west. Reeves also had a book, the like of which I had never seen – T.A. Coward's *The Birds of the British Isles*. This was the forerunner of the Witherby Handbook and the Peterson field-guide: for me it became the 'bible' of ornithology in those distant days.

The robbing of birds' nests is so outmoded and frowned upon today that it may be hard to realise that sixty years ago it was absolutely normal and acceptable for children to make collections of eggs in the same way that they collected postage stamps or match-box labels or cigarette cards. Indeed at various times I collected all those things. Life at a boarding-school seemed to foster the collect-ing urge, partly from rivalry and partly from a shared enthusiasm, but also perhaps for the pleasure of having a distinct personal treasure in what was otherwise a commonwealth.

Under Reeves's leadership four or five of us would set out to search first of all through the surrounding areas that were classified as 'within school bounds' and later we broke 'out of bounds' to explore further afield. If we were caught out of bounds we were caned but it was a reasonable risk and a spice of danger is not always unwelcome. I began to experience what became a life-long pleasure – the movement away from the orderly man-made world to the wilder untamed scenes of Nature; the sharpening alertness of one's senses; the absorbed concentration on each significant detail of sound or movement; the sudden flash of colour and the excited recognition of what had come into view. It is the same pleasure that the hunter has always known, and I take comfort from Thoreau's words, as nearly as I can recall them, 'We hunt in order that we may learn to love; and when we love, we no longer need to hunt.'

The countryside round Cranleigh in 1923 had scarcely begun its transformation into a fashionable dormitory for commuters: it preserved much of its traditional character. 'Wildness' is a relative term, and if Ewhurst and Abinger were hardly comparable with arctic tundra or Arabian desert they were at any rate more rural than East Sheen, and Pitch Hill had qualities that Richmond Park knew not. Mine had been an essentially suburban childhood, with the Sussex coast as my alternative landscape. The England of downland and forest, heath and coombe and moor, had been a closed book to me until at Cranleigh I did turn at least the first few pages.

The best day in the school year was Ascension Day when all school rules were suspended and it was the custom for each house to have a lunch arranged in the village to which it traditionally made this annual journey. You went as you pleased, started when you chose and had no obligation except to arrive in time for lunch at the village inn and return to the school for supper. With my newly found interest in birds this was a day's walking to cherish, going freely over the sandy heath, climbing hills among the pine trees, calling or beckoning to each other when we caught sight of something interesting – a kestrel's nest perhaps or, on one occasion, a red-backed shrike's.

Further encouragement came from a well-known naturalist of that time, Captain Knight, who visited the school with his celebrated eagle 'Mr Ramshaw' and showed some of his own film of birds. He was the first lecturer in my experience to advance beyond the magic lantern for his illustrations – a sign that the motion picture was becoming a part of our everyday life. To my parents it had been a sensational novelty but I had grown up with a vague awareness of the cinematograph from my earliest years – in the music halls the last item on the bill would sometimes be the 'bioscope' showing a brief film. I was taken at a tender age to the Albert Hall to see *The Four Horsemen of the Apocalypse* and a stunt-film of Harold Lloyd's in the days before he used his name and was known simply as 'Winkle'. I saw *The Birth of a Nation* at the Royalty Kinema in Richmond, with a pianist giving his all to enhance the terror aroused by the Ku Klux Klansmen. And then there were serials at our local 'flea-pit' – *The Perils of Pauline* with the intrepid Pearl White, and my special hero Eddie Polo in *The Broken Coin*. Each weekly instalment culminated in a crisis of suspense, with Pearl tied down on the railway-line or Eddie manacled in a dungeon with the water rising, until that frustrating moment when the words flashed on the screen the awful questions 'Can Pearl save herself?' and 'What will Eddie do?' and we knew that next week's pocket-money would have to go on finding out. There were even prizes to be won for the best forecast of what Eddie would do.

My interest in movies took a sudden emphasis when my father gave me a projector. I cannot think what possessed him to do it except that he considered it a great bargain. It had been salvaged from a fire in a cinema and part of the wooden casing was charred. As it used a carbon-arc lamp and flammable film there was every prospect that it would soon be on fire again. The only place we could set it up to operate in was the attic, which had no windows and a single door approached by a ricketty staircase. As a death-trap it would have defied the combined wits of Pearl White and Eddie Polo together. I reckon I was about fourteen at the time. Among guardian angels mine was one of the busiest and most successful.

I decorated the attic with surplus posters that the local cinema manager let me have, found a source of supply of short lengths of films and taught myself to make acetate joins in torn or damaged film. Gradually I accumulated bits of early cowboys like William S. Hart and Chaplin comedies until I could make up programmes of an inconsequential sort that lasted for several minutes. The attic cinema was my own private kingdom and I spent many hours up there, alone or with Basil as my helper, until enthusiasm began to wane in the way that schoolboy enthusiasms usually do.

Chapter Four

THE social transition from war to peace is an uneven, haphazard business varying greatly in duration and personal intensity. For me the departure from Bognor to the new chapter of school-life at Cranleigh was as near as I could come to the crossing of a frontier. If the food was still lamentable it was no longer so from wartime necessity. The school tuckshop had as much chocolate and sugar and jam for sale as one could afford to buy. After the great sprouting of war memorials the pervasive atmosphere of adult anxiety seemed to disperse.

In the holidays the fading of wartime evidences was slower. The wounded men in their blue uniforms were a part of the everyday scene in Richmond, where the Star and Garter had become a convalescent home. There were many civilians who liked to be known – and some who insisted on being known – as colonel or major or captain. And there was the arbitrary personal imagery of war that persisted. Inconsequentially a few memories continued to resonate after the event and even now preserve their macabre vitality as, for examples, the 'Old Bill' drawings of Bruce Bairnsfather and a jingle that we sang in our childish games:

> O the moon shines bright on Charlie Chaplin,
> His boots are crackin'
> For want of blackin'
> And his little baggy trousers want a mendin'
> Before we send 'im
> To the Dardanelles.

I can have had no idea of where or what were the Dardanelles. At a deeper level, though, I retained a momentary glimpse of horror when the father of one of my friends was invalided home with 'shell-shock'. His wife brought him in to our house when an air-raid started. The firing of the anti-aircraft guns in Richmond Park suddenly unnerved him and he crawled under the dining-room table, weeping and crying out. The studiously cultivated calm 'in front of the children' suddenly broke. We were all – adults and children alike – at a loss to know what to do. It had not occurred to me that fathers had so much in common with children – were not a race apart but could cry and scream as much as we did.

A more personal wartime memory that lingered like a terrible hallucination in the first peacetime years was of an occasion when I was alone, riding my bicycle. There was a general rumbling sound and I began to realise that there was nobody about in the street although it was mid-morning. Someone called out from a window 'Get home, sonny – quick.' I began to pedal faster and faster. The sudden stillness and emptiness, the disappearance of people and the absence of movement created an eerie atmosphere. The rumbling sound became menacing. Where was everybody? As I came up East Sheen Avenue I saw my parents at the gate waving frantically. We hurried indoors and stood in the hall by the inner wall which was supposed to be the safest if the house collapsed. What was in progress was the first daylight raid by German warplanes – a daring exploit in which they followed the line of the Thames up to Richmond. When our first sense of alarm had calmed down my father took me up to a flat section of our roof where we watched the Fokker planes in a clear sky, with little cloudlets of explosives bursting near them as the gunners fired at them. And still the memory of that frantic cycle ride along the empty avenue preserves its reality with all the added imaginative force of a classic nightmare.

There was one deeper and more enduring shadow than my childish experiences to contend with in the aftermath of the war, involving my Aunt Jessie. She had seen her fiancé go off to the Front, had heard from his companions of the man walking forward into No-man's Land – and disappearing. The one word that haunted and continued to haunt so many young women in the 1920s was 'Missing': not dead, not alive, but missing. Absent without explanation.

In earlier years she had been a deputy mother to me. Now the position was altered: with a rueful humour she began to call me her 'little husband'. We were much in each other's company during the school holidays when, for instance, my parents might go away for a few days leaving me in Jessie's care. Our choice of an outing, depending on the weather, would be to go for a row on the Thames or to a theatre matinée in London's West End. If we chose the river we went to Hampton Wick, where she kept her dinghy. This little boat was to Jessie a symbol of her independence. Her two sisters had the secure position of married women: she had to make do without husband, capital or professional qualification, in a world which still offered few opportunities to the genteel spinster beyond the traditional ones of 'companion' or 'governess'. She had made herself financially independent by creating her kindergarten and junior school; and from its slender profit she had bought the one astonishing luxury that was triumphantly her very own – the dinghy. In a life that was never easy she had her regal moment when she put the picnic hamper in the stern, slid the oars in the rowlocks and pulled away upstream.

In our theatregoing we could normally find matinée seats in the pit for half-a-crown. Our tastes were in no way specialised and our choices probably made up a broad mixture of 'strong' drama and comedy, but – with the benefit of hindsight – it is not difficult to identify the fresh element that typifies the early twenties. The new favourites we discovered – Jack Buchanan, Nelson Keys, Beatrice Lillie – were a different breed from the great names of music hall. Impresarios like Charlot, de Courville and Cochran were bringing on a new style of revue and cabaret artiste displaying wit, elegance, sophistication and a rejection of sentimentality. It is too glib to say that all public sentiment had been drained away in the war years, for there are springs of sentiment to be found at any time; but it was certainly the fashion to polish the surfaces of life so as to reflect smartly satirical images.

The accompanying cynicism was often shallow but it was widespread and insistent. My own straw in that wind was a gramophone record played every night by our house prefects in the dormitory at Cranleigh. One of them had a portable gramophone and, I begin to suspect, only this one record. For perhaps a year it was my nightly lullaby –

> O the Hotel Pimlico
> Is the place where you should go –
> You can even take your wife
> But, on your life,
> Don't let them know.

The message was plain enough. Down with boring old virtue!

I was fourteen or fifteen at this time, coming rather late to puberty, trying to sort myself out and bring many impressions and influences into a degree of coherence. I had no lack of conventional ballast available in my family inheritance, but it was an inert kind of ballast. My father had discovered that the Congregationalist chapel did less to refresh his spirit than did a round of golf on a Sunday, so my mother's firmer adherence to the Church of England had steered me through the service of Confirmation to a quiet pleasure in the rituals and ceremonies of the school chapel. I liked the cool stone surfaces, the slow processions, the repetitions of familiar words, the choral intertwinings of our singing voices – and I suppose I 'believed' in a Laodicean way.

At a less spiritual level I had an unquestioning loyalty to King and country, knew that anything made in Britain was better than anything made abroad and that the British Empire was a force for good throughout the world. On this last point I received added confirmation when the music master announced that the choir's annual outing would be to the Empire Exhibition at Wembley. This was indeed one of the marvels of my youth, a city of fantasies created from nothing in a place nobody knew existed. We wandered from pavilion to pavilion, collecting samples and leaflets, until we had addled our minds with a superfluity of Indian tea, Australian wool, South African oranges, Rhodesian tobacco, New Zealand butter and goodness knows what else. The world was ours to enjoy – or so it seemed at Wembley in 1924.

There were other delights there, not perhaps striking quite such a high note morally but undeniably appealing. There was a headless woman. So she was described, though in truth she was a woman in two disconnected parts, with her breathing head resting on a sword while her torso lurked nearby. I lingered, hoping to detect a trick. Mirrors possibly? I never knew. I wished she might wink but she remained impassive. There was more action at another stand which was furnished with two beds, each containing a girl dressed only in a nightie. A well-aimed ball, striking a target, operated a pivot which tipped the beds sideways – and out tumbled the girls on the floor. They looked as bored as I am sure they were, one chewing an apple, the other reading a book, while the last of our pocket-money went in hopes of the elusive naughty glimpse.

Nineteen-twenty-four was to be a memorable year for me in another way. My father and Uncle Frank had bought two adjoining plots of land on the outskirts of Guildford, in the parish of Merrow.

We were to leave East Sheen for one of the two new houses that an architect-cousin of my mother's had designed. To part from Basil and my other boyhood friends was a sadness but there was no denying the advantages of the move. With Frank's family next door I should have three boy-cousins for company. Each house had an acre of ground on the chalk downland ridge that extended from Guildford to the celebrated beauty-spot at Newland's Corner. Our outlook was across a valley of farmland to the little chapel of St Martha's on the Pilgrim's Way. There were lapwings tumbling in the sky and wild rhododendrons on the hillside opposite. It was *real* country, like the countryside round Cranleigh that I had become used to. The lane, which was the only approach to the new house, became almost immediately a rough cart-track until it was eventually lost altogether on the open downs.

I hoped we should have moved by the time the summer holidays started; but first I had to take the exam for the Oxford and Cambridge Schools certificate. This was roughly equivalent to the more recent 'O' level, with the further condition that 'Distinction' in five approved subjects – rather than a mere pass – qualified for exemption from Matric. As I was considered a clever little swot I had nothing much to fear, and indeed all went well until we came to History, which was divided into two papers – one of a general nature, the other concentrated narrowly on a special period. The general one presented no problems but, when the Special Period paper was distributed, there was instant pandemonium. The Period was not the one we had been studying over the previous year. Our history master was sent for, the syllabus was consulted, and the awful truth dawned that he had simply assumed that this year would be as last year and probably the year before as well. That the examiners might think it time to make a change had not occurred to him. He had put their syllabus aside, unread.

Poor man, he urged us to believe that our general grounding was good enough for us to scrape through if we applied ourselves to the task with a will. He was probably right but it was a lovely summer's afternoon, we had the perfect alibi, and boys have sometimes a cruel taste for revenge. I scribbled away briskly and handed in my paper with an hour in hand, which I could translate into an unexpected hour's tennis.

It is the consequence rather than the mishap which justifies the tale. My total history mark was a comfortable pass but just missed 'Distinction', which meant that I had to take Matric as a separate exam if I wanted it. For some reason the word 'Matric' had a magical quality among employers, and in this my father was typical. I had meanwhile moved into the Upper Sixth to start work on the Higher Certificate but there was a Matric exam – London Matriculation to name it correctly – in the autumn term, and this I could take. There was only one condition to be observed: I had to be not less than sixteen years old. The exam was in September and my birthday is in October. At the material time I was still only fifteen. I was doomed therefore to sit as an external candidate in London during the Christmas holidays – a stroke of poetic justice, no doubt.

It was a very strange holiday altogether. Work on the new house at Guildford had been greatly delayed. It was still not ready for occupation. The old home in East Sheen was sold and possession had to be given. I returned from Cranleigh to find my parents living in the Hotel Stuart on Richmond Hill. This in itself was pleasant enough, for the hotel was already coming into a festive mood – with Christmas imminent – and the surroundings could hardly be more congenial. The hotel faced the Terrace, which was recovering some of its pre-war charm as a fashionable promenade, with a breath-taking view from the Terrace of the Thames winding away towards Petersham. At the top of the Hill was Richmond Park, offering so much to be explored. In the other direction it was only a short walk to the Royalty Kinema.

All this was excellent but had somehow to be reconciled with the hard fact that I had to do considerable revision of my school-work for the exam in early January. This mainly involved working over exam papers of previous years to make myself familiar with the general style and method of the London examiners. Consequently there I sat each day in one or other of the hotel rooms, an incon-gruous schoolboy figure crouched and concentrated over a miscel-lany of textbooks and papers while the adult residents moved about round me and either ignored me or looked at me in a puzzled way.

One man in particular was intrigued by the oddity of my presence and began to interest himself in what I was doing. I have long since forgotten his name so I must invent one for him – and what in the circumstances could be better than 'Mr Petersham'? His interest quickly took a practical turn and he said he would like to help me. We arranged to meet each morning at an agreed time and place.

Mr Petersham was a graduate of Trinity College, Dublin, and a man of many blessings; he was tall and handsome, rich enough to need no employment but to live as he pleased, with an extremely smart and pretty wife who dressed well and smelt nice when she came near me. I admired and envied Mr Petersham. I also found him something of an enigma, probably because I had never known what the newspapers described as 'a gentleman of private means'. In my world men ate a rather hasty breakfast and set off to do something. Mr Petersham ate a leisurely breakfast and did not set off anywhere. His only morning appointment seemed to be the one with me. Mrs Petersham made few demands on him before midday, when they both felt it was time for a drink.

With my teetotal background I knew very little about people's drinking habits but I had a suspicion that Mr Petersham occasionally drank rather a lot – perhaps from a lack of anything better to do. Not that he was ever the worse for drink, or 'disguised in liquor' as the saying goes, but my mother hinted that in the late evenings he might be just a bit 'squiffy'. By that time I was in bed of course.

What is so fascinating about the contacts between human beings is that they can be superficial and static over ten years or intensely penetrative within ten days – and so often unpredictable in their matchings and mismatchings. As Mr Petersham and I sat in the hotel lounge reading and translating Latin to each other we formed a highly improbable bond of intimacy. I was particularly fond of Latin as a subject and to sit with this cultured and cultivated man, discussing Cicero or the *Aeneid* as between equals, was a new and exhilarating experience. As for his part, I can only guess. Did he forget me in a week, a month, a year? – it scarcely matters, but I fancy that strange Christmas interlude revived in him something that he had not wished to lose but had mislaid.

With the festivities of Christmas and New Year over, the day of the exam came upon me. I travelled into London to take my place in a vast hall where I seem to remember a biplane suspended from the high ceiling. Around me were candidates in great variety including at least one bearded elder. I was to hear in due course that I had passed but in the meantime the question of my future had to be faced before I returned to Cranleigh and settled down to the two years of specialised work which would culminate in Higher Certificate and a place at Oxford. That was the prospect as my housemaster and my form-master saw it.

My father saw it differently. For a business career the right preparation was to go to a public school until sixteen or seventeen and get Matric, after which one should be ready to start 'real' work. The masters at Cranleigh hinted that scholarships were possible if there were financial difficulties, but the principal difficulty was not financial. My father had left school at fourteen. None of his friends had gone to university. Oxford and Cambridge were not a part of our world. Boys who went there were apt to get a very exalted idea of their own importance and to look down on their own parents. I could begin to see myself as a monstrous cuckoo in our unpretentious nest.

There was a further consideration of a severely practical kind. The two partners in Alexander Hawkins & Sons of London Road, London – my father and his brother Frank – had between them five sons, among whom it should not be impossible to find the firm's next generation. However, the two eldest had already gone their separate ways. From the City of London School my brother had gone to an agricultural college and thence as a farm-pupil. From Caterham School my eldest cousin had followed his bent for motor-car design and gone to Lagonda's. I was the third in line. If I went to Oxford I could be reckoned as lost to the ironmongery business. That at any rate was the logic of the 1920s.

For my part I had no clear sense of purpose at this stage. I enjoyed the whole paraphernalia of learning, the feel and smell of a new textbook, the beckoning invitation of a clean sheet of paper; but equally I was ready enough to give up school-life. I had just begun to find in myself an instinctive nonconformity. I have a rebellious streak, a readiness to protest, which makes me ill suited to a highly institutionalised form of society. The public-school ethos, which I at first accepted uncritically, had become irksome.

The form my protest first took was nothing if not original. I wanted to disturb the pious solemnity of the house-captain and his prefects by doing something which was subversive but not illegal. In the holidays I persuaded my mother to make me a night-cap – literally a pointed flannel cap of traditional style. On the first night of term, as we prepared to get into bed, I put on my night-cap. I was ordered to remove it and refused to do so. There was no rule against the wearing of night-caps – admittedly because no one had foreseen that such a rule could ever be needed, but nevertheless there was no such rule. It was an absurd quibble and an absurd gesture, I must allow, but absurdity was the weapon I needed. In a dormitory of fifty identical beds at identical distances and with identical coverlets the sight of my night-cap was a cheerfully defiant eccentricity.

The matter of the OTC was more serious. It was an unquestioned assumption that any public schoolboy would wish to be trained to take his commission as an officer in the armed services if the occasion arose. I certainly did not question it at first. I drew my uniform, did my regulation drill and enjoyed the annual field-day at Tidworth. My disaffection came on gradually till I decided to resign. I was told I could not resign as I had signed a pledge, or sworn an oath, or done something binding originally. I then discovered a vaguely pacifist conviction and refused to carry a rifle. Under pressure I claimed that my doctor would give me an exemption because of my deformed arm. From what appeared to be a deadlock there was only one solution – the band. I was transferred to the care of the Band-master to be trained as a drummer and excused from arms drill on unspecified medical grounds.

If this appears to imply a dawning political consciousness in me I must dispel it with another bizarre confession. By some means I had acquired a leaflet issued by an embryo fascist organisation, which was commanded by an army officer who resided in the Tower of London. The date, let me emphasise, was 1924, when Oswald Mosley was a rising Labour politician and the name of Adolf Hitler was virtually unknown in Britain and positively unknown in Cranleigh. Fascism was something new-fangled in Italy only.

I decided to join the fledgling body of British fascists, partly because I liked the idea of a semi-secret society conducted from the Tower of London but mainly because it offered an attractive tie in black and silver at a price I could afford. This was handed to me by the county organiser, another but lower-ranking ex-officer who lived in the village of Cranleigh. At speech day, when the venerable Duke of Connaught handed me the form prize, I was wearing this mysterious tie and wondering if my local commandant was in the audience.

My membership developed no further. The tie became creased and soiled, and through 1925 my school career was losing momentum and drifting to a conclusion. When it was finally established that I should not be staying long enough to take Higher Certificate I was allowed to choose which classes I wanted to attend and to make up my own timetable. The English master gave me a key to the school library and encouraged me to spend as much time there as I liked. For some reason I fastened on the Jacobethan dramatists and read my way through the contemporaries and successors of Shakespeare one by one – Tourneur, Dekker, Webster, Marlowe, Jonson and the rest – until I had absorbed a whole poetry of lust and satire and violence, and was well-nigh drunk with the power of language. It was a lovely blazing way to finish.

I was now sixteen – three months short of my seventeenth birthday, to be precise, and no longer a schoolboy. I had a head full of history, Latin, French, and English literature but no idea of a suitable vocation. I was easily persuaded to 'give the business a try'.

My brother meanwhile had decided that there was no future for him in agriculture and he had gone into the City to work for a firm of insurance brokers: he became eventually a Lloyds underwriter.

My first step was to attend a business college in Guildford, which my father thought a necessary preliminary. The change in atmosphere from Cranleigh was a distinct shock. It was a severely unpretentious establishment with modest aims, concentrating mainly on shorthand, typing, elementary book-keeping and the jargon of business correspondence. The majority of pupils were girls hoping for employment as shorthand-typists: their presence was a more welcome factor in the contrast with Cranleigh. Surreptitious notes began to pass, flirtations followed and a mixed hockey team became the college's most enthusiastically supported activity. On Sundays I cycled the long flat road from Guildford to Ash Vale for an inarticulate conversation with the girl who sat in the front row of our weekday classroom. It was a way of beginning the real life of an ex-schoolboy, riddled with the nameless guilt, taboos and sexual hang-ups which were the stigmata of that epoch.

A term at the college was clearly sufficient to equip me for my first sight of the world of ironmongery. However, it was thought inadvisable that I should appear as a complete novice on the scene where I should one day be the 'guv'nor', so an informal sort of apprenticeship was planned for me at the premises of one of my father's friends. There I could sweep the floor and fetch the tea, metaphorically if not actually, in a safely anonymous way.

And so it came about that, one winter's day, I travelled to Clerkenwell to meet Mr Walker of the Willen Key Company and to have lunch with him at his club in City Road. Mr Walker was a bluff, plainspeaking man – a bit of a rough diamond – who had built up a successful business very rapidly by working extremely hard. He reckoned he had worked as many hours in twenty years as most men spread over forty, so he could now spend only a couple of hours a day supervising the business and leaving the detailed operation to a manager. For the rest of the day he normally played golf.

I doubt if he really thought I was the 'right stuff'. He was too shrewd a judge for that. But he had a friendly warmth of feeling for my father and was ready to be helpful. He himself had no sons and therefore no problems of that sort. He gave me a reassuring handshake and told me to report to his office, first thing on Monday.

Chapter Five

ON my first day at the Willen Key Company I was put in the care of the manager, Mr Armstrong, who was at that time preparing a new edition of the firm's catalogue. I quickly learned that 'catalogue' was an inadequate word for what proved to be a large hardback volume of perhaps 150–200 pages, with illustrations of every imaginable kind of lock and key as well as associated objects such as door handles, hasps and staples and the like. I was to sit in the manager's office and sort out the electros from which the illustrations would be printed. It was an oddly appropriate start for an author's career.

In person Mr Armstrong was everything a manager should be. He was a powerfully built man with a large head, which seemed reluctant to withdraw from the capacious bowler hat that he invariably wore. Black was the colour of his hat, his jacket, his striped trousers, his shining boots and his moustache. The one relieving colour in his heavy presence was the gold of his watch-chain. His temper had a short fuse but he kept it well controlled. His feeling for the proprietor was one of grudging admiration mingled with an occasional resentment on difficult days that Mr Walker was on the golf-course while his manager was beset with mounting problems. In the main he took life philosophically, reflecting perhaps that he had come some way to hold his present august position. He took a pride in his house and garden in one of the more desirable northern suburbs and he had the comforting knowledge that he was much respected in the business community – as the manager of the Willen Key Company might properly expect to be. His general character of solid worth and firm-footed stability must have been a valuable foil to the rough and more mercurial talents of Mr Walker.

The office area had two other inhabitants. There was Miss Cook, a middle-aged lady of impressive quickness and brightness who had been Mr Walker's close assistant for many years in what he tended to treat rather scornfully as the 'paper work'. And there was Miss Drewry, a young typist of a very respectable sort whose father was one of the firm's travellers. There were other typists downstairs, beside the trade counter, but Miss Drewry had been given a more elevated status because of her parentage and her ladylike manners. I realised that there was a more than symbolical importance given to the flight of stairs up to our office area – or I should say, not the 'stairs', but the 'apples and pears' since the warehousemen were great exponents of Cockney rhyming slang. The first time I was asked 'Going up the apples?' by someone wanting me to take some invoices upstairs I betrayed my ignorance as a 'foreigner' so completely that I was regarded almost with pity.

Travelling from Guildford to the City Road in Clerkenwell was indeed rather like an expedition to a foreign land at first. From our new house at Merrow to Guildford was a steeply downhill journey of three miles in the morning and an even more steeply uphill one in the evening. If I went by car with my father and my uncle in the morning I had to synchronise with them in the evening or walk. The alternative was a bicycle, which became the usual method. From Guildford to Waterloo was a railway journey by the newly electrified line from Guildford's London Road station; and then the Underground to Old Street and the final walk past the Black Cat cigarette factory, the fish-and-chip shop, the blank-faced warehouses and the sleazy café where the waitress in black bombazine liked to tease the customers with a glimpse of her tits as she leaned over to swab the spilt tea on the marble table-tops. It was all very different from the green valley and quiet downland I had left at daybreak.

The journey became even more difficult in May of my first year at work, 1926, when the General Strike took place. I had not yet begun to take any interest in politics so I had no understanding of the issues involved. My brother volunteered to drive a milk lorry, which was based in Hyde Park, and we were caught up in the broadly adventurous attempt to keep life going as normally as possible. By one means or another I got to some part of south London each day and walked across the city to Clerkenwell. The strike did not appear to arouse any sympathetic response inside the Willen Key Company, where work went on without any interruption that I can recall. At that period the locksmiths and warehousemen had no union loyalties and tended to regard the strike as the private concern of the big industrial unions, in which they themselves were not involved.

To me, at seventeen, it was a nine days' wonder that was quickly forgotten among the urgent matters that seize the attention of teenagers in any generation – fashions in dress and popular entertainment and the first intoxicating tastes of adult independence. I was a ready victim of the craze for Oxford 'bags' – the nearest I was to get to Oxford. I wanted to master the Charleston and used to practise its knee-twisting steps while I waited each day on railway platforms. In one form or another American music was coming to dominate – jazz, the big stage band of Paul Whiteman, the sentimental waltzes of Irving Berlin and with them two new sounds, the saxophone and the ukulele. The Ta-ra-ra-boom-de-ay of the old music hall and the sets of lancers that my parents liked to dance were swept away in the new styles of the twenties; and, like chewing-gum, they were American. In the Lyons Corner Houses, where you might once have found a piano trio competing with the clatter of crockery, it was now the young saxophonist playing 'The Birth of the Blues' who was watched admiringly by ladies with time to spare.

The ukulele was a different matter. It came in with the Hawaian sound and was adopted by my generation much as the skiffle players after the second war adopted the guitar. The ukulele was cheap, easily portable and could be mastered instantly by anyone with fingers and the capacity to memorise three simple chords. Its sibling, the banjulele, had a fuller tone and is remembered now, if at all, through its two celebrated executants – George Formby and 'Two Ton' Tessie O'Shea. I plumped for a banjulele and enjoyed being mournful with 'What'll I Do?' and 'All Alone'. There was a little shop near Willen Key which sold sheet music, and the shopkeeper used to let me take away three songs overnight on approval, provided I brought them back next morning and bought one of them. I expect he knew I had copied out the words and the finger positions of the two rejects, but at the time I felt guiltily triumphant in my low cunning.

While I was settling into my working life in London I was also becoming acclimatised to permanent home-life at Guildford, after the years as a school-boarder, and I became more intimate with my brother. He too was living regularly at home now. The seven-year gap in our ages was less significant at this stage, even if only briefly: he was already contemplating marriage and a home of his own. On winter weekends we went tobogganing together. The wooded northern slopes of the downs were so shaded from the sun that a heavy fall of snow lay for several weeks. The difficulty of steering a safe course through the trees and bushes on a steep slope added to the excitement.

Another interest we shared was the wireless, which was establishing itself as a normal feature of home-life. The dance music of the Savoy Orpheans, relayed from London's prestigious Savoy Hotel, gave us a new sort of access to the smart world of high society. Our local dance bands in Guildford had now to consider that they were playing for dancers who knew the latest hits at the Savoy. The BBC was even experimenting with the tapping feet of a chorus-line of dancing girls in a revue called *Radio Radiance*.

Quite a different pleasure was to be had from picking up the signals of foreign stations. Each year new ones came on the air and our receivers improved in range and strength. Our original stalwarts were France's PTT from the Eiffel Tower and the Dutch station at The Hague. Two memorable newcomers were Radios Toulouse and San Sebastian. We picked up Toulouse when it was transmitting test signals and asking any listeners to report reception. Stan and I wrote to Toulouse and had a reply indicating that we were their most distant listeners at that date. San Sebastian I recall particularly for the extremely beautiful voice of the woman announcer identifying her station as 'Radio San Sebastian in el monte Igueldo'. I fancy she was the first female announcer in Europe – an unexpected innovation to come from Spain. The appealing loveliness of her voice was much talked about at the time: listeners tried to pick up the San Sebastian signal in order to hear her.

A yet greater prize was an identifiable signal across the Atlantic. This was just possible and counted as the supreme triumph among wireless enthusiasts. Because of the time difference, and the need to have the full darkness of night well established at both ends of the signal's path, it was not worth starting to listen before midnight. The favoured time was between 2 and 3 a.m. Many a night Stan and I sat listening intently, with a heavy accumulator freshly charged beside the set in case our receiving strength weakened. WGY Schenectady and KDKA Pittsburgh were our likeliest quarries as we tuned the set through the mush of atmospherics and cracklings in the hope of a distant human voice. I cannot pretend that we really succeeded. Once or twice there were the faintest snatches of what might have been words. Our spirits rose and we redoubled our efforts, straining to catch even the slightest intelligible sound, but the broadcasters of America never quite reached their willing audience in Guildford.

Our sense of participation in a technological advance was all of a piece with the general buoyancy that had succeeded the stagnation of the wartime years. My father and Uncle Frank became the joint owners of a six-cylinder Buick motor-car and for the first time we travelled at sixty miles an hour. A mile in a minute! It was difficult to believe such a thing to be possible. Yet what was impossible? Alan Cobham had just flown an aeroplane to Capetown and back, and was about to make a similar flight to Australia. We were attuned to marvels.

There was precious little excitement, however, to be found in my daily task of compiling the new Willen Key catalogue. After the first stage of novelty one electro came to look very like another. I began to seize any opportunity to go downstairs, if only to spend a few minutes with the warehousemen and the locksmiths. Their world seemed so much livelier than the politely insipid atmosphere of the upstairs office: they shouted, laughed, talked bawdy and argued with a zest and openness that were uncommonly attractive to me at this moment when I was beginning to emerge from my middle-class cocoon. I asked Mr Armstrong if I could spend more time 'below', to broaden my experience of the business. He consented readily enough as he had no very clear idea of what he was supposed to do with me. Work on the catalogue proceeded in a desultory way which left vacant hours when I could explore the rows of fixtures from which the warehousemen extracted the goods to fill each customer's order; or I could go to the bench where the locksmiths worked.

There were two locksmiths – William and Horace. William, a genially bubbling Cockney, was always to be called William, never Bill. Horace, a quiet and deeply thoughtful man, had the problem of a name that is somehow unsuited to working-class conventions – like Lionel, which has to be tactfully converted to Len. Horace was always known as Horry. I often wondered, and still wonder, about the family circumstances in which the young Horace grew up. He was completely at ease in the world in which he now found himself and yet he preserved a detachment from it, in a curiously bookish way. The range of his knowledge, and of his ignorance, were alike unpredictable. He read a lot and liked to discuss the larger world of ideas, though not in any topical or narrowly political way.

The tools of the locksmith's craft are simple: a vice, an assortment of files, a cutting wheel, some blank keys and a candle. The work consisted mainly of cutting new keys to replace ones which had been lost. If one of the original keys survived it would be sent in for matching. If all had been lost the lock would be sent and a new set of keys cut to operate it. The work came in from ironmongers and builder's merchants all over the country, and at a steady flow which kept William and Horry comfortably busy. They shared a long bench and enjoyed conversation while they worked.

I liked to be with them, partly for the friendly chat and partly for the pleasure of watching skilled craftsmen at work. There were reservations, however, on their side. Like any other craftsmen locksmiths have their technical secrets which are not shared in any casual way. I was expected not to look too closely at certain moments, and at other times they would turn their backs to me while their hands were manipulating a lock. Their motive I well understood. Occasionally a customer, collecting at the trade counter a cylinder lock which he brought in without keys and which now had its new set, would put a five-pound note on the counter and ask to be told 'how it was done'. The reply tended to be blunt and not particularly cordial.

The warehousemen were in a different class from William and Horry. If I seem to refer frequently to 'class' it is because the class-structure sixty years ago was so finely tuned and widely honoured that such comprehensive labels as 'working-class' or 'middle-class' were hopelessly crude and imprecise. Within the main divisions there were subdivisions, tenaciously guarded and rigorously applied. Speech, income, vocation, neighbourhood, dress, family connections, eating habits – all interacted in the final status. The warehousemen were a mixed lot – a tall blond Swede, two East End Jewish brothers and a teenage apprentice, under the tentative authority of Mr Miles, an impassive and somewhat enigmatic character whose outlook on life was soured by the fact that his wife would only 'let him' once a year, on Christmas morning. This he confided to me, as I am sure he confided to any sympathetic listener. Not surprisingly he pursued various pornographic interests in a discreet way. Much treasured was a battered copy of an erotic poem which he had carried in his wallet for years and which he assured me was by Byron.

Each morning Miss Cook gave Mr Miles the orders which had come in by post, either directly from customers or from the firm's reps – the commercial travellers out on the road, whom we seldom saw. The day's work was to assemble and despatch the goods ordered and to handle the incoming crates of fresh supplies from manufacturers. It involved a lot of 'humping' of boxes, shouting of messages and clambering up and down the fixtures. The two brothers, Sid and Perce, kept up a flow of banter in their almost impenetrable rhyming slang and local catch-phrases, occasionally stirring the imagination of Mr Miles with tales of the girls they had groped in the cinema the previous night. In their early twenties they had an unquenchable ebullience, full of good-natured humour, which did not relax until the midday break when they settled down with the others round a packing-case which did duty as a card-table. Here they played Banker for half-pence, in a solemn mesmeric mood, with the incantation to 'nish me one' which I heard so often and never understood.

The big Swede was known to everyone as Puck. His real name had been hard to pronounce so it was soon forgotten. I suppose Mr Walker knew it but he would come halfway down the stairs and shout 'Puck!' when he wanted him. The nickname sprang from the Swede's own brand of English. If he felt menaced he would shout, 'I puck the best one of yer then – I puck the lot of yer.' It became a bit of a joke as everyone grew used to him, but he was not a man to cross. He was over six foot, powerfully built with a body as hard and obstinate as stone.

The others liked to affect an air of virility and physical strength but when there was an exceptionally big case to shift they tended to stand about, commenting on its unusual weight and general awkwardness until someone fetched Puck. He would put his great hands on the case and grin in a rapt sort of way, mumbling to himself 'Eyup then' – as a man might talk to an animal – until suddenly the case was securely on the trolley.

The other inhabitants of 'downstairs' were the two typists who worked in a glass-sided hutch beside the trade counter. The one I recall was Miss Treherne, who was neither young nor old, and neither 'refined' nor unrefined. She had in fact a problem in determining her own identity and therefore in establishing clear relationships with others. She was sometimes ladylike and sometimes not: at times skittish, at other times sedate. One evening as we were all preparing to leave she had some sort of verbal exchange with Puck, who promptly picked her up, put her over his knee, spanked her bottom, set her back on her feet again and walked away. Poor Miss Treherne – she found herself contending with so many unexpected emotions and impulses, from rage to mild astonishment, that they somehow cancelled each other and she failed to find any coherent response at all. The only part of her that had been more than trivially hurt was her dignity and she was not sure how much that mattered. She just said 'Goodnight' with a slightly indignant shrug and departed.

My time at the Willen Key Company was not to be of long duration but two pleasant events were still to come, both of them involving the locksmiths with whom my friendship was deepening. Their natural caution had recognised me as a bird of passage and a member of the 'boss' class, even if I was not an actual spy; but the day came when William, turning his back to me in the usual way as he handled a cylinder-lock, suddenly turned round again and said, 'Come here and I'll show you.' In its context it was a moment of great significance. He was admitting me to the mystery of his guild just as much as if some elaborate ritual of initiation were being enacted.

Observing is not quite the same thing, however, as performing. My attempts to apply my newly acquired knowledge were painfully inept until by degrees my fingertips acquired the sensitivity that the technique demands. William and Horry encouraged me patiently until I became proficient enough to work unaided.

My pride in this unexpected achievement must have prompted my father to recall that he had inherited a strange heirloom from the Great Exhibition of 1851 in the form of a mammoth padlock, weighing perhaps a quarter of a hundredweight or more. It was stored away in some remote corner of the London Road premises and had long since lost its key. There was no way of opening it. It could never have served any practical purpose, because of its bulk, and had clearly been made purely to display the highest flights of the locksmith's art.

When I mentioned its existence to William he responded to it as a personal challenge: the thought of making the key that would open it seized his imagination. The great padlock was transported from Southwark to Clerkenwell. As a first step William designed a blank key of the size and shape to fit the keyhole, and this had to be made specially since it was far larger than any commercially available blank. Meanwhile the padlock lay on the bench, the object of admiration and astonishment to all who saw it.

William's method of working, when the blank arrived, was to complete his normal day's stint and then to devote about an hour each evening to the padlock. So far as he was concerned it was a labour of love, not to be confused with the business of earning a day's wage. He relished every moment of his battle of wits with the old Victorian master-craftsman who had put all his cunning into the lock's internal structure. It was not a task to be hurried. Several

47

weeks passed while the key took on, under William's files, the character of an intricate piece of fretwork or fine tracery. From time to time he held the key in the candle-flame, inserted it in the lock and felt the points of refusal and frustration as it failed to turn, until the moment came when the key freed itself from the last resisting ward and pushed back the bolt. William pulled the hasp up to liberate it. The padlock was open. It was a moment of triumph, to be savoured still in the memory.

The effect on me of William's action was greater than I realised at the time. It undoubtedly reinforced my growing conviction that the only employment worth having was one which engaged your interest, your ambitions and your talents. I was to follow that path later but at this time I had no clear ambition and no comprehension of what talents – if any – I might possess, beyond my ability to open a cylinder lock without a key. I was simply drifting into an inheritance for which I had no appetite. Such interests as I had lay outside the negative but inescapable world of 'nine till six'.

In some of my interests – girls, for instance, playing tennis and dancing the Charleston – I shared the normal pursuits of my Guildford contemporaries. More original was my persisting and deepening interest in the theatre. I became a regular reader of *Theatre World* from its first issue, while I was still at school. The first bonus of my new life as a wage-earner in London was that I could now go to theatres on my own initiative. Hitherto my opportunities had naturally enough depended on the choice of theatre that my parents made; and this in turn depended in large measure on Bert Fry.

Mr Fry was a tailor and an old cycling club buddy of my father's. He shared a house in Clapham with Miss Brebner, who was a dressmaker and I expect had also been a member of the cycling club. At an early stage in their lives Bert Fry and Edith Brebner had been betrothed. The shared house at Clapham symbolised the happy conjunction of professional and conjugal interests which, alas, was marred by some dramatic rupture that was never explained and never healed. Miss Brebner retired into the upper part of the house, which Mr Fry was forbidden to enter: he had his kingdom in the lower half. The thought of selling the house and setting up separate establishments was evidently too complicated and troublesome to entertain, and they had almost come to depend on each other as inexhaustible topics of malicious conversation with their friends. To be parted after so many years of guerrilla warfare could well be a greater deprivation – bereavement even – than if they had been married.

As a tailor Bert Fry was dull and unenterprising but he had a clientele of sorts and it included a number of box-office managers and other contacts in the theatrical world. From them he received complimentary tickets for those theatres which were struggling to keep going in the face of half-empty houses. In such circumstances it was the custom discreetly to 'paper the house' with free tickets, to give the illusion that the play was attracting large audiences. As an outlet a tailor was a good practical choice since his beneficiaries would at least be presentably dressed.

It was thanks to Bert Fry, therefore, that I saw many of the least memorable flops of the period, but also some of the better productions which were coming towards the end of their run or had been slow to catch the popular fancy; but in addition from 1926 onwards, with a few shillings in my pocket, and my day's work in London ended, I could make for the West End and join the queue for the Pit at the theatre of my choice. It was the first taste of emancipation.

Three things stand out in retrospect from that first year of independent theatregoing. Pride of place must go to the Irish dramatist, Sean O'Casey, who shattered the general cosiness with *Juno and the Paycock* and *The Plough and the Stars*. His winning of the Hawthornden Prize provoked an astonishment which emphasised the extent to which the theatre had become divorced from any literary values. When, if ever, had a dramatist last won the Hawthornden? Next I recall Tallulah Bankhead's triumph in *They Knew What They Wanted*, which had won for its author, Sidney Howard, the Pulitzer Prize in New York. My third and quite different reason for gratitude is that I was privileged to see the Aldwych farces – which one is immaterial, for I saw them all.

Where the theatre was liveliest was in American musical comedy and cosmopolitan revue. This was the time of *No, No, Nanette*, *Mercenary Mary* and the Astaires dancing in *Lady, Be Good*; of the Russian *Chauve-Souris* company and the bold blending of revue talents which was C.B. Cochran's hallmark. In straight drama the standard was generally mediocre and safe enough to survive the ludicrous interventions of the Censor. It is an odd fact that the older writers who influenced my generation – Yeats, Hardy, Joyce and D.H. Lawrence – all flirted with the theatre but treated playwriting as a secondary medium and never enjoyed any recognition from London theatregoers. In the winter of 1925/6 Hardy's own dramatisation of *Tess of the d'Urbervilles* failed at the Garrick Theatre, despite a warmly acclaimed performance by Gwen ffrangçon-Davies as Tess.

In this artistic doldrums the racy vigour of O'Casey's language had a revolutionary impact. Here were poet and dramatist fused in one. I suppose my schoolboy love of the Jacobethan dramatists was rekindled by *Juno and the Paycock*: when its successor, *The Plough and the Stars*, was announced I was determined to see the first performance. I joined the Pit queue as early as I could and made my first acquaintance with a special bunch of theatregoers – the 'first-nighters'. It was their boast that they attended the opening night of every new production. They greeted each other as fellow members of a club who met frequently but only in this context. I am tempted even to liken them to colleagues on a magisterial bench for they addressed their conversation mainly to the verdict they would reach when the curtain fell at the end of the 'trial'.

The talk otherwise while the queue stood patiently waiting was all about recent productions and what the critics had said, flavoured with bits of gossip about favourite actors and actresses. Once inside the theatre the first-nighters would identify the arrival of the usual opening-night celebrities and the more recognisable newspaper critics – among them Hannen Swaffer, a notable Fleet Street character whom I had begun reading regularly. His comment on the stage costume of a leading actress as 'more navel than millinery' had recently enraged her admirers and amused everybody else.

For me one of the pure unalloyed pleasures in life resides in those last moments of expectancy before the rise of a theatre curtain. With no apparent cue given, the buzz of conversation begins to falter and die down. Until that moment we in the audience have been a most heterogeneous body of people, but suddenly we take on the unity of a shared adventure which may lead us into emotions great and small and of untold diversity. As the house-lights fade and the curtain stirs we admit the magic of an unseen conjuror: and if we have queued outside the theatre for a couple of hours the pleasure is that much sharper.

The first night of *The Plough and the Stars* ran much longer than was anticipated. The latest possible moment for catching the final passenger train to Guildford came and went. I sat spellbound. Not till I die can I forget the voice of Arthur Sinclair crying out, 'D'ye want us to come out in our skins an' throw stones?' Dramatically it was devastating. At the end we stood and cheered. I think we realised that this was no common event but a landmark in stage history.

I eventually got back to Guildford's main station by what we knew as the 'milk train'. On the long walk home in the small hours my memory tells me it was snowing. It seems improbable in the month of May but not impossible. What I remember with certainty is the glow and radiance of the performance that still totally obsessed me as I plodded on up that interminable hill.

The duped waitress in *They Knew What They Wanted* could be described as twentieth-century Chicago's answer to the Tess of Victorian Wessex. Here again was the obscure and hopeful innocent – more worldly-wise than her predecessor but no less vulnerable – and drawn in a vernacular dialogue with the theatrical force and directness that Hardy's lacked. For Tallulah Bankhead it was the perfect opportunity to justify the 'Tallulah fever' which swept London and must now be so difficult to justify or explain. Her appearance in Noël Coward's *Fallen Angels* and Michael Arlen's *The Green Hat* had identified her with the 'fast' set in café society. She was reputed to be audacious and unconventional offstage and she was undeniably beautiful in the sexually challenging way that one recognised again later in Marilyn Monroe.

Her opening nights were attended – and interrupted – by a claque or impromptu fan-club of girls in the gallery who greeted her stage-entrance with calls of her name, cries and shrieks and the generally hysterical response that we have come to expect in today's fans of the latest pop idol; but in 1926 this was a distinct novelty and made her undeniably newsworthy. Was she bathing in the nude by moonlight at Maidenhead or dancing through to dawn at the Café de Paris? The journalists of the gossip columns were ever alert.

For my part I was totally enslaved. I cherished her signed photograph, went to her first nights and joined the crowd at the stage-door afterwards, waiting for her to come out. When she did so eventually, she would linger for quite a while talking quietly and individually to some of the girls about their own lives and concerns. The contrast between this inexpressibly beautiful and *soignée* woman and the homely group of Cockney kids clustering around her was touching. Physically she was a perfect blonde with soft corn-gold hair folding about her temples; her skin had an underlying fairness and whiteness which accentuated the warm touches of colour in her cheeks and the red of her mouth. The low, husky, crooning voice was as unique as her romantically exotic name. Her body had a subtly articulate sensuality which set her apart from most of the British actresses of the time. I wonder if it was my good or ill fortune to be a mere seventeen-year-old then – so immature but so impressionable.

They Knew What They Wanted was produced by Basil Dean, who probably enjoyed greater prestige than any other producer. His next production was to be a dramatisation of a currently successful novel *The Constant Nymph*, in which he proposed to cast Tallulah opposite John Gielgud, then at the start of his career. What a duet that might have been – but the plan went awry and Tallulah moved to another management which mainly wanted her to appear in various stages of undress in light comedies. She returned to America to make films and was never seen on the London stage again.

Considered in retrospect the Aldwych farces are now regarded as a golden age of the genre, and rightly so. Some of their qualities are easily recognised: they had the benefit of ensemble playing by a highly integrated company, any one of whom could make the running or 'feed' a colleague as the action demanded, and they could make an effect with exhilarating economy. As an example of what can be done with only two words I recall a moment when Tom Walls entered an empty stage by the french windows. It was a night scene and he was visibly merry in liquor. The room door opened and the accusing wife in dressing-gown entered to confront him. 'Hubert!' she said, 'You're drunk!' There was a pause while Walls's fuddled mind struggled to come up with the totally convincing rebuttal. At last he seemed to have it. He drew himself up with dignity and uttered two words – so nearly triumphant but so fatally inculpating – 'Nonstance, Constance.'

More recent farces have seemed to go for broader, less subtle effects and to concentrate more narrowly on being 'naughty' in the realm of the obvious taboos, which were in any case becoming weaker. I believe the Aldwych 'characters' had a much deeper and more comprehensive rootedness in the social context of their time and drew strength from that fact. There was then a distinct working-class morality, to be outraged by 'goings on'. There was likewise a provincial puritanism, alert to be shocked. In family life the tension between generations was accentuated in the aftermath of the war and I believe this underlies the key characters played by Tom Walls and Ralph Lynn, who were not just 'funny men' but, in an oblique way, parable figures of the 1920s. Walls was the father-figure, corrupt, worldly-wise, by turns tyrannical and bibulously amiable. In the war he would have been the epitome of the base-wallah satirised so venomously by Siegfried Sassoon; now in peacetime he was safely back in the economic and social saddle, troubled at times by angry women but otherwise secure. Ralph Lynn was the ineffectual heir-apparent, the stage's conventional dude, the 'silly ass' who is one of the period's archetypal figures: his apotheosis is as Bertie Wooster in the world of P.G. Wodehouse.

I suspect therefore that the legendary splendour of the Aldwych farces owes a debt, not only to the dramatist's wit and the actor's craft, but also to these cryptic identifications with the personas of underlying social forces – and potent ones, moreover. To my surprise they illuminate more clearly than most of my theatregoing in those days the rebellious but ineffectual world of my teenage years. Laughter can sometimes take us open-eyed into territories where we are at other times blindfolded.

Chapter Six

LEAVING the Willen Key Company and joining the family business meant a change of scene for me from Clerkenwell to Southwark; and one needs perhaps to be a Londoner to appreciate the difference. The long stretch of the City Road running away to the north of Old Street into Clerkenwell as I knew it in 1926 had nothing to show of any interest. It was remote from the atmosphere of the City proper and even more remote from the Thames. There were no interesting buildings or refreshingly open spaces to be discovered in a lunchtime stroll.

By contrast Southwark, still keeping its ancient name as the Boro', had many features of note. The great cluster of Thames bridges – London, Blackfriars, Waterloo, Westminster and Lambeth – all lead to a common junction at St George's Circus, which stands at one end of London Road, with the Elephant and Castle at the other. The premises of Alexander Hawkins and Sons are at the St George's Circus end, still today where they have been since 1844 despite the fact that so much of the vicinity was destroyed by wartime bombing. I look now in vain for the Elephant and Castle as I used to know it and for the old music hall, the South London Palace, but I recognise the broad outlines; and the shop next door to ours is still selling Mr Leete's paint.

It soon became a part of my job to be out and about in the neighbourhood, keeping in touch with our regular customers and looking for new ones. Each of the 'bridge' roads had its own character and one or two special features that interested me. Lambeth

Road showed me the grounds of Bedlam – the Bethlehem Hospital – and, further on, the Archbishop of Canterbury's palace where my business took me to call on the butler down long stone-floored passages. In Waterloo Road blind workers wove wicker baskets and Lilian Bayliss ruled the Old Vic. The Westminster Road introduced me not only to Big Ben and the Houses of Parliament but also the new County Hall where our electricians were working, as Uncle Frank had won the electrical contract there.

Blackfriars Road had strange charms. In my great-grandfather's time it had promised to be a fashionable area – part of what he knew as the 'carriage trade'. The grimy forgotten squares in the side-roads still spoke of a minor gentry who had arrived hopefully and departed long since. The Surrey Theatre was a last relic of that vanished era – a ghost theatre near St George's Circus which had been closed and boarded up for many years. I managed to find a means of entering it and saw an astonishing sight – layers of dust everywhere, festoons of cobwebs hanging from the circle, patches of fallen plaster, sagging and rotting curtains, rust and decay on all sides. Thus it had stood in the deepening silence of its desolation because the owner – nursing some implacable grievance, so I was told – would neither reopen the theatre himself nor permit anyone else to do so. Another remarkable building in Blackfriar's Road was the Ring, built originally by the Victorian preacher, Charles Spurgeon, in a circular shape so that there were no corners for the Devil to hide in. I knew it in quite a different guise, however, as a popular setting for boxing matches and later for all-in wrestling.

The Boro' Road ran down into the heart of the Boro' – to Bankside and the Pool of London, to Barclays brewery and the offices of the hop merchants. Why it became the centre of the hop trade I do not know. Perhaps Mr Thrale had something to do with it. It was so important a feature of the district that our telephone exchange was named 'Hop', our number being Hop 6682.

The characteristic scent of Bankside was the odour of spent brewers' grains stacked outside the brewery – a heavy, sweetly malted odour. Bankside in the main was a surprisingly sleepy, old-fashioned area. I liked to find somewhere to perch along the low parapet wall overlooking the river and make pencil-sketches of the buildings on the opposite bank, the massive warehouses of Upper Thames Street with the Monument rising behind them.

To be enclosed within that great bending, curving bow of the Thames as it passes through the very heart of London was South-wark's great attraction for me. In every direction the river added its own dimension to the scene. Even if I turned my back on Waterloo and Blackfriars and walked along London Road – or, better still, boarded a tram – to continue past the Elephant and Castle into the New Kent Road I had yet another Thames bridge ahead of me, Tower Bridge. This route took me into Southwark's neighbour, Bermondsey, which seemed to me to be perhaps the most Cockney area of all. There were unmistakable industrial smells there, the jam and pickle smells of Crosse & Blackwell's factory and the tannery smells of the leather trade, but there were also residential areas with rows of narrow houses and native inhabitants that preserved much of the atmosphere of Dickensian London. The Tower Bridge Road swarmed with life, bustling, joking, swearing, trading, fighting and just simply being itself with a total indifference to the rest of the world. I remember watching a street-market when there was bad blood between two young costers: as the exchange of abuse rose in pitch the bystanders instinctively stopped what they were doing and formed a ring enclosing the two angry, shouting men as they threw down their jackets and faced each other. They fought with bare fists but by a code of conduct which was well understood. The blood flowed and when one fighter was indisputably winning he was pulled back from his victim; the crowd broke up contentedly and the silent, watchful traders suddenly began shouting their wares again. It was all a family matter, one felt, on a tribal scale.

My own family connection with the district was one of quite a different sort. I can imagine my great-grandfather living over the shop, but my grandfather bought a property at Worcester Park which became the family home and, during my youth, was occupied by one of my aunts. To three generations of us, therefore, Southwark was the place of work to which we travelled as commuters. We were not indigenous but the bond was a strong one nevertheless. In my own case it has mainly a dynastic character. Standing beside St George's Circus is the Royal Eye Hospital, of which my father was a governor and keen supporter. Turn into the Boro' Road and immediately there is the public library, with my grandfather's name carved on its foundation-stone. I retain at least that degree of relationship – and something deeper to the library itself, or rather to the librarian in 1927.

He was a Mr Robison, if I recall his name correctly – a quietly courteous bespectacled man, with greying hair and the breath of an obsessive tea-drinker. He had the good librarian's intuition which recognises a novice in search of some personal Grail with few clues for guidance. In the most unobtrusive way he would come up beside me, as I browsed along the shelves, and put a book into my hands with the murmured comment, 'I think you might enjoy this one.' As he discovered the way I responded to particular authors his suggestions became more discriminating. He was the first man to whom I could talk about my growing interest in books and authors. The debt I owe him is great.

One of his early selections for me was D.H. Lawrence's *Twilight in Italy*, then newly added to Jonathan Cape's Travellers' Library, a very attractive series which I began to collect. The volume of Lawrence's Italian essays may now seem an unlikely way to make a first approach to him, but its effect on me was overwhelming nevertheless. The book spoke to me with a directness I had not encountered before. To see European civilisation through Lawrence's eyes was to see it in terms that I could grasp and make my own. To explain his remarkable influence on my generation is not easy but there can be no doubt of its power. At the time when he had left England with Frieda, his future wife, and was making his own discovery of Italy in the months on which *Twilight in Italy* is based he wrote to Edward Garnett, 'I think, do you know, I have inside me a sort of answer to the *want* of today; to the real, deep want of the English people, not to just what they fancy they want.' It was with that conviction that he won the loyalty of many whose literary values were formulated in the twenties.

Two other discoveries in the Boro' Road library were H.L. Mencken and Theodore Dreiser – my first experience of living American authors. Mencken's boisterously aggressive prose would put courage into the most timid pen, so I found him a healthy model to copy. Dreiser's novels, in their massively turgid way, accumulated an emotional force which was not to be denied – at least by me – particularly in *An American Tragedy*. Before long I was writing Menckenesque open letters to all my favourite aunt Sallies, Lawrentian atmospheric landscapes and poems, and the early chapters of a novel in which Dreiser and Lawrence each had an involuntary hand.

The Boro' Road library was not my only oasis. There was also Morley College, offering short courses of evening lectures by eminent speakers. Two I remember are Gustav Holst and Robertson Scott. I knew nothing at the time of Holst's reputation as a composer, but as a champion of music and expositor of its glories he was magnificent. Robertson Scott, the founder–editor of *The Countryman*, seemed to me in later years to be a rather phoney and pretentious figure but at the time he was an impressive speaker who helped to give definition to my feeling for the countryside.

I developed a taste for lectures and used to subscribe each year to the Fabian Society's winter series. The point of subscribing for the whole series was to make sure of a seat for the final one, which customarily was by Bernard Shaw and would certainly be sold out in advance. Shaw, with the stimulus of a full house and an enthusiastically responsive audience, was a superb orator. His musically lilting voice, with its Irish brogue and fine diction, was a pleasure to hear in itself: the easy confident humour and the lively play of his wit were inimitable. He made it impossible to doubt the unalloyed wisdom of every word he uttered, and when his formal address was concluded he relished the exchanges with those who were intrepid enough to challenge him with a question. The only other speaker I heard who could captivate an audience so completely – though in a totally different manner – was Lloyd George, whom my father took me to hear at the Queen's Hall during my schooldays. The Welshman was all fire and passion, lion-maned and histrionic like an Old Testament prophet, alternating tense pauses with brisk salvoes of words that burst about us like fireworks. It was my second baptism. The first was in the Christian faith, this was in the nonconformist radical tradition of Liberalism. In the general election of 1929 – the first since I had left school – I followed family practice by working in the committee rooms of Mr Strauss, the Liberal Member for Southwark.

Meantime I was being absorbed in the day-to-day running of the business. There was much to learn, starting with the secret code in which cost prices were written on the stock: it was based, in exemplary Victorian style, on the words 'God be with us', each letter of which represented a number. The stock itself, in the manufacturer's original boxes or in brown-paper parcels tied with string, filled innumerable fixtures which ranged along every wall from floor to ceiling of the four premises behind the shop-windows; further stocks of a more bulky sort were stored in the cellars. Once a year, when the shop doors closed at the usual time, we settled down to the gloomy task of stock-taking. Night after night we unwrapped parcels, opened boxes, shook off dust, counted and relabelled, made lists of items for disposal and made resolutions to reduce the vast assortment before next year's ordeal came upon us.

It was not a very businesslike business, by modern standards. We tended to hold on to remaining lots of things, year after year, in case there might be a call for them. Seekers after the rare, the outmoded and the obsolete travelled great distances buoyed up with the knowledge that one place remained in London where they might yet find what they sought – and we were that place. My father took a pride in our reputation in that respect. The slow turnover did not worry him.

Such prosperity as we enjoyed came principally from the development of special forms of trading suited to the changing times which the founder could hardly have foreseen. The local retail trade had become negligible as the residential areas sank into decline and near-poverty. What mattered most was the electrical wiring of new London schools and telephone exchanges, the supply of components for the wireless boom, the esoteric trade in the peculiar fitments – tit-pins and the rest – that blindmakers and shopfitters wanted, and the domestic hardware called for on the new suburban estates that were pushing London's outskirts deeper into Kent and Surrey. It was in this context that I tried to hit on something fresh that might happily coincide with my private interests. The outcome eventually was a fledgling department concentrating on the needs of cinemas and theatres, as my special care. I had thus a daytime foothold on the fringe of the performing arts, which already occupied so much of my evenings. It was my passport to the West End. The batteries in usherettes' torches might not be the most glamorous part of showbiz but they were a part of it nevertheless.

The idea began naturally enough in Southwark itself. One or two of the leading stage designers had their workshops in the Boro' and looked to us for tools and the miscellaneous items – screws, hinges, nails, etc. – that they used in the construction of scenery. The cinema boom culminated in the erection at the Elephant and Castle of the largest cinema in Europe, the Trocadero, complete with 'mighty Würlitzer' organ and a stage which mounted a live show lasting an hour or more as an 'interlude' between films. Goodness knows how many people the Trocadero could seat – I believe it was five thousand. Such a momentous innovation on my doorstep, as it were, was a clear signal of the course I should pursue.

A smaller version of the Trocadero followed, the Trocette in Tower Bridge Road; and similar buildings elsewhere established a new social feature in the poorer districts of London. For a very modest sum they provided what many homes lacked – warmth, comfortable seating, wholesome surroundings and a sort of snug privacy. The Trocadero was open for twelve hours a day continuously: it is no reflection on the quality of its entertainment to say that many of its patrons valued it as much for the respite and relief it offered from the squalor they normally endured. That was a lesson I learned in a single sentence from a CID detective who said to me, in a plain matter-of-fact way, 'Incest is not a moral problem in Southwark: it's a housing problem.'

The rise and fall of the cinema in Britain is a fascinating topic. When I visit the United States I am impressed by the fact that the conversation of my friends there concentrates on the latest motion-picture in preference to anything on television: in Britain it is quite the reverse. The town in which I live lost its cinema at about the same time as it lost its railway-station. We have moved – I don't say advanced – from a steam and celluloid culture to a petrol and electronic one.

In that fast-moving history the Trocadero represents for me the golden age of the cinema, with its larger-than-life screen idols, its fan magazines, its ballyhoo and its fantasy. Its perfect symbol was the Würlitzer organ, coming up dramatically through the floor with its console rotating in the spotlights and the organist, Quentin Maclean, already playing as his head came into view. The great organ notes filled and shook the building until, with equal suddenness, the console swirled down out of view and disappeared, leaving behind a sense of fairyland grandeur.

The scope of the stage-show I can best illustrate by a personal anecdote. I chanced to read a brief newspaper account of the bankruptcy of Tom Burke, known as the 'Lancashire Caruso' and one of the few British operatic tenors of any note at that time. I suggested to the manager of the Trocadero, Mick Hyams, that he might offer Burke an engagement in some form of tribute to him as part of the stage-show. The response was to mount a full-scale production of *Cavalleria Rusticana* – as the week's 'interlude' between the two feature films.

The more usual type of interlude tended to take over an element of the old music hall and feature the popular singers of the day, but with the difference that they were now almost invariably American. I used to time my business meetings with the stage manager so that I could stay on and stand in the wings to watch the performers. The most memorable were the Mills Brothers, Louis Armstrong and Sophie Tucker. The Mills Brothers pioneered a kind of close harmony which depended on the meticulous control of their own sound-reproduction equipment: it was a complete and somewhat unwelcome novelty for the stage staff to have their authority usurped by the Mills Brothers' own sound-engineer, who travelled everywhere with them and took charge of their act technically.

The young Louis Armstrong was the most explosively exuberant personality onstage. Not for him the restrained bow to the audience in acknowledgment of their applause: when he hit a final triumphant high note on his trumpet he followed it with a great shout and set off at high speed round the stage on a lap of honour, leaping in the air and punching with his fist like a footballer who has just scored a cup-winning goal. Sophie Tucker was less flamboyant but no less exciting in the way she steadily built up a rhythmic vibrancy as her performance developed. It was uncanny to watch. I stood quite close to her as she happened to favour the side of the stage nearest to me. She used very little movement, standing four-square and compact, a very solid figure beginning to rock, beginning to sway a little, beginning a slow rippling movement unobtrusively but firmly in her body as a heavy rhythm took possession of her. The number inevitably was 'Some of These Days'. The voice was harsh and gritty, at times with an almost growl-like timbre. 'You're gonna miss your red-hot momma some of these days' – as she sang the sweat was running down her and the hard beat of the rhythm became more insistent. Like all great singers she had that curious and invaluable gift of somehow gathering a momentum in her singing until you felt that the very walls of the building must bend in the face of her final assault. At the end she just hammered her way home to an ovation and then stood still for a moment, utterly spent, until she seemed to return to her normal self from some rapt inner state to which her singing had taken her.

From my childhood days I had known London's West End simply as 'theatre-land', with a further acquaintance on a minor scale at Christmas time with the famous toy-shops – Hamley's and Gamage's particularly. My new business life broke fresh ground, taking me to the offices of cinema and theatre owners in Leicester Square and Oxford Street, Soho and the Strand and the many side-streets whose names I gradually learned. The blue plaques on buildings, commemorating historically famous residents, brought London's past alive for me. I was reading voraciously at this time, on buses and trams, in restaurants and cafés and wherever I could be undisturbed for a few minutes: the discovery that Blake had lived in this house, or de Quincey in that one, reinforced the reality of their writings and added depth to my reading of them.

In the loneliness of my first attempts to mark out a literary path for myself to follow I craved the companionship of others in like circumstances. They were not to be found among the friends at Guildford with whom I went to dances and played tennis, nor in the acquaintances of my daily work. It was by chance encounters that I formed my first precarious alliances. Frederic Bontoft, a pianist and composer, happened to make the same railway journey as I did once a week and we began to look forward to this opportunity to talk. He had broken away from his family and was hard pressed to make a living but he had a flat, with a piano, and used to play for me sometimes. To have Chopin played at something like concert standard was a vivid new experience. I bought one of Bontoft's short piano compositions and revived my very limited familiarity with the instrument to play it slowly and awkwardly, but to my own satisfaction. As a man he impressed me with his blunt Yorkshire manners. I admired his single-mindedness and his obstinate defiance of the difficulties that beset him. There was in him, moreover, that specifically bohemian quality which now beckoned to me so irresistibly.

More obviously bohemian was Almon Clark, an Australian playwright, who lived in Soho's Gerrard Street. At this time, 1929–30, Gerrard Street showed a variety of faces to the world. It housed the Gerrard telephone exchange and some highly respectable business offices, including those of Turner Film Productions and the Bulman Back-projection Screen Company with whom I had business dealings. It also housed London's best-known night-club, the Forty-three, run by the celebrated Mrs Meyrick and sometimes raided by the police. It had shops with rather sleazy residential accommodation above them, and in the street itself were always several prostitutes walking their individual beats, with heavily made-up faces and their continually inviting murmur of 'Dearie'.

Al and his father lived in a bedsitter over one of the shops. Their window looked on to Gerrard Street and they found an endless interest in watching the prostitutes. This was to them the stuff of life: it was what they had come to London for. Al's father had originally had the ambition to become an actor but an unexpectedly early death in his family had put him under an overwhelming pressure to sacrifice his personal ambition and take charge of his family's business, on which several female relatives – his mother probably among them – depended utterly. With reluctance he had done his duty, as he saw it. The business prospered under his management, until he could now – at last – withdraw from it and live as he pleased.

It was his pleasure to live in this frowsty bedsitter in Soho, watching the whores as they strolled beneath his window, and pursuing the remote bohemian fantasy that he had nourished, patiently and quietly, over the past thirty years in Australia – reliving now those old ambitions through the plays that his son was writing. When a new work was completed Al's father would wrap it neatly in brown paper and take it to the stage-door of one of the nearby theatres and try to persuade some well-known actor to read it. Rejection meant nothing to him. 'I've left it with Matheson Lang this time,' he would say, 'I'm sure it will appeal to him.' It never did – but Henry Ainley was next on the list, and the list was long.

It was easy for me to identify with father and son, both. The emotional and financial pressures of the family business – how well I knew them and the hopelessness of escape! Al's freedom to write, and to be taken seriously in doing so, was so exactly what I wanted that I became a sort of non-playing member of the enterprise, discussing every stage of his work in close detail and feeling myself involved in it. My business customers in Gerrard Street must sometimes have wondered why I attended so assiduously to their least whim. Any pretext to visit them was most welcome.

I used sometimes to go to a little café in Gerrard Street which was frequented by the prostitutes when they were, as you might say, off duty. Their whole manner and demeanour were quite different then. They were relaxed, glad to rest their feet and usually enjoying a boisterous humour among themselves. They ignored the other customers among whom, on one occasion, I met an unusual trio from Belfast – two men and a girl. The girl's name was Cherry, the men's I forget. All three were of about my age and were aspiring writers. We struck up a friendship and they invited me to a house they had rented in Welwyn Garden City. They had not a single stick of furniture: we sat on up-ended orange boxes and slept on the floor. They read their poems aloud and we talked poetry. I had recently acquired D.H. Lawrence's *Collected Poems*, which I was devoutly imitating, but I had very little knowledge otherwise of contemporary verse and I was eager to learn from them. They gave me a little pocket anthology in blue paper covers, published in Belfast at an incredibly low price – a few pence only – which was to prove a gift of great worth to me. Most of the poems were by names unknown to me. There was a strong American element – Amy Lowell's 'Red Shoes' I remember and Carl Sandburg's 'Cool Tombs' and Vachel Lindsay. But most of all I was captivated by a poem entitled 'Rhapsody on a Windy Night':

> Every street lamp that I pass
> Beats like a fatalistic drum,
> And through the spaces of the dark
> Midnight shakes the memory
> As a madman shakes a dead geranium.

The compelling rhythm took possession of my mind, like some catchy tune that it is impossible to shake off. I had never before met anything like it. The powerful incantatory form, the bold imagery, the strange juxtapositions of ideas – these to me were revolutionary in their impact. Clearly I had a lot to learn, for the name of the poet was wholly unfamiliar to me: T.S. Eliot.

Chapter Seven

WITH the ending of my teenage years I felt a deepening sense of
alienation from my parents, from their way of life and all it
represented. I expect I was insufferably priggish and full of self-
conceit, but my phases of frustration and despair were real enough. I
can see my father now as a good-natured and well-intentioned man
but at the time he was the oppressive symbol of a philistine world in
which golf and bridge were the highest pleasures.

The move to Guildford had not been quite the success that he had
wished. The daily journey was irksome, the setting too rural, and an
acre of sloping chalk downland was undeniably difficult to transform into a neat and formal garden. There were ominous portents
also of financially testing times ahead as the industrial depression
intensified. Uncle Frank intended to stay on but my father sold his
house and moved to a smaller one at Surbiton, where a new housing
estate was being developed. There we settled, with my newly
married brother a short distance away.

It was some consolation to renew my boyhood familiarity with
Richmond Park. When there was a heavy fall of snow my brother
and I fetched out our toboggan, to revive an old enthusiasm, and set
off to the Park. There was quite a crowd, old and young, on the
slopes. We stayed until I was cold and wet and suggested going
home. Stan answered me and I suddenly realised that I could not see
him. When I asked, 'Where are you?', he replied, 'What do you
mean? I'm standing in front of you.' I said, 'Stan, I think I've gone
blind.'

Snow-blindness – which is what it was – I had never heard of. I assumed that, like Job, I had been singled out for some malign act of God which was beyond my comprehension and irreversible. I had to come to terms with the thought that I would never see anything again. I lost consciousness: my brother laid me on the toboggan and towed me to the Park gate. When I came round I was lying on the floor of a doctor's surgery, in front of a fire. My relief at the dawning realisation that I could see the fire is beyond description.

The snow-blindness was precipitated by the fact that, in my late teens, I had grown at an inordinate rate, adding nearly a foot to my height. I had therefore to be convalescent for a while, which gave me a splendid opportunity for uninterrupted reading. I joined the nearest public library and developed a craze for social anthropology, starting with Westermarck and working through surveys of every primitive tribe represented on the library shelves. My father meanwhile observed sadly that I had not asked him to bring home the weekly trade papers – *The Ironmonger* and *The Hardware Trade Journal* – which he felt I should have wanted to see during my enforced absence from the business.

In these last adolescent years of uncertainty I assumed differing personalities experimentally in the same way as my mother tried on hats – to match a mood or emphasise an affinity. I suppose I wanted to explore, while there was still time, the kind of person I might become or avoid becoming. It was that stage of life when each new impression, new experience, new emotion can be almost unbearably vivid – a time when superlatives outnumber comparatives. It was a time too of extraordinarily complex and potent dreams and nightmares which seemed to carry over into my sleeping the daytime introspections and forebodings that I confided to a secret journal.

One night I had a horrifyingly graphic dream in which I committed a murder. I awoke with the conviction that I must somehow get out of the house without arousing my parents, and then disappear to spare them from knowing what I had done. I dressed, packed a bag with a few clothes, tiptoed out of my room and began to creep slowly down the stairs. I had nearly reached the front door when it suddenly dawned on me that I was innocent and had nothing to fear. The murder was a dream only and I was now awake and liberated from it. I sat down on the stairs and wept with relief.

There were inevitable tensions between the different styles of living – different worlds almost – that I was trying to reconcile. I can best identify them now in terms of place: Surbiton, Guildford, Southwark and London's West End. For many other young men and women of my generation the tensions were similar – only the places were different. Surbiton with its surrounding areas was booming in the late twenties: ideal homes for commuters were springing up in hundreds. It was all part of the scene I already knew from my business dealings with the speculative builders in the Kent suburbs, cheerfully cynical men who described their creations as 'Queen Anne fronts and Mary Ann backs'. The knowledge that two of my literary idols, Joseph Conrad and Thomas Hardy, had been numbered briefly among Surbiton residents in earlier days did nothing to mollify my dislike of the place. To me from force of circumstance it seemed a place of exile, by contrast with Guildford which looked now like a paradise lost. In the new home I had bed and board and the smooth surfaces of family life which I knew would be ruffled if I mentioned any of my true interests.

Finding Surbiton to be either barren or hostile I clung to the friendships I had made in my own age-groups at Guildford and spent much of my leisure with them in what looks to me now like a dream world of pleasure and privilege – simple pleasure and modest privilege. We were certainly no *jeunesse dorée* in the aristocratic or wealthy sense, but we were free from the practical worries and anxieties that beset the greater part of mankind. To be convincingly miserable was something we should have had to work at. It would not have come naturally. I ought to have been content with what I certainly enjoyed in the company of Miss Joan Hunter-Dunn – or was it one of her cousins? No one has portrayed that vanished world with such fond accuracy as John Betjeman and there is no denying the sweetness, the romantic sweetness, that leavened its absurdities. At the mid-point between the two wars the superior middle-class style in the Home Counties seemed to imply that few problems remained to be solved and would not be intractable. The old war was a fading memory and we were sure there would not be a new one.

London Road, Southwark, was different again: this was how the world conducted its business, in peace or wartime, in boom or slump, this buying and selling, estimating and bargaining, checking goods in and despatching goods out, in the weird jargon of trade correspondence. By degrees I became accustomed to it until it was almost like entering a second home to walk through the main shop door, flanked in the first stage by counters on either side, with the shorter electrical counter beyond forming part of a central well or quadrangle in which Miss Mabel sat at her typewriter. Right at the back were the two glass-fronted offices of the partners, my father and my uncle, with a connecting door between them.

A place was found for me in the central quadrangle between the switchboard, with its distractingly pretty telephonist, and Mr James, who handled all the blind-makers' trade. 'Farmer' James he was called because he looked and dressed and smelt like an old-fashioned farmer and had a smallholding out in the country where he rose in dawn and darkness to start his day's work. He was good at handling blindmakers, some of whom – like other independent craftsmen – were apt at times to go off on great drinking bouts and forget to pay their bills.

In front of us sat Miss Mabel, though 'sat' is an inadequate word. Anyone can sit but Miss Mabel presided. She set the tone in the territory between the partners' offices and the trade counters. She was no taller than 'six pennorth of coppers' as the phrase went, but she could rise in her dignity to a Britannia-like presence, before which strong men quailed. Among other things Miss Mabel abhorred bad language. She was like 'poor Charlotte' in *Far from the Madding Crowd* – 'never a damn was allowed, mind – not a single item of taking in vain'. Although she had a surname, for use in official documents, she was known to everybody as Miss Mabel and the respect due to her was acknowledged by even the more primitive of Southwark's inhabitants. When they came into the shop they sensed that this frail, trim figure, in her freshly ironed blouse and skirt, with her hair drawn firmly back into a bun, had enough spirit to quell a mutiny if need be.

From the central area a wide doorway led into adjoining premises which were frequented only by the staff – quiet dusty warehouses; dim cellars; a workshop with a forge; and a sort of enlarged sentry-box beside the goods entrance, inhabited by one of my mother's brothers – Uncle Bob – who had found here a refuge from the disappointments of life. One of my father's finest qualities was his quiet acceptance of the role of unofficial guardian and benefactor in various forms to my mother's brothers and sisters. The role of head of the family came naturally to him and extended to all the staff at London Road. Paternalism, in the old-fashioned way, is much derided but in a small undertaking, where everyone knew everyone else, it made for a contented stability: the personal loyalties were mutual and strongly held. It was my personal dilemma that I felt miscast in the role I was expected to play; but while I remained in the business I grew increasingly to appreciate the atmosphere of community which prevailed. It was that, as much as anything, which was difficult to leave.

Above the shop frontage were a few rooms, one of which was

kept for my father and uncle to use as a dressing room if they were going to some formal evening function. It also served as a sort of overflow office when our accountant paid his annual visit. Much of the time it was empty and locked. As I had a key I made the room my private bolt-hole, where I could write in privacy when I had the leisure to do so – at lunch-time, for instance. It was a small poorly furnished room with a wash-basin, a table, a couple of chairs and a single window looking on to a drab jumble of roofs and walls; but I prized it as a sanctuary where I could simply be myself, thinking my own thoughts in peace and dreaming that I might save enough money to go to Italy or France and visit D.H. Lawrence. I suppose my plan was no more than a fantasy as I had not even taken the first practical step of discovering his address and writing to him; nor did I realise how ill he was in the summer of 1929 when I went to the exhibition of his paintings at the Warren Gallery in Maddox Street.

The visit to the exhibition was a typical interlude in a day's business in the West End. Picture galleries were part of the magnetic pull that drew me so willingly to cross the river from Southwark. I had found my way first to the National Gallery and the Tate, and then to the smaller galleries where contemporary artists exhibited.

Coming from a narrow background and with a largely untutored mind I found my open university in the West End, from Soho to Piccadilly. The bookshops of Charing Cross Road and the distinctive food-stores of the foreign communities were necessary parts of the civilising character of the capital city. In such cosmopolitan scenes I felt liberated and inspired. The art galleries, museums, theatres and concert halls of London were to me what the temples of Mecca and Jerusalem might be to others; and when the police raided the Warren Gallery and seized as 'obscene' some of Lawrence's paintings – along with one or two William Blake drawings – I felt it to be an act of sacrilege.

Fortunately I had visited the exhibition during the few days before the police action. My copy of the catalogue amuses me now with its excise stamp which levied two pence from me as a form of entertainment tax. The sixteen oil paintings and a further nine in watercolours were not masterpieces, but nor were they without talent; and they had a secondary value from their associations with Lawrence's literary themes. Their erotic qualities would seem very restrained today. Even in 1929 they would probably have passed unremarked had they been the work of an obscure artist and not of the man who was then the object of a campaign of vilification. While *Lady Chatterley* stayed out of reach the appearance in London of the paintings offered the pretext that Lawrence's detractors could seize. In so doing they widened further the gap, as I saw it, between my generation and the implacably censorious 'old gang'. Lawrence had become our rallying point.

The anarchic turbulence of my feelings at this time found a curious and slightly comic expression a few months later – on 20 October 1929, to be precise – when my twenty-first birthday was to be celebrated. As was the custom there would be a social function combining the basic features of a wedding reception and a private ball, to which all one's friends and relatives were invited. A hotel ballroom and a band were engaged for the night, menus and guest lists were brooded over, and suddenly I felt the need to make some gesture which distanced me from the whole conventional rigmarole. At a suitable moment I wanted my musician friend, Frederic Bontoft, to give a piano recital – some Chopin, one of his own compositions and the Myra Hess arrangement of 'Jesu, Joy of Man's Desiring' were among my requests that I remember. It was, to say the least, an unexpected interlude in the night's dancing. Our guests sat and listened in well-mannered but baffled silence, Fred earned a fee that he desperately needed, and I fancy there was some relief that my eccentricity took such a relatively harmless form. The mandatory singing of 'For He's a Jolly Good Fellow' went off without a hitch.

I came of age therefore just in time to greet the new decade. It is a bogus journalistic device to pretend that the arrival of a new year or a new decade automatically initiates important changes in the style and quality of people's lives, but one can nevertheless recognise something of the kind in the transition from the twenties to the thirties. It was the moment when the wartime children, my contemporaries, were pouring into the adult world from universities and colleges in growing numbers, examining their heritage and formulating their hopes and intentions. The directions they might choose to follow were the new political challenge. As I look back now to 1930 I recognise two events which epitomise that historical moment. One was a letter which appeared in a literary periodical in the summer. The other, preceding and possibly precipitating it, was the death of D.H. Lawrence.

When Byron died young men wore a band of crape on their hats. In March 1930 the news that Lawrence had died at Vence was received in Britain with an equally intense desolation of spirit. Hats were going out of fashion but the aura of black crape was unmistakable and oppressive. By this time I had read virtually everything

Lawrence had published and was deeply influenced by him. I did not know that he was 'consumptive', as victims of tuberculosis were then described, so his death at the relatively early age of forty-four came as a numbing surprise – so unforeseen and unforeseeable that it was difficult to believe.

What was the nature of Lawrence's ascendancy over my contemporaries? Clearly it was something more than his literary merits as a novelist and a poet: these remain valid for later generations. To us he spoke with a particular urgency that responded to our preoccupations, gave us fresh leads in our thinking and our feeling and pointed to new directions that opened hopefully ahead of us. This is more obvious in the area of sexual morality where he was acclaimed – and with comparable vehemence opposed – as a liberating force. From *The Rainbow* at an early stage in his career to *Lady Chatterley's Lover* at the end he was harried and censured by a host of prodnoses, watch committees and self-appointed guardians of public morality. He broke the silence that the old gang were trying to maintain with their squalid little censorships.

The provocative air of 'naughtiness' in the Bright Young Things of the twenties was little more than the froth on the small beer of bourgeois respectability. For the great majority the realities of life continued to be repressive. Marriage tended to be delayed until the man was at least in his mid-twenties and this was indeed a condition of employment among bank clerks, for example. Pre-marital sex could exact severe penalites socially. The sale of contraceptives was considered disreputable: the largest chain of chemists' shops, Boots, refused to stock them.

In an old notebook I find a report of a police-court case which I copied from a newspaper in or about 1930. It has haunted me down the years in its pitiless triviality, which has nevertheless an eloquence from which there is no comfortable escape. It reads thus:

> Man charged with theft at Cardiff Police Court: 'I want to state that it was an act of desperation that caused me to do it. I went to see the branch manager to ask him to give me a rise or any assistance as to rising to another position, as I am only earning twenty-eight shillings and sixpence. I am actually drawing 24/5 on a Friday, and it has become necessary for me to get married. I plead guilty to the charge.' (Age 22, employed by General Electric Co.)

Poor young man! For him it had 'become necessary to get married' at the age of twenty-two. He should have contented himself with furtive acts of masturbation and wet dreams, like his more prudent contemporaries in the holy silence of frustration: at least he might have kept out of gaol and hung on to his starvation wage.

It was Lawrence who seemed to us to challenge that web of malevolent circumstance, and to do so moreover as a direct successor to that other novelist and poet whose later novels – *Tess of the d'Urbervilles* and *Jude the Obscure* – had aroused equally stormy controversies. In many ways Hardy was Lawrence's immediate ancestor. In the preface to *Tess* Hardy observed that 'any shifting of positions, even the best warranted advance, galls somebody's kibe. Such shiftings often begin in sentiment, and such sentiment sometimes begins in a novel.' This concept of the Novel as potentially an antenna capable of sensing the first impulses to a change in social attitudes was certainly supported by the evidence of Hardy's own novels; and it was seized upon and developed more explicitly by Lawrence when he wrote, in *Lady Chatterley's Lover*,

It is the way our sympathy flows and recoils that really determines our lives. And here lies the vast importance of the novel, properly handled. It can inform and lead into new places the flow of our sympathetic consciousness, and it can lead our sympathy away in recoil from things gone dead.

It was in this larger context that Lawrence was to be so influential, and not narrowly as an evangel of the sexual permissiveness of a later generation. If a single sentence can epitomise his essential philosophy it might be this, from his *Studies in Classic American Literature*:

Eat and carouse with Bacchus, or munch dry bread with Jesus, but don't sit down without one of the gods.

It was that sense of a sacramental quality in life that he awakened in us and made us wish to restore. The ideas associated with it are easily recognised as shaping forces in the newly emerged writers of the thirties, notably W.H. Auden. If the desiccated rationalism of Wells and Shaw suddenly became *vieux jeu* it was due as much to Lawrence as to anyone.

In political terms too his writings were similarly disturbing, if in a more cryptic idiom. The ten years from 1912 to 1922 were for Lawrence an intensely personal experience of the European transformation that the Great War precipitated. He left England for

Germany and Italy in 1912, while he was writing *Sons and Lovers*. His wife was German and he returned to the Continent in 1919 after the wartime years in Britain, during which he was associated with Bertrand Russell in opposition to the war. In 1922 he left Europe for Australia where he at once began to write *Kangaroo*. To compare *Sons and Lovers* with *Kangaroo* is to measure the enormous gulf between their two worlds and to realise that Lawrence's comprehension of what had happened and was happening in Europe far exceeded that of any other British writer at that time in imaginative penetration. It was his sophisticated, experienced and often intuitive sense of what was simmering and fermenting beneath the surface of public events that gave him his unique charisma. To make the point plainly I need only add that *Kangaroo* was written before Mussolini's fascists made their march on Rome: any Roman who had read Lawrence could have been expecting them.

The other event in 1930 that I now recall was obscure and ephemeral indeed if set beside the death of Lawrence, but for me the two are closely linked. During that summer there were others beside myself who felt that we had lost a vital leader and were now more than ever isolated and unable to find any cohesion. It was in this time of despondency that a literary weekly, *Everyman*, published a letter under the heading 'The Revolt of Youth' which had surprising consequences. The letter was written by E.M. Barraud and was in effect a call to her fellow readers to stir themselves in some concerted way.

The response was remarkable. According to Geoffrey Trease in his autobiography, *A Whiff of Burnt Boats*, 'Letters of support poured in, filling the columns week after week. There were too many to publish, and some were too good for the wastepaper basket. They were S.O.S. messages from the isolated. The editor handed the whole lot over to his original correspondent and suggested that she was morally bound to do something with them'.

What was happening was a sort of spontaneous combustion among a frustrated student class who so conspicuously lacked what the red-brick universities were able to give later, in the fifties and sixties – education and the opportunity to exchange opinions. I read *Everyman* and instinctively reached out to this promising outline of a cohesion based on assumptions that I could share. An informal meeting was announced and I went to it. The decision was taken to found a new society – the Promethean Society – and to publish, in the Society's name, a magazine. Its title was to be the *Twentieth Century* and it would appear monthly.

The initial excitement sprang simply from being in a large room full of articulate young men and women with shared ideas and ideals and now with a keener sense of purpose stimulated by the *Everyman* correspondence. I have vague recollections of meetings at Gowerdene House in Gower Street and at Bogey's Bar in Southampton Row which crystallise into memories of particular friendships formed then – with Trease himself and 'John' Barraud among the pioneers of the Society, with Hugh Gordon Porteus, Bill Warbey, George Pendle, Tony Barlow and – more particularly in this context – Jon Randell Evans, who edited the *Twentieth Century* during the four years of its existence. Most of us cherished literary ambitions of one sort or another but were novices in the arts of publishing: Jon Evans stood out among us as a professional among amateurs for he was a publishers' reader and as 'Hugh Macmillan' a literary agent as well, so he was clearly a citizen of that world the rest of us were trying to enter. We could not have wished for a better editor. He treated the talents of others with sympathy and encouragement, his own with a self-effacing modesty.

My sudden accession to this company of like-minded contemporaries led on to other friendships. Three poets whom I link with these early meetings were Randall Swingler, John Pudney and George Barker. I recall Hugh Gordon Porteus showing me some remarkable poems submitted by a youth of sixteen, when I had become one of Evans's editorial auxiliaries; that unknown young poet was George Barker. He made his début in the *Twentieth Century* and I must have met him shortly afterwards.

However, I run ahead of my story. In March 1931 the first number of the *Twentieth Century* appeared. It described the unpremeditated origins of the Prometheans, proclaimed their emerging purposes and offered membership for a nominal fee of one shilling. 'There are now', it claimed, 'active groups in almost every big city in the country.' Its contributors included Paul Rotha on Cinema, Fenner Brockway on Disarmament and from George Pendle the first evaluation in England of Ortega y Gasset; but the prevailing tone was set by W.H. Auden in his poem 'Get There If You Can', with its minatory closing couplet:

If we really want to live, we'd better start at once to try;
If we don't, it doesn't matter, but we'd better start to die.

The second number also included a poem, a somewhat scurrilous piece of invective against Lord Beaverbrook and his Empire

Crusade. I can hardly refrain from mentioning it since I was its author. It was my first appearance in print. I read it now with little relish but it preserves nevertheless that moment of elation which comes only once in every author's life – when for the first time he or she steps from the anonymous audience on to the literary stage and makes a bow. I must have felt I had found my true vocation.

Chapter Eight

In the aftermath of Lawrence's death, with the realisation that I had missed my opportunity for going abroad to meet him, I used my summer holiday instead to make a sort of consolatory pilgrimage to the Cornish village of Zennor. I knew he had lived at a cottage on Tregarthen Farm at Zennor during the war and had written there the sequence of poems entitled *Look! We Have Come Through!*: one of the finest of these poems, 'Manifesto', is inscribed 'Zennor'. So in late July 1930 I arrived, with my tent, at Tregarthen Farm, the home of the Hockings – two brothers, two sisters and their aged mother. More than a dozen years had passed since they last saw Lawrence, and their final recollections would have been of his expulsion from Cornwall by police order on an unsupported suspicion that he and Frieda might be enemy spies! The Hockings were evidently surprised by the extent of his fame as I now described it to them. He must have passed completely out of their thoughts in recent years, until they perhaps read a newspaper report of his death.

Lawrence's cottage was one of a pair on the hillside, known as Eagle's Nest. It was a good name for such a lofty isolated spot on the open moor. The cottage itself was tiny, just one room upstairs and one down. The woodwork still showed traces of Lawrence's royal blue paint and I could persuade myself that something of his presence still lingered. The cottage had no occupant at the time, which made it easier for me to people it in my imagination with Lawrence and Frieda and their neighbouring friends, Middleton Murry and

Katherine Mansfield, and Philip Heseltine – better known by his pseudonym as the composer Peter Warlock.

It was my first sight of this remote Cornish landscape, as it had been also for Lawrence. It is part of Old Cornwall, which is the name for the last treeless miles of the peninsula thrusting into the Atlantic – so exposed and gale-torn in winter that no tree can survive here. The hillside is clenched like a fist, stony, craggy, strewn with boulders and brilliantly coloured with gorse and heather, bracken and foxgloves. I had never seen anything like it – so romantically wild, so charged with a visual poetry. It seemed impossible that such scenes could belong to the same country as Southwark and Guildford and Soho. I was enthralled by that first encounter with the far west and have remained so ever since. To cross the Exe and move through the western moors towards the Land's End is to experience a subtle change of key.

Life at Zennor in 1930 still followed traditional patterns. Fish landed locally was more plentiful than meat. There was a tin-mine at work in the next village, Pendeen, where the monotonous rhythm of the pumps in the shaft kept the visitor awake at night, while the inhabitants contentedly slept: what would wake *them* would be the threatening silence if the pumps stopped. On the surprisingly fat pastures the cows yielded a milk rich in cream, as I learned during the days I spent with the Hockings.

The two sisters milked the cows. I thought them strikingly beautiful in a distinctive Cornish way – their eyes so darkly brown as to seem black, their features softly rounded, their hair extremely fine and lustrous. It is the general darkness of complexion that I remember and the silken delicacy of their hair in flowing folds and loops. They moved with the slow easy movements of those who spend their days in the open among animals. I enjoyed the sight of them as they came up slowly with the cows to the farm buildings, and then their composure as they sat to the beasts and drew down the milk from the udders.

The elder brother, William Henry, was physically very like his sisters, with the same glistening Cornish darkness, the same shining black depth of eye; but without their gentleness of voice. William Henry had a sharper edge to the Cornish accent, a burr of masterful authority as befitted the head of the family. He is thinly disguised as John Thomas Buryan in *Kangaroo*, where Lawrence's love for him is expressed unfeignedly. The other brother, Stanley, was in some ways the odd one out. He alone had gone away from Zennor, had been out and about in the great world – even as far as Canada, I

77

believe. Back home again he seemed slightly restless, as if he could no longer immerse himself as deeply in Cornishness as the rest of the family.

While the brothers and sisters busied themselves about the farm the old mother remained immobile beside the kitchen range, tending the permanently and forever stewing pot of black tea that the Cornish love – or used to love. She was happy to have me sit with her and talk about Lawrence. She recalled – as others have done – his delight in the 'ordinary' offices of daily life: for example, the baking of bread or saffron cake. When she was baking he liked to sit beside the range, finding a keen pleasure in each stage of the procedure and somehow giving it a sense of occasion, of achievement. She had liked that about him, particularly. She fished out a long-handled fork and passed it to me. 'Mr Lawrence was very fond of that one – used to like making toast with it.'

As the days passed other little domestic objects were brought out for me to inspect because of their association with Lawrence. There was the chair he normally sat in, an old bureau he occasionally made notes at, the miscellaneous flotsam recovered from the cottage after the sudden departure. And then Stanley handed me an exercise book that Lawrence had given him. 'Some of his writing,' he said.

It was indeed. I soon recognised sections of the essays that had eventually appeared in 1924 as *Studies in Classic American Literature*. Lawrence had begun writing these 'Studies' at Zennor and I suppose he had made a typescript of this draft, or redrafted it, and given the superseded notebook to Stanley. I explained to Stanley that it might be worth quite a lot of money; that I myself was not a collector but that there were collectors who would make offers to him and he should be on his guard to get a fair price if he decided to part with it. I hope he wasn't swindled.

My stay at Zennor was necessarily brief, but those few days were full of vivid detail that flood back into my mind now. I recall the head of a seal swimming near me and looking at first like a dead dog's head, for I could think of nothing else that it might be. My notion of normal seaside life, as I knew it at Bognor or Bexhill, did not include seals. A whale or a shark would not have seemed more improbable. Walking the moors and the narrow lanes I came on the ruined stone walls of abandoned cottages – suddenly pathetic touches of desolation in the flowering profusion of the natural world. The pub at Zennor was called the Tinner's Arms but the heart had gone out of Cornish mining and some of the old native families had abandoned these crumbling homesteads.

78

When I went to a local fête it was the young men and women from the farms who put some life into the proceedings. For them the great event was 'Pitching the Sheaf', a test of skill and strength that I have not seen elsewhere. The sheaf was a tight bundle of rushes and it had to be pitched with a hay-fork over a bar supported between two uprights, like the bar athletes use for the high jump or – more comparably – the pole vault. Inch by inch the bar was moved upwards until only the champion could send the heavy sheaf flying high and clear over the top. The prize, appropriately, was a new pitch-fork and the admiring glances that champions attract.

Returning home I settled down to an outwardly uneventful winter in the oddly assorted dual role I had created for myself as ironmonger–poet. During working hours I was at my desk in Southwark or calling on my customers. At other times I was exploring the new world of the Prometheans, arguing, debating, kicking around fresh ideas that excited me; or withdrawing into the quickening solitude where my own writing took shape and my literary ambitions leaped imaginary hurdles. There was so much to be done. I read on buses and trams and trains and in cheap lunchtime cafés. I filled notebooks with sudden impulses and calmer reworkings.

Among the Prometheans I picked up the crusading temper of the time. I learned the names of the sexual gurus who were going to bring the light of sanity into the darkness of repression and taboo – Havelock Ellis, Norman Haire, Helena Wright. I discovered the hope that Social Credit might solve our economic problems. I caught the urgency of a pacifist ideal and a will to disarmament. And I did not question the presumption that all right-thinking people were to be found on the political left. In the winter of 1930/1 I was intellectually very much a child of my time. I felt I was moving into the centre of things where momentous events were about to happen. The petty details of the family business seemed an irrelevance, in comparison.

And yet – add the dimension of hindsight and the picture changes. Add, to be precise, Wilhelm vom Brück of Velbert in the industrial Ruhr, and the family business seems far from irrelevant. Mr vom Brück was in the business of manufacturing the special types of hinges and other small metal fittings that were used in the furniture trade. I could find customers who wanted such things and I had become interested in the idea of importing from Germany. In the early thirties Mr vom Brück and I were business associates, there-fore. He came to London several times a year and I grew to know him quite well and to like him. He was in middle age, a war veteran of moderately conservative views, with the typical loyalty of an old soldier towards President Hindenburg, who embodied – in his eyes – the hope of German stability. When Hitler first appeared in our conversation he was dismissed scornfully.

The furniture trade was in a particularly interesting state at this time. It was being revolutionised by mass-production methods and by the new marketing technique of hire-purchase. Chains of shops selling cheap furniture on what became known as the 'Never-never' system of payments seemed to spring up overnight. It was a trade in which Jews were prominent. Two of the largest chains were Drage's and Smart Brothers, both Jewish. The proprietors of Smart Brothers were not brothers and their name was not Smart: they were Mr Teller and Mr Goldberg. My Uncle Frank, on the electrical side of our business, did a great deal of work for Smart Brothers but never had a written contract from them, nor needed one: he impressed on me that, with such men, a Jew's word was indeed his bond and would infallibly be honoured. I mention this here for a reason which will shortly become apparent.

The principal factory to which I sold Mr vom Brück's products was situated in an unlikely place which has for me an inescapable symbolism. It was in the grounds of the Empire Exhibition at Wembley. Barely half a dozen years had passed since I had seen Wembley in all its glory. To my schoolboy self, it had then been the ultimate expression of all the patriotic sentiments in which I had been nurtured. No little lad on a choir outing could have had more conventional ideas, or have sung 'Land of Hope and Glory' more devoutly and yearningly than I did. Now it was all different. The Palace of Industry, the Indian Pavilion and the rest of the Exhibition buildings had become factories, warehouses, offices. The ornamental grounds were neglected, the whole place had a makeshift, transient atmosphere. The pompous façades were flaking and peeling. Nobody talked much about the Empire. Our thoughts were nearer home.

The furniture factory at Wembley was part of a different empire – the great commercial and industrial empire of the Wolfson family. My negotiations were with Charles Wolfson: he and vom Brück, when they met, had an easy rapport and an evident respect for each other's abilities. Everything augured well. Indeed everything was well for a year or two. What impresses me now is the gradualness and the inevitability of what happened.

Although I was less than half his age vom Brück seemed to like to confide in me: partly, I think, because I warned him in advance of Britain's going off the gold standard. What possessed me to come up with this gem of economic soothsaying is quite beyond my comprehension, but it saved him a lot of money and it earned for me an oracular reputation which was certainly unmerited. At first he talked to me about the growing violence in the Ruhr and then the open gun-battles in the streets between the communists and Hitler's Brown-shirts. He held to his middle ground, to his faith in the old Field Marshal and the rule of law, but the polarisation began to tug at him. What if only the Nazis could subdue the Reds? The question was not yet spoken but it was in his mind.

Mr Wolfson similarly was troubled with new thoughts. Anti-Semitism was in itself no new thing, but what was happening in Germany was increasingly ominous. As the sense of outrage grew there was a rising conviction among British Jews like himself that, if only for their own self-respect, they must cease to trade with a Germany that tolerated Hitler and his racist doctrines. It was in an atmosphere of mounting and irresistible pressures that I found myself eventually in the Exhibition grounds at Wembley, walking with vom Brück to Wolfson's office in a last bid to preserve our trading relationship and the contract which enshrined it.

Our dilemma had in it the seeds of so much that was to follow. These were two fundamentally decent men forced by events to pursue a course of action that neither had wished to contemplate. It violated Wolfson's probity to renege on a contract. It violated vom Brück's pride to concede that Germany was sinking into the depths of infamy. And I was inescapably trapped between them since their contracts were not with each other but with me as the broker linking them. That we resolved our dilemma without recourse to the law is pleasing to recall; what signifies is the larger portent of what was to come. It was my first insight into the way Europe was heading.

In 1931 and 1932, however, it still seemed possible that Hitler might be checked. That he might even be 'in the fullest sense a Man of Peace' was a view suggested by Wyndham Lewis's book, *Hitler*, to its reviewer in the *Twentieth Century*. Anyway continental Europe was not Britain and we had our own preoccupations. Financial difficulties brought down the Labour government and the consequent election in October 1931 gave a landslide victory to the coalition national government, with Ramsay MacDonald continuing as Prime Minister but now dependent on Tory support. Those of us whose political views were naively idealistic were beginning to come up against unwelcome realities.

My fellow Prometheans held fast nevertheless to the privilege of youth which refuses to lose sight of the larger and further horizons of utopia. On Thursday evenings at 102 Gower Street the topics ranged from the desirability of a world-state to the defence of Epstein's latest sculpture, Genesis, against the attacks of the philistines. A Federation of Progressive Societies was about to co-ordinate all our reforming impulses in the grand design of a new social order. The *Twentieth Century* would become the voice of this Federation.

A more down-to-earth development was an advertisement in the June 1932 number announcing that 'a good BOOKSHOP is being opened this month by a Promethean at 4 PARTON STREET, RED LION SQUARE, LONDON W.C.1.' It was entirely in character that a month later a further advertisement exclaimed 'Not last month but THIS month! ARCHER'S is opening!'

And open it eventually did, to the great benefit of many. Its proprietor, David Archer, has earned himself a place in the literary history of the thirties which none who knew him would wish to deny him, for he was the kindest and most unassuming of men. His bookshop attracted his fellow Prometheans as his original clientele and by degrees a wider circle of young writers and their friends. From selling books to publishing them was a short step and one which comes naturally enough to booksellers. In nearby Red Lion Street Lahr's Bookshop had established its Blue Moon Booklets with titles by T.F. Powys, Rhys Davies and H.E. Bates. David Archer specialised in hitherto unpublished poets – the riskiest of commodities. In his short career the three he launched certainly justified his encouragement and went on to vindicate his judgment: they were David Gascoyne, George Barker and Dylan Thomas. Each made his début as a poet in a slim volume from the Parton Press.

The shop has long since vanished. Parton Street itself is no more – erased from the map by post-war planning of the neighbourhood. It was a short side-street off Southampton Row, leading to Red Lion Square. On the opposite side of the street was Meg's Café, which became the sitting-down complement of the bookshop. After first calling in at Archer's to chat with David, look at the latest books and journals and find a friend or two with time to spare, it was convenient to cross over to Meg's and settle down to a more substantial conversation over a cup of coffee.

The first impression David Archer gave was almost one of self-parody. He was so nearly the effete, effeminate young gentleman who was being sent up in a dozen stage comedies, with his languid manner, his willowy figure, his exaggerated upper-class voice. It was almost too much, even perhaps an imposture – but no, the pedigree was Wellington and Cambridge, with a high-ranking military father in the background. As he came into sharper focus it was the discriminating taste and the sheer generosity of spirit that stood out, supported by a quiet determination to go his own way.

Considered in any limited and conventional manner as a shop-keeper David was not a success. His friends 'borrowed' new books and failed to return them. Debts were apt to be forgiven by him though not to him. The stock tended to erupt in bouts of anarchy. The phone was either being used by someone unable or unwilling to pay for doing so, or it had been cut off by an unsympathetic Postmaster-General. None of this made the least impression on his equanimity. He remained the most even-tempered and cheerfully optimistic of companions.

In the same year that Archer's Bookshop opened – 1932 – I met D.H. Lawrence's widow, Frieda. How I managed to do this I can no longer recall. I suppose someone presented me to her, at a party probably, as a passionate Lawrentian who had recently been to Zennor and had up-to-date news of the Hockings there. Whatever the chance that brought us together, we quickly formed a friendship. Perhaps she had time on her hands while she stayed in London. She invited me to visit and certainly I was quick to seize every opportunity to be with her. She had come to London for several reasons. There were obvious business matters to discuss with Lawrence's publishers and his agents. The loss of Lawrence's will gave rise to legal problems. She also wanted to see the children, now grown up, of her previous marriage and to renew old friendships. She stayed for some months and it was my good fortune that she took me under her wing and put me in touch with some of the principal figures in Lawrence's life.

Twenty years earlier Lawrence had written of Frieda that 'she's got a figure like a fine Rubens woman but her face is almost Greek'. She was still strikingly handsome, her features clean-cut – the nose particularly – but the Grecian quality seemed to me subordinate to the obvious Wagnerian overtones. The leonine mane of tawny hair and the heroic carriage of the head needed only a bronze helmet to authenticate the mythic German heritage. When she laughed, as she often did loudly and heartily, there was no doubting her open-hearted zest for living. Her favourite praise of another person was to say that he or she was 'somebody', meaning somebody to reckon with. Frieda herself, by that yardstick, was certainly somebody.

In London she stayed at the Kingsley Hotel in Bloomsbury. I used to visit her during her afternoon siesta. She lay on the bed propped up against pillows and we talked, in a surprisingly easy way. She did me an immediate kindness by telling me how fortunate I was – not unfortunate as I had believed – that I had not made the journey to meet Lawrence. 'You would have expected the man you know through his books,' she said, 'but you would have met a dying invalid, often fretful and perhaps refusing even to talk to you if he was feeling too weak to do so.'

She valued me, I think, as a representative of the new young generation in England that Lawrence had wanted to get through to but was not sure if he had done so. During the twenties he could have had only a fragmentary and specialised contact with the post-war English attitudes that were emerging while he was in Australia and New Mexico. Perhaps for this reason, when a film producer invited her to Paris to discuss his proposal to film *Lady Chatterley's Lover*, she took me with her as a sort of critical checkpoint. When her mother gave her two letters that Lawrence had written to her in German Frieda suggested I collaborate with her in translating them as I could imitate Lawrence's style in English. Sometimes we discussed my literary ambitions or the likelihood that she would marry again.

On such topics we passed the afternoon until her bedside phone rang. 'It's Kot,' she would say, 'you'd better go down and have tea with him. Tell him I'll come down later.' This, with a great chuckle of merriment. Downstairs I went to find Koteliansky sitting in the lounge and smoking one of his strange Russian cigarettes. These seemed exceptionally long until you realised that half the length consisted of an empty cardboard tube, with the tobacco in the front half.

Koteliansky was a friend from Lawrence's pre-war days. He was a heavily built man, deep-voiced and still with a Russian accent despite his long residence in England. As a professional translator he had introduced Lawrence to Russian literature at an early stage, particularly to Dostoievsky, who greatly influenced Lawrence. At the time when we had tea together he was bitterly scornful of those of Lawrence's friends who were rushing into print with what he considered unseemly haste to present *their* Lawrence. He told me he had preserved many of Lawrence's letters and other papers but would allow nobody to make them public.

Koteliansky's disapproval of the *Lady Chatterley* film project could be taken for granted. He would consider it the ultimate vulgarity. Frieda was undeniably tempted, partly by the prospect of having the title role filled by her daughter, Barbara, an attractive blonde in her mid-twenties who certainly looked the part though she had no acting experience. Barby, as Frieda called her, was one of the party of five who set off to Paris to meet the producer and see his latest film, which was causing a sensation in Paris with hostile crowds protesting outside the cinema.

The reason for these demonstrations of public disapproval was the surprising one that the film showed an explicitly sexual scene: surprising at least to me because I had not thought of the Parisian public as puritanical in that way. The film itself was heavily symbolical in the central European manner – beautifully photographed stallions in misty meadows, a mournful husband driving a car through pouring rain and swallowing aspirins as he peered anxiously through the windscreen, intercut scenes of his wife with her lover culminating in a fragmentary orgasm expressed in a hand, a shoulder, part of her face, a leg. 'She really did it, you know,' said the producer, 'on the studio floor. It was treated very reverently.' He repeated the words with becoming piety. 'Very reverently – only the essential technicians were permitted in the studio.' He wanted it to be understood that *Lady Chatterley* would be treated just as reverently.

We watched in silence and Frieda seemed at first to be impressed, but as the turgidly symbolical sequences grew more portentous she began to laugh and I felt I could relax from my state of alarm. I suppose mine was a puritanism of a different sort, a wish to defend Lawrence's work from crude exploitation.

How long Frieda remained in England I have forgotten. I recall her now in a timeless way as an intervention in my life of startling intensity which began abruptly and unexpectedly, and ended equally abruptly when she returned to New Mexico and began a new chapter in her life with her *bersaglieri* husband, Angelino. During the time I knew her she enlarged my world in many ways. It so happened that we both needed a confidant at that time: although we were so oddly matched in age and background we somehow found a rare accord. The one tangible souvenir I have of those afternoons in the Kingsley Hotel is a letter from Frieda which reminds me that I was on the point of ending a relationship with the first woman I had deeply loved, and that I was writing a novel which I hoped Frieda – in the name of Lawrence, as it were – would endorse in a foreword. Having revealed my private unhappiness to nobody else I apparently asked her to destroy my letter, to which hers came in reply:

Dear Desmond,

I thought your envelope was *Medley* & then it was you & I was so glad. I felt so grateful to you & a bit guilty that I talked to you as I did because perhaps you are too young, that I burden you – but then in that other world, if you are a natural citizen there, then it is all right & *such* a joy!

Yes, poor Emma Goldman, ideas, theories, love of humanity, it's all my eye, an extension of your own self – the fun begins in the awareness of another being if there *is* anything to be aware of. What is Lawrence's value really [is] his *awareness* of all things around him –

I was unhappy & bitter when we met, so were you, & then because we were lucky enough to be a bit aware of each other it all seemed light & was no more – like a miracle! One isn't an anarchist, because one is more engaged in sticking to that other golden city than in destroying their old stuffy town. Why bother about last year's dead leaves when we have new ones to make this year? I went home & wrote a most awful letter to Angelino, letting all the bitterness out so I can love him again.

Yes, we shall always know each other now, it's quite safe – with a real generosity I felt from you. I felt cross with Lawrence too, there he loved humanity more than me, humanity did *nothing* for him, but I did & my soul laboured for him – and he gave it to *them* – I had never thought that before – I may be wrong & selfish – it may have been the greatest he could do for us both – but I don't like humanity, I only love individuals – I may be quite wrong, but that's how I feel.

Barby is just ringing me up, she'll be here in half an hour so I'll burn your letter. Isn't it a pleasure to know this secret of *another* life, one does feel secretive about it – not the 'dirty little secret', but the real secret of the other life – And one musn't betray it, that is the sin against the holy ghost. And I think Lawrence would say to you: watch it, watch it carefully that they don't destroy you – know your enemies! One is so affectionate when one's young.

Of course I'll write an introduction to your book if you want me to. Will it help? Won't they only say you are a Lawrence fan?

my love to you & my goodwill –
        You'll be alright –
                    Yours ever –
                            F.

Chapter Nine

THE two Lawrence letters that Frieda and I had translated were published in the *Twentieth Century* in January 1933 – the twenty-third monthly number of what had become a substantial and influential periodical. During 1932 it had published W.H. Auden's 'A Communist to Others' and a group of notes on Auden's work by Stephen Spender. It had also been the subject of a sensationalist piece in the *Daily Express* under the heading '250 young rebels challenge the whole world'. It was as yet the only forum for my intellectual contemporaries: the many 'little reviews' of the thirties generation did not gather momentum until after *New Verse* appeared at the beginning of 1933.

The title of Auden's poem is symptomatic of the way the tide was running. Its prevailing mood was reinforced by the 'Christmas Carol' in the December issue. As a measure of our disillusion it is worth reproducing (see overleaf).

Our seniors might yearn for the return to pre-war politics and the reformist impulses of Liberalism, but we had no pre-war memory. Asquith and Lloyd George were ghosts in our world. With the rise of a narrowly defined and dogma-ridden Labour Party the clearly obsolescent two-party system was disintegrating in a series of fissions in the political left. In September 1922 I happened to attend the debate in the House of Commons when Archibald Sinclair led the Samuelite Liberals out of the coalition government and crossed the floor to join the Opposition – a dramatic and moving occasion for anyone who could appreciate a classic defence of the Liberal

Christmas Carol

In England there are 2,986,940 unemployed.
,, France ,, ,, 264,509 ,,
,, Germany ,, ,, 5,279,666 ,,
,, Italy ,, ,, 949,408 ,,
,, Austria ,, ,, 275,825 ,,
,, Holland ,, ,, 508,977 ,,
,, Belgium ,, ,, 855,876 ,,
,, Denmark ,, ,,˙ 317,794 ,,
,, the U.S.A ,, ,, 10,000,000 ,,
(approximately)

In England, police baton hunger marchers.
In Germany, " shoot at sight " orders are given to the police.
In the United States, a candidate for president is clubbed and arrested.
In India, 350,000,000 people are held in subjection.
In the Far East, hostile armies are still massed.
In Geneva, seat of the Disarmament Conference, there is martial law. The League building is guarded by machine guns. Troops fire on bodies of workers, killing many of them.

Peace on Earth, Goodwill toward Men

In England — 85,611 applicants, during October, were refused all unemployment benefit.
— 243,522 applicants, during October, received reduced benefit.
— 744,814 applicants, during October, received Poor Relief: an increase of 32.9% on the same figure in 1931,
— 16,000 workers received, during October, wage cuts to a total of a £1,500 weekly wage reduction.
— 130,000 workers were, during October, involved in trade disputes.
— in October, the percentage of unemployment in

Iron Ore and Mining ...	...	...	...	was	49.4%
Lead, Tin and Copper Mining	...	...	...	,,	56.6%
Steel and Iron Melting and Forging	...	...	,,	46.6%
Marine Engineering ...	...	...	...	,,	50.8%
Shipbuilding and Repairing ...	...	...	...	,,	59.5%
Public Works Builders	...	...	...	,,	45.0%

— in eight months, by refusing unemployment benefit in 161,495 cases and reducing it in 289,726 cases, the Exchequer has saved £8,000,000.

BUT — the annual expenditure on armaments is £150,000,000.

HOWEVER:

MR. J. H. THOMAS: " I think the bottom has been reached." (February, 1930).
Lord MELCHETT: " There is an upward trend." (June, 1930).
Daily Express: " By the immutable laws of economics, it cannot go on for ever." (July, 1930).
SIR ARTHUR DORMAN: " We have seen the worst." (August, 1930).
FEDERATION OF BRITISH INDUSTRIES: " We have reached the bottom of the trough." (Nov. 1930).
SIR HERBERT AUSTIN: " I am confident that 1931 will see an improvement." (December, 1930).
SIR WILLIAM MORRIS: " We shall have a revival of trade within six months." (January, 1931).
FEDERATION OF BRITISH INDUSTRIES: " The worst of the slump is over." (May, 1931).
Morning Post: " More signs of trade boom." (September, 1931).
SIR HARRY MCGOWAN: " The dawn is breaking." (February, 1932).
Daily Mail: " The dark cloud has passed." (March, 1932).
SIR HENRY BETTERTON: " We have turned the corner." (March, 1932).
MR. L. S. AMERY: " We are beginning to get out of the wood." (June, 1932).
SIR WILLIAM MORRIS: " I see prosperity right ahead." (August, 1932).
SIR ROBERT HORNE: " Our noses are round the corner." (September, 1932).

So a Very Merry Christmas to You.

principle of free trade, but I realise now that disarray was to be the normal condition, during my lifetime, of the opponents of the Tories.

When the 'Christmas Carol' appeared the Labour Old Guard under Ramsay MacDonald was in alliance with the Tories in the self-styled National government, except that MacDonald's right-hand man, Philip Snowden, had departed with the Liberals. The leadership of the residual Labour opposition had passed, *faute de mieux*, to dear old George Lansbury, who was full of windy sentiment and not much else. The Liberals were split into those who followed John Simon in support of the government and those who followed Herbert Samuel and Sinclair in opposition to it. At the same time an ex-Labour minister, Oswald Mosley, had established his British Union of Fascists. It was against that background that we read and discussed Auden's 'A Communist to Others'. He spoke our language. The political topics that held our attention were associated only incidentally with the conventional parties. How could one take seriously Ramsay Mac, 'Honest Stan' Baldwin, Sam Hoare, Halifax and the rest?

Besides contributing poems, articles and book reviews to the *Twentieth Century* I found myself involved in its distribution also. I had the use of a small car, an Austin Seven, for my business journeys: it was not difficult to arrange my life so that once a month I toured the streets of central London, stopping at the bookshops to deliver copies of the new issue. In the early days the magazine circulated mainly among members and at meetings, but as its reputation grew it found an increasing readership through the bookshops. The stock was held by David Archer so I would drive first to Parton Street and load the back seat of the diminutive Austin with a pile of freshly printed copies and set off to Zwemmer's and the Bomb Shop in Charing Cross Road, Stoneham's in the Strand and the numerous other bookshops in that civilised London of long ago which displayed in their windows the periodicals that a literate public bought – the *Criterion*, *Life & Letters*, *transition*, the *Bookman*, the *London Mercury* and now the *Twentieth Century*.

There was a feeling in the air that these were revolutionary times. The eventual drift into war was as yet no more than a dangerous possibility, to be resisted. If the latest poems contained a deal of doom-laden imagery they had also their equal share of a rhetoric of hope – even of a new Moses and a new Promised Land. Western Europe might be in a bit of a mess but all those Russian tractor-drivers on sunlit horizons seemed to point to a better future.

National planning and comradeship were the magic formula.

And, above all 'newness'. 'Make it New' was Ezra Pound's injunction. 'New' became one of our favourite words. 'Modern' was another. We were self-consciously a *new* generation creating *modern* literature. The footprints ahead of us, that showed the way, were those of Lawrence, Eliot, Auden – men of our own day. We enjoyed therefore a particular buoyancy and sense of freedom. One of the penalties of coming late in the long history of a civilisation is that one is dwarfed and constrained by the weight of tradition, by the long shadows of former glories. William Shenstone was conscious of that in 1761 when he wrote, 'The taste of the present age is somewhat higher than its genius.' However, taste loses its zest and turns sour, until a revolutionary spirit stirs the pot and adds some new ingredient. It was the feeling that we had the good fortune to be living in a period of radical change and innovation that made London in 1933 so exciting a place. Admittedly the sheer gusto of youthfulness puts a spring in one's step anyway, but I think it was more than that. The twenty-five years from 1910 to 1935 saw a drastic realignment in all the arts in Europe under the imprecise but useful heading of 'modernist', applied impartially to Picasso, Stravinsky, Eliot, Joyce and their peers. The newest and humblest recruit felt an exhilaration in enrolling beneath such banners. Without discounting all the miseries of the world – perhaps even because of them – we were on an up-beat.

My personal circumstances were caught up in the general atmosphere of change. After what I can best describe as a trial-marriage which had failed I went to live with Tony and Ruth Barlow. Tony was a fellow Promethean and – as K.E. Barlow – a contributor to the *Twentieth Century*. He and Ruth had a flat overlooking Shepherd's Bush Green, though 'overlooking' is a figure of speech only. The single window that faced the Green was totally covered by an advertisement hoarding which kept their spare bedroom in permanent darkness. This was no drawback in my case as all I wanted it for was to sleep in. The blocked-up window kept the rent down and none of us had much money. Tony was a medical student, engrossed in the final stages of qualification as a doctor at the Middlesex Hospital. Ruth, completing her theatrical training at RADA, was looking hopefully to casting directors for a day's crowd-work in the film studios or a walk-on part in the West End. I had persuaded my father to halve my salary, which was modest enough anyway, and to release me for half the week to concentrate on writing: it was a good and workable compromise which suited us both.

It was the first time I had lived in London, as distinct from the city's suburbs or its outer commuter-belt. From Shepherd's Bush I could walk to Hyde Park, Marble Arch, Oxford Street; I came to believe, and still do, that London withholds the best of itself from all except the pedestrian. There is so much to see that is immobile and too easily hurried past. Among the great spectacular sights that everyone shares there are also the personal discoveries that reflect an individual taste. For me a pleasure lingers from my first sight of Epstein's Rima on the W.H. Hudson memorial in Hyde Park; or from finding the Admiral's Cabin, one of Joseph Conrad's favourite haunts, a basement café down a flight of stairs in the Strand. For everyone it is normal to retain some warmth of affection for the scenes of one's youth but I extol the virtues of London in the thirties with more than common conviction. It was still a city scaled in proportion to human beings, not ants; and its character was of, and for, its indigenous population.

So there we were, the three of us, in the flat behind the Guinness advertisement over the estate agent's shop, happily preparing to astonish the world in our different ways and talking interminably about all the subjects that start with capital letters and are the proper concern of mankind. From being a trio we quite often turned into a quartet, with the addition of one of Ruth's actress-friends, Nancy, who had the special gift of being almost boisterously cheerful in the face of every adversity. When she was professionally 'resting' she earned a few shillings by modelling at the Hammersmith Art School. In the company of Nancy and Ruth my long-standing interest in the theatre took a practical turn. I decided that we must take our destiny in our own hands and launch ourselves as a theatrical enterprise. The immediate necessity was to find a play with just four characters – two male and two female.

It was my task, as the budding author, to go to the public library and examine the literature of world drama in search of a suitable piece to exercise our four talents. I returned in triumph – with Ibsen's *Ghosts*. Tony was obviously made to play Pastor Manders, Ruth would be dignified and distressed as Mrs Alving, I had no doubt of my suitability as Oswald, and Nancy would be pert and sexy as the maid. In that season of bounding confidence the knowledge that Tony and I had never acted anywhere was brushed aside. Rehearsals started in the all-purpose living room and we even got as far as making enquiries about renting Chelsea town hall for a night's performance. Perhaps it was the cost of that which quenched our ardour; or possibly it was the harmonium overhead. It may even be that spring displaced winter and brought other things to do. Whatever the reason our conscientiously prepared version of Ibsen's famous drama was seen by nobody but ourselves. I am sure we were the better for it.

The harmonium belonged to a young woman who lived in the flat on the top floor and had a passion for playing 'The Sheikh of Araby' and one or two hymn-tunes slowly and repeatedly. After what seemed like the seventeenth encore of 'There Is a Green Hill Far Away' Tony would shout up the stairs his demand to know how he was supposed to concentrate on the memorising of medical text-books in the circumstances. This brought the young woman to the head of the stairs, equally eager to learn when she could play her harmonium, if not on her return home after a hard day's work. A state of beautifully balanced deadlock was thus achieved.

Green hills far away in Sussex were one form of escape for us from the merciless harmonium. During this year, 1933, and the next I was in the company of friends who liked to go out of London at weekends to camp in tents or uninhabited cottages. It was a new trend in our generation, influenced partly by the pre-Hitler 'youth movement' in Germany. Thirty years earlier my parents would have gone touring with their cycling club at weekends but, if they stayed away from home overnight, it would have been in a proper bed at an inn or a guesthouse. Had they thought of a tent it would probably have had to be the heavy army-type bell tent and not the portable lightweight that was available to us.

Tony and Ruth had made a friendly contact with a farmer near East Grinstead on whose land we spent our weekends, beside a little stream which was pleasant to lie in on hot days. What it lacked was a pool of some depth so we decided to dam it at a strategic point. This involved finding and carrying large boulders and devising plugs for the interstices. It became a project of the highest importance to us and quite incommunicable to anyone else. As each weekend approached our thoughts centred on some fresh plan to improve the dam. We were scarcely arrived before Tony was splashing upstream, clasping some immense boulder he had dislodged somewhere. Through the intervening years the thought of that dam shines now as the purest action of the creative impulse, unalloyed by the least suspicion of any base motive.

Another friend of these weekend expeditions was John Pudney, who greatly influenced my life at this time. John had begun to make a mark as a poet; a first collection of his poems, *Spring Encounter*, was due to appear in a series published by Methuen, The Gateway Poets, which included the work of yet another friend of this time, Randall Swingler's *Difficult Morning*. The verse of John Pudney is largely forgotten today, I fear – as is Swingler's – but the best of his wartime poems survive in anthologies and deserve to do so. I was certainly impressed by his early work, which had a direct influence from Auden, who had been a dominant figure during their schooldays at Gresham's. As the younger of the two John had taken his cue, in writing poetry, from Auden's example and instruction.

Unlike Auden he had not gone on to university. When I first met him John was working for one of London's leading estate agents and, like me, tended to be out and about in the streets of London on business, with the opportunity to drop into Archer's Bookshop and Meg's Café. His most prized possession was a Scott Flying Squirrel – a motorbike of considerable glamour and unusual design, on which I rode pillion when we set off on a Saturday for nowhere in particular, with the knowledge that we could sleep in a farmer's barn if nothing better offered – though what could be better than a bed of hay on a summer evening? We talked of poets and poetry incessantly, read and criticised each other's poems, and sustained each other's determination to find some more congenial way of earning a living. Quite soon John left the estate agents to join the staff of the BBC.

The friendships that I owe to him are numerous and varied. There was David Cleghorn Thompson, one of Methuen's literary advisers. There was an astonishing Australian singer, Nelson Illingworth. There was A.P. Herbert, one of the great characters of the time, whose daughter, Crystal, John married. I suppose I just hung on to John's coat-tails and found the whole background of my life transformed in no time. Cleghorn Thompson had been appointed Controller of the BBC's Scottish Region at a remarkably early stage in his career, despite the fact that he was not the sort of Scot that John Reith might be expected to choose. His was the romantic Highlander style expressed in the tasteful manner of a dilettante who could versify and compose in a gracefully facile way. In his company you could imagine Bonnie Prince Charlie brought up to date as a 'greenery-yallery Grosvenor Gallery' sort of young man. When he forsook Scotland and advanced on London he was replaced by a sober-sided antithesis, more congenial to Reith and pleasing to the elders of the kirk, the Reverend Melvin Dinwiddie.

In London David Cleghorn Thompson quickly established himself as the radio critic on a national daily, in addition to his work at Methuen's. He had a house in Sussex where his manservant listened to the wireless programmes that David was too busy to hear but would need to write about. He also had a room in Fitzrovia, on the floor above the flat that John Pudney shared with two of his friends in Charlotte Street. This room was kept by David as an occasional *pied-à-terre*. At various times he gave me the use of it and it became for me a second home to Shepherd's Bush.

Nelson Illingworth was one of London's originals in the thirties. Born and bred in Australia he had enjoyed great success as a baritone in America before settling in a top-floor flat beside Oxford Circus. Here he began each day throughout the year by going to Hyde Park and diving in the Serpentine. He showed no desire to sing in public and confined himself to coaching one or two professionals. He was quick to befriend musicians from overseas, particularly refugees from Nazi persecution. In Nelson's flat I first heard Iso Elinson play Chopin, before his broadcasts and recordings established him in British musical life.

In appearance Nelson was tall, lanky, not thin so much as narrow – a rearing column of a man, crowned with a wide-brimmed hat. His personality was warm, loud, outgoing, vigorous in the Australian way with expletives and seeming to have volcanic sources of enthusiasm which erupted at any hour of the day or night. He enjoyed the company of his juniors, bullying and rousing us in a genial way, addressing us impartially as 'boy' and making his flat an open house to us. A meal with Nelson was entirely predictable: it would be curry. It took him hours to prepare, with innumerable sorties to and from the kitchen punctuating his conversation. The kitchen was tiny and, as he bred Siamese cats in it, there was no knowing what unusual ingredients might go into the curry.

The particular object of his pride was his collection of operatic recordings. Caruso, Tetrazzini, indeed all the great names of the first quarter of the century were there. He taught me to appreciate them and would leave me alone in the flat at times to play the gramophone to my heart's content. I knew *Norma* in the voice of Rosa Ponselle thirty years before I had the opportunity to hear Joan Sutherland in the role at Covent Garden.

The Herbert household on the Mall at Hammersmith was on a different scale altogether, with teenage children adding their newly pressing interests to the expanding fame and esteem of their father – A.P.H. of *Punch*, champion of the rights of authors, campaigner for divorce reform, independent Member of Parliament and best-selling novelist. In the literary and theatrical life of the thirties Alan Herbert was one of the most courted figures in London. As a versifier of Gilbertian wit he worked with C.B. Cochran in revue and musical comedy after his earlier association with the triumphant era at the Lyric, Hammersmith, under Sir Nigel Playfair's management.

It was as a friend of his two eldest daughters, Crystal and Jocelyn, that I became a frequent visitor. When A.P.H. was at home he tended to be busy writing or in older company, but he could be a splendid companion when he relaxed with us. I picture him most vividly at the piano or on his boat, the *Water Gypsy*. In such circumstances one saw him at his most endearing. Gathering us round him at the piano he would lead us in *The Beggar's Opera* which we must all have known by heart from constant repetition.

The river, from Hammersmith to Westminster, was almost an extension of A.P.H.'s home territory. The garden of his house ran down to the water's edge, so he could embark from his own jetty. During his years in the House of Commons he must have been the only member who regularly made the journey to Parliament by boat, as his own helmsman.

The proximity of the river had an added significance in the Herbert household on one particular day in the year – the day known to Londoners as Boat Race Day. The annual race from Putney to Mortlake between competing eights from Oxford and Cambridge stirred the loyalties of millions who had never been to either place: for no discernible reason we were all 'Oxford' or 'Cambridge' and wore a dark or light blue ribbon. The race is still an event which attracts the television cameras, but I doubt if London responds as it did in my youth when normal life halted during the race and the subsequent celebrations in the West End made Boat Race Night as wild and unrestrained as New Year's Eve.

The Herberts' party for the race was therefore something to remember. Not only did their house command a splendid view of the river, but it was a view which included Hammersmith Bridge; and students of the race's history knew the strategic significance of that. The first boat to pass under Hammersmith Bridge was virtually certain to win the race. It was the point at which the contest was won and lost, and where therefore the well-informed spectator most wished to be.

To my still innocent eye the spectacle of so many celebrities crammed into a private house was almost awe-inspiring. Not all names which were famous fifty years ago would repay their dropping now but collectively they represented the political, theatrical and literary eminences of London in the thirties. For an unsophisticated observer it was somehow comforting to learn that H.G. Wells or Arnold Bennett or Gordon Selfridge was a human being of more or less normal dimensions, who could compete quite sharply for a plate of sandwiches.

This was the great party of the year but there were lesser ones at the Mall where one had a better chance to get to know individually some of the Herberts' friends: Lawrance Collingwood, for example, who was conducting at Covent Garden at that time, and the sculptor Leon Underwood, who liked to join us in our improvised dancing. Lance Sieveking, who was pioneering avant-garde radio drama with Tyrone Guthrie's plays, was sometimes there; so too were Charles Laughton and Elsa Lanchester. In 1933 Laughton was acting at the Old Vic with Flora Robson in the vintage season that Tyrone Guthrie directed.

Gwen Herbert, Alan's wife, took a party of us to see Laughton in *Measure for Measure*. He was ideally cast as Angelo for he had a particular ability to suggest a character endowed with fine qualities and yet unable to master some inner corruption. Flora Robson was no less perfectly cast as Isabella: no other actress could radiate such a resolute dedication to the ultimate moral principle. The intellectual and emotional duel between them was a masterpiece of acting, such as one is fortunate to see even once in a lifetime. I recall particularly an inspired moment when Laughton advanced to a spotlit apron with the stage in darkness behind him and started the soliloquy which begins by asking 'the tempter or the tempted, who sins most?' and goes on to recognise that it is Isabella's modesty which provokes him to possess her: that he is driven to 'desire her foully for those things, that make her good'. He sees himself in an open struggle with the Devil, crying out

O cunning enemy, that, to catch a saint,
With saints dost bait thy hook!

and at that moment of crisis Laughton suddenly checked and turned his gaze slowly and deliberately to look back over his shoulder. There was a quick indrawing of breath among the audience as, for a moment, we seemed to see a second and satanic figure standing in the shadows behind Laughton. 'O cunning enemy' – it was a stroke of pure genius.

After the performance we went round to Laughton's dressing room to congratulate him. There were five in our party: Gwen Herbert and her two daughters, Crystal and Jocelyn, with John Pudney and myself. Laughton had only one other visitor, who was already there when we arrived – a middle-aged man, very correctly dressed in a conventional way, reclining in an easy chair and saying nothing while Laughton removed his make-up and chatted with us. Our attention was naturally focused on the actor, until he said, 'Oh I forgot to introduce you' and turned towards his other guest. 'This is Mr T.S. Eliot.'

What passed after that, I forget: probably no more than the small talk appropriate to such circumstances. I must have been tongue-tied with sheer disbelief. Until that moment I had no idea what Eliot looked like although I had a powerful sense of his presence in my reading of his poems. The case of Lawrence was quite different for I was familiar with photographs of him almost as soon as I began to read him. I had seen no photograph of Eliot, no portrayal of any sort, nor could I have anticipated that I should meet him in this somewhat bizarre manner. It was its total unexpectedness that made the event so startling. I still cherished the naive assumption that poets looked like poets, or at least did not look like bank managers.

An air of paradox inevitably accompanies thoughts of Eliot. When Frieda Lawrence sent me to visit Middleton Murry the conversation turned to the contemporary poets I admired, and Murry said 'When I was your age I reckoned to know the new poets of that time and I was sure that it would be one of my acquaintance who would have the greatest influence on your generation. But never in my wildest dreams did I expect it to be Tom Eliot.'

It seems a strange judgment now, but Murry was no fool: his astonishment was generally shared on the elder side of the generation gap. For them it was as if a hundred-to-one outsider had won the Derby as Eliot's influence spread through the new readership of the twenties and thirties. But 'Tom'? I hardly forgave Murry that vulgar familiarity, as it seemed to me. Would he next refer to Lawrence as 'Bert'? It so happened that my three literary heroes all used concealing initials – D.H. Lawrence, T.S. Eliot and W.H. Auden – and I was not then prepared to rub shoulders with the great in such a free-and-easy way.

Lawrence I had failed to meet. Auden I had not yet met. The chance encounter at the Old Vic gave substance to my mental image of the poet who made me rethink everything I had ever thought about the nature of poetry. My own copy of Eliot's *Poems 1909–1925* is the third impression, published by Faber and Gwyer in 1928. I bought it at the Poetry Bookshop in Great Russell Street in 1930 or 1931 and, as I look now at my youthful annotations, I can experience again the sense of entry into a new field of language. It was not simply the borrowings from other nations and the arcane allusions, but the use of a vocabulary which seemed to be alienated deliberately from conventionally 'poetic' usage:

Polyphiloprogenitive
The sapient sutlers of the Lord
Drift across the window-panes.

This was not the language to which the Romantics and the Georgians had accustomed us. It had a harder surface. It was, for want of a better word, more 'intellectual'. Yet at the same time there was the easy conversational tone of:

Let us go, through certain half-deserted streets,
The muttering retreats
Of restless nights in one-night cheap hotels
And sawdust restaurants with oyster-shells:

With it all, and underlying all, the subtly rhythmic tone of voice that communicated a stoical pity which lay beyond grief. When I try to identify what it was that Eliot's poems signalled so strongly to us at that time, I think he showed us that a compassion could be compounded of ironies. That was something we needed to discover.

Chapter Ten

By the end of 1933 my principal loyalty was still to the *Twentieth Century* but I had begun to find other editors who would print my work. The editor of the *New English Weekly* gave me a book to review – the first of many – and so too did Gerald Barry, whose *Weekend Review* intended to compete with the *New Statesman*. What I valued even more was the acceptance by the *Listener* of one of my poems, for at that time the weightier periodicals gave little encouragement to the new generation of poets. The *Listener* was the exception to the rule, thanks to the pioneering spirit of its assistant editor Janet Adam Smith, who had been put in charge of this section of the journal. To have a poem printed here was a special mark of distinction among the coffee-drinkers of Meg's Café.

Four months later a poem by Dylan Thomas appeared for the first time in the *Listener*. Shortly afterwards Janet invited us both to tea at her flat in Ladbroke Square – our first meeting. There was one other guest, Michael Roberts, who was engaged to Janet and later married her. Dylan and I knew him by reputation as the ringmaster of the university poets grouped round Auden. His introduction to the symposium, *New Signatures*, had been recognised as a sort of manifesto for them. Outside his literary work he was a schoolmaster, which gave him a general air of authority reinforced by his being a few years older than the rest of us – not quite an uncle figure, more an elder brother.

The tea-party, for all its friendliness, was inevitably intimidating as a kind of initiation ceremony. Back in the street Dylan and I agreed that what was required next was a beer, over which we vowed to meet again on some future visit of his to London. I was left with an impression of a tweedy figure in a porkpie hat, a voice bubbling and loquacious, and a readiness to laugh. We both had plenty of things to occupy us, however, and a year was to pass before I saw him again.

What occupied me particularly at this time was the beginning of a correspondence with T. S. Eliot. In February 1934 I sent him two pieces of opaque atmospheric prose which I hoped might be suitable for the quarterly he edited, the *Criterion*. His letter of rejection was not as discouraging as it might have seemed at first glance:

> I have your letter . . . enclosing two sketches or fragments. While they are interesting, I am afraid that they are too incomprehensible to be effective in separate publication. You, of course, have a general notion, at least, at the back of your mind, in the light of which these are fully intelligible, but as they cannot mean very much to me without knowing more about them, I am afraid that they would mean still less to our readers.
>
> As for these, and also for the matter of reviewing, I suggest that it would be best if you rang up my secretary here and made an appointment to come and see me one morning.

I must have phoned immediately, for the appointment was made to take place within a week. I decided to take with me an essay on the relationship of poetry to drama, and some examples of my book reviews. As I walked up Southampton Row to Faber's offices in Russell Square I felt elated. The prospect of a private audience with the editor of the *Criterion* aroused in me feelings that a pilgrim to the Vatican would understand.

Eliot's office was at the top of the building. I suppose there must have been a staircase but the only recognised way of approach was by a lift of antique design, the like of which I never saw, before or since. It was so counterbalanced that, when empty, it remained stationary, but with a nervous trembling expectancy, like a virgin in dragon country. To set it in motion the passenger grasped and pulled a heavy vertical rope which extended through the floor and ceiling of the compartment. This provided the impetus for the ascent which was accompanied by such strainings and groanings of rope that one might have been aboard a windjammer rounding Cape Horn.

In the little attic room that had probably been a maid's bedroom in the earlier residential history of the building, Eliot had just enough space for a large desk, his own swivel-chair and an upright chair for his guest. Two visitors would have been difficult, three a crowd. What I recall most clearly was a pervasively serene courtesy which seemed to belong to an earlier century than our own. Eliot gave you his whole attention, with no distractions or interruptions; nor did he betray any sign that his was a busy life, with much to be fitted into each day. I think he genuinely enjoyed conversation *tête-à-tête* and actively wished to explore his guest's mind in an unhurried way.

I cannot pretend to recall the details of that first conversation, but it is a certainty that we talked about the theatre, about our previous meeting in Charles Laughton's dressing room, about the essay on the theatre I had brought to submit to him and about Auden's play *The Dance of Death* which was at that very time going into rehearsal with the Group Theatre, its text having been published by Eliot's firm a few months earlier. I had reviewed the book in the *Twentieth Century* and was to comment on the theatre production in the *New English Weekly*. That Eliot's own thoughts were turning increasingly towards the theatre I did not then know.

Eventually the open-fronted lift, like an airborne sentry box, creaked and squeaked its ropy way down to the firm ground of Faber's hall and I departed to await the outcome of Eliot's perusal of the papers I had left with him. An interval of some weeks would not have been unreasonable but to my astonishment he wrote almost immediately:

I like your essay on the Drama, and I like your reviews. If, as I suggested at our meeting, you will send me from time to time suggestions for books that you would like to review, I hope that we may find something for you soon.

I think that I could use your essay on the Drama also, but as you wrote it some months ago, and as you expressed a certain dissatisfaction now, I think that I had better let you have it back, as you may find that you wish to some extent to recast it. Please let me have it again as soon as convenient.

Thus began an association with the *Criterion* and its editor which was to my incalculable benefit. I worked over my drama essay again and resubmitted it in time to appear in the October issue, under the title of 'The Poet in the Theatre'. Its general thrust was not to suggest that the plays of the time would be improved by transliteration from prose into verse, but to urge poets to create a new sort of drama in their own terms as poets. In essence I was heralding the work to come in the next few years from Auden, Eliot, Spender, MacNeice, Christopher Fry, Ronald Duncan and others.

The Group Theatre was an important focus of these innovations. Its initial drive came, I believe, from Rupert Doone with the support of Robert Medley. Doone was primarily a ballet dancer, Medley a designer. As the Group developed it attracted a strong and versatile management team which included Stephen Spender, Benjamin Britten and John Piper. In addition to its theatrical productions it organised lectures and exhibitions and aimed to attract a club membership, much as the more dogmatically left-wing Unity Theatre did. While the conventional playhouses of the West End struggled with the idiocies of censorship and the problems of financial backing this alternative theatre of the clubs captured much of the vitality of a new generation.

At the first performance of *The Dance of Death* Auden enjoyed a hero's reception: at one point a topless dancer in a Polynesian grass skirt whirled and spun her way along the line of the audience to land felicitously in his lap, to general applause. I had a rather surprising conversation with him as he knew I had recently been to some political demonstration about which he wanted to hear the details – particularly the conduct of the mounted police. I don't now recall what the demonstration was about: probably it was a march to protest outside the German Embassy. I was not a particularly zealous demonstrator and I had no deep-seated antagonism to the police, so I was unprepared for Auden's insistence that the key to revolutionary success lay in the morale of the police force. In street demonstrations it was vital, he felt, to neutralise or in some way counter the mounted police.

This may have been a modish attitude that he affected briefly but it made a sharp impression on me, to whom a public protest was one thing and a strategy of concerted street-fighting was something else. At least it emphasised the dilemma at the core of his play, which was to find a literary way through to the moment of climax when Rupert Doone completed the bourgeoisie's dance of death and Marius Goring, as Karl Marx, entered with two young communists to close the performance with the words 'The instruments of production have been too much for him. He is liquidated.'

It was probably the nearest Auden came to a personal identification with Marxism. Coincidentally the *Everyman* magazine started a weekly series on 'Life in Nineteen-thirty-four' under the general title of 'The Modern Point of View', and here the first voice to be heard was Stephen Spender's:

> The hope of the world no longer lies in Capitalist governments, it lies in the will of the common people. Whether they wish to or not, governments seem compelled to go on arming: in this respect they are prey to the interest of the secret armament international. . . . And that is where the people – *das Volk* – comes in. For war provides the situation in which the interests of the Capitalists and the workers really separate. . . . it is not to the interest of the English worker to kill the French or German worker. Because the interests of the workers of all the world are fundamentally the same. In this lies our hope of peace. The weapon with which the workers may fight war is revolution.

That was dated 30 March 1934, and it fairly represents the mood of its time. We were much preoccupied with that sinister image of the 'secret armament international' which could only be countered effectively by another form of internationalism – the uniting of the workers of the world. The issue was formulated as a conflict between national loyalties and class loyalties. We looked, with some uncertainty, for our real enemy. Was it to be a resurgent Germany led by the Nazis in another clash of patriotisms, or a conspiracy of 'merchants of death' peddling weapons for capitalist profit? Might it be neither of these, but perhaps an evil banking system enslaving us financially or even one of the passionless and seismic movements of history which, inch by inch, transform social institutions? In a time of such uncertainties writers looked for a firm and recognised platform from which criticism and satire could be directed at public events; and it was Marxism which seemed best suited for that purpose. It was absolute and unequivocal, where so much else was contingent. It was also, in British intellectual life, relatively new and imperfectly understood, which gave it an uncharacteristic adaptability. For Auden, Spender and their like-minded contemporaries it put on stage some intellectual furniture that it was reasonably safe to sit on, without fear of its collapsing.

While I lived in London, and particularly when I was occupying Cleghorn Thompson's bedsitter in Charlotte Street in the mid-thirties theatregoing was a constant interest of mine. Having been brought up in the outer suburbs I particularly relished the pleasure of walking home after the fall of the curtain. Charlotte Street, lying north of Oxford Street and parallel with Tottenham Court Road, is an easy stroll from Shaftesbury Avenue. Remembering past scrambles to catch the last train to Guildford or Surbiton I became even more convinced that the way to enjoy London was to live in the midst of it, as a pedestrian.

For my purposes Charlotte Street was an ideal centre. Across Oxford Street lay Soho and the main concentration of theatres. Beyond Tottenham Court Road lay Bloomsbury and its literary activities. Frieda Lawrence was no longer at the Kingsley Hotel, but Bloomsbury Street had a new significance for me: here were the offices of *Time & Tide*, owned and edited by Lady Rhondda. In the thirties *Time & Tide* ran a strong third to the *New Statesman* and the *Spectator* among the literary weeklies, with such diverse talents as Malcolm Muggeridge, Norman Angell and Sean O'Casey among its more regular contributors: the idea that it was written 'by women, for women' is a latter-day myth, without foundation. After the closure of the *Weekend Review* I went to see Ellis Roberts at *Time & Tide*, who gave me a book to review, with the charming comment 'I can't refuse a contributor to the *Weekend*, which I greatly admired.' It was the beginning of an enduring association with *Time & Tide*, though Ellis Roberts himself soon departed and my commissioning sessions were with Lorna Moore, a freckled redhead with a nice glint of mischief who later became a BBC producer.

Running westward from Charlotte Street was Mortimer Street, leading through to Portland Place and Broadcasting House. In 1933 Broadcasting House was still a novelty, with Eric Gill to be seen working on his sculptures of Ariel and Prospero on the front of the building. Another well-known figure was on view in the restaurant window of the Langham Hotel opposite, where Sir Henry Wood sat over his lunch each day and looked across to the Queen's Hall. The mid-thirties were an exciting time in the musical world as the BBC's patronage and the growth of its listening audience made themselves felt. The Proms were saved from imminent collapse. The concert-going public was drawing recruits from outside its traditional sources, from those like myself whose tutors were the wireless and the gramophone. Among the revolutionary aspects of the decade some prominence must be given to this upsurge of musical interest. Standing in the promenade at the Queen's Hall became for me as exciting as queuing for the pit at a theatrical first night.

Vintage musical occasions of another sort take my thoughts back, not to Covent Garden as one might expect but to the Alhambra. Like the Queen's Hall, the Alhambra is now no more, demolished to be replaced by a cinema. It stood in Leicester Square, adjacent to Jones's restaurant, where stage people congregated to exchange gossip and hope to find work. The theatrical agencies were hereabouts, where an authentic Minnie Higgs might enter hopefully and come out as Ottoline Du Barry with a half-promise of a place in the back row of the chorus at next season's panto in Derby. Normally the Alhambra was a music hall where one might see the Houston Sisters or Talbot O'Farrell topping the bill, but in the summer of 1933 it was taken over by Colonel De Basil's *Ballets Russes de Monte Carlo*. For those of us too young to have known the great days of Diaghilev this was a wonderful Indian summer of that tradition and those talents. The décor included work by Picasso and Miro. Among the dancers were Massine, Lichine, Baronova and Woizikowsky.

Hitherto the only ballet-dancing I had seen was in miscellaneous music-hall programmes which sought to raise the tone of the entertainment by introducing a romantic *pas de deux* as a brief item. To be able to walk from Charlotte Street to the Alhambra any evening and join the queue for the cheap seats to see *Petrouchka* or *Jeux d'Enfants* was a totally new experience. Like opera it is a world that one must discover in one's own way: the fusion of several arts is the supreme conjuring trick. I was content to marvel at this bringing together of movement, colour, shape, drama and music within the whole vocabulary of the human body. As I write these words I see again two visions in particular. One is of Massine as the miller in De Falla's *Three-cornered Hat* – the epitome of the macho male, arrogant, flame-like, glittering with the sharpness of his vitality, thunderously heeled and with steel-bladed arms, menacingly proud and triumphant. The other is of the empty street in *La Source* when the tramp-figure of Leon Woizikowsky suddenly appears up-stage in a whirling confusion of torn and tattered garments. As he begins to dance his way down-stage the scarecrow muddle of his presence takes on a mocking, teasing quality. Each movement of his body seems to outrage a convention. He is the irredeemable outsider, the lord of misrule, the king of *je m'en foutisme*.

Such are the recollections, dimmed perhaps but far from enfeebled, which make light of the passing of half a century since those days when I could believe the world was my oyster. Nor need that be quite so metaphorically a figure of speech, for a commonplace feature of the time was the modestly priced oyster bar. In a side-street off Shaftesbury Avenue De Hem's specialised in the combination of oysters and draught Guinness: I even doubt if they sold anything else. You stood at the bar to be served with a dozen Whitstables and a pint of the black stout as a quick snack on a theatregoing evening. Why oysters should since have become such a preposterous luxury is beyond my understanding. After all, Dr Johnson used to feed his cat on them.

A particular advantage of living in the heart of London was to be there on Sundays. Without the daily tide of shoppers and workers the mood of the city was quite changed. There was a serenity, a spaciousness, a composure in place of the nervous, fretting hurry of weekdays. On fine Sunday mornings I liked to stroll down Oxford Street to Lyons's Corner House at the Marble Arch where they served a newly invented meal which combined breakfast with lunch: after which I went across to Speakers' Corner in Hyde Park. This was a wonderful intellectual mish-mash, ranging from the fanatical to pure farce and constantly punctured by the sharp wit and bawdy interruptions of the listening crowds. On the soap-boxes were the devout believers in every creed, as well as the agnostics and the atheists; and with them the pedlars of political systems and the impassioned orators who wanted to stop somebody from doing something. With them also were a few nondescripts who had mistaken their vocation and one or two colourful characters who simply enjoyed playing to the crowd. There was Prince Monolulu, the racing tipster, and a largely naked man with a fur loin-cloth who used to pound his hairy chest with his fists and shout: 'I'm a cave-man!'

Sunday evenings in Hyde Park had a very different feature – community hymn-singing of an impromptu sort. It seemed to start with a small group: the familiar tunes attracted passers-by who gradually formed a 'choir' of perhaps two or three hundred. There were no accompanying instruments, just the swelling up of voices as each fresh tune was recognised. During the pauses in the singing an easy comradeship developed. I remember a conversation with a man who was a wayfarer, as distinct from being a tramp. He walked the length and breadth of the country, as a seasonal casual worker. His calendar was a sequence of places where he could find a few days' work. He liked the independence, the ever-changing scene, the fresh acquaintances; and if he passed through London on a Sunday he liked to sing a few hymns in Hyde Park. He was now on his way to Lincolnshire where the potato-growers would pay him a few shillings for his labour.

One reason for my Sunday stroll to the Marble Arch for 'brunch' was the inability to do anything more than boil a kettle in the bedsitter at No. 88 Charlotte Street. I became something of an authority on the restaurants, pubs, tea-shops, coffee stalls and

Corner Houses within walking distance and – no less important – within the reach of whatever money I had in my pocket. Charlotte Street had a variety of bars and restaurants at its southern end, as indeed it still does. In the street itself and spilling into its junction with Percy Street and Rathbone Place were three pubs, the Fitzroy Tavern, the Marquis of Granby and the Wheatsheaf. They were much frequented by young writers and artists and provided the settings, the throne-rooms, for two women who held court nightly as bohemian celebrities. One was Nina Hamnett, whose torso Henri Gaudier-Brzeska immortalised in the sculpture now in the Tate Gallery, and who gave to her autobiography the appropriate title *Laughing Torso*. The other was Betty May, a model associated particularly with the work of Epstein and known to everyone as Tiger Woman. You could not be considered a genuine habitué of Charlotte Street until you had listened to Nina's anecdotes of the Parisian art-world and crossed swords verbally over a glass with Tiger Woman.

The more expensive restaurants tended to be on the east side: L'Etoile, Auguste and – T.S. Eliot's usual choice – Antoine's. More suited to my pocket were Schmidt's and Bertorelli's on the opposite side. Schmidt's has long since gone but it has one imperishable memory for me from the early summer of 1934 when I had a lunch-date there to meet a Miss Dorothy Pantling, of whom I knew very little more than that she was connected in some way with the British Institute in Paris and had suggested that I might perhaps lecture there. I accordingly invited her to lunch, having decided after careful deliberation that Schmidt's would be just a shade more impressive than Bertorelli's but still within the range of what I could afford.

To meet her I had only to walk down Charlotte Street from No. 88 so I busied myself with other things until past midday when I suddenly realised that I had very little cash and certainly not enough to pay for lunch. Could I borrow some? In the flat below there was no sound: John Pudney and his two flatmates were out. I thought quickly of other possibilities but without success. There was only one solution that I could see. In or near Rathbone Place there was a pawnbroker's shop where my watch should raise a loan of a pound or two. Luckily there was still time to get there and back to Schmidt's before we were due to meet. I hurried along Charlotte Street towards Rathbone Place and as I was passing Schmidt's a voice said, 'My, my – we are both punctual, aren't we? I wasn't expecting you yet.' It was Miss Pantling.

Our lunch together must have been one of the oddest meals

imaginable. She can hardly have failed to notice that I hung on grimly to the menu and was deeply absorbed in it though I seemed to have an aversion to everything it offered and ate very little. I was of course calculating at each stage how to keep the final bill within the inadequate sum of money I had in my pocket. It was touch and go to the very last. Coffee? Yes, she would have a coffee. A liqueur with it perhaps? This was a terrible gamble, but – thankfully, no. What of myself? I proclaimed my love of coffee but, alas, it was very bad for me. I had had to give it up temporarily. Just one coffee therefore. I asked for the bill in a flush of triumph. I must still have had twopence ha'penny in hand when we stepped back into Charlotte Street and parted.

The pleasant consequence of this meeting was that I was invited to collaborate with Miss Pantling in preparing a course of lectures on the contemporary English novel to be given in Paris at the British Institute. She would give the bulk of the lectures weekly during the winter, using my notes, but I would go to Paris to give the two lectures that were to be devoted to D.H. Lawrence. The British Institute, in the rue de la Sorbonne, was a part of the University of Paris: the lectures were primarily for Sorbonne students but would be open to the general public.

Shortly after the meeting with Miss Pantling I moved out of Charlotte Street to rent a bedsitter of my own, which John Pudney had offered me. His work at the estate agents' involved dealings with a Soho landlord who specialised in accommodation for prostitutes. Having his own reasons for wishing to appear in a more public-spirited way this landlord decided to convert one of his buildings into a warren of tiny bedsitters for male students – a sort of secular YMCA which he named University Chambers. It was useful for provincial and foreign students at the polytechnic or one of the colleges of London university and for other miscellaneous young men like me. In each room there was just enough space for a narrow bed, a table, a chair, a wash-basin and a wardrobe – not the ideal setting in which to entertain my future wife, but it had to suffice. She admitted later that the invitation to dinner at University Chambers had not immediately suggested perching on the edge of a bed to eat baked beans on toast.

I had first met Barbara at the Trocadero cinema, when I called there in the usual way on business. She was a cashier, in charge of the box-office. It was an unlikely occupation for someone with such a wholly theatrical pedigree. Piecing together our fragmentary conversations I learned that her father was a comedian, her mother a singer and she herself had been cradled in the proverbial prop-basket. The pattern of family life had been determined by the summer season entertaining the holiday-makers at Yarmouth and the winter pantomime in one of the big cities. At other times they were touring or 'resting'.

She was still a child when her mother died, and her father married a teenager. The young bride was far from being the conventionally cruel stepmother but could do little to help Barbara, who tended to be left behind with landladies who quickly found that the promised allowance for the child's maintenance failed to arrive. As soon as she could do so Barbara launched herself on her own stage career and had established her independence by the time her father shot himself. One way and another it was a tough apprenticeship.

Her ambition was to see her name on the posters of the London Palladium. Having achieved that, she decided that her kind of theatre would be swept away by the rise of the cinema. The answer therefore was to win a foothold in the cinema world. The Trocadero at the Elephant and Castle was the symbol of this latest trend in the revolution that was transforming popular entertainment, so there she went and there I met her.

We started our married life in the autumn with the pleasant prospect of a slightly delayed honeymoon in Paris when the time came to give my lectures on Lawrence at the beginning of December. Our first home was in Clapham where we rented a couple of rooms. On Saturday nights our great excitement was the butcher's auction. In those days the Sunday joint was the universal custom for all but the poorest – roast on Sunday, cold on Monday, minced on Tuesday. Consequently the shoulders of Canterbury lamb from New Zealand and the other prime joints of meat that were not sold when the shops shut on Saturday night were going to stay in the butcher's shop until well into next week – unless he could find some last-minute customers. As the shutters began to go up the butcher came to the front of his shop, holding up a joint and calling to the bystanders to bid him a price for it. You could expect a bargain but there was also a warm, friendly, laughing and bantering mood that somehow rounded off the week in a very pleasant way.

My first lecture in Paris was on 8 December, the second a week later. We arrived in the city at daybreak. First impressions are often the most vivid and the Paris that comes back to my mind now was sparkling and clear in the light of the rising sun. By contrast with London's general haziness and the occasional sulphurous opacity of the traditional 'pea-soupers' Paris had a beautiful clarity in that wintry sunshine. I realised the price we paid for the British love of open coal-fires.

Giving the lectures was something of an ordeal. I was ready enough to express my literary convictions on paper but addressing an audience was quite different. My only previous experience had been unsought, when Stephen Spender asked me to deputise for him at a poetry circle in one of the London suburbs. With a foreign audience there was the added complication of the speed at which to speak. We decided that Barbara, sitting at the back, would rest her chin on her right hand if I went too fast, and on her left hand if too slow. Unfortunately she became interested in what I was saying, relaxed her concentration on the signals and made several involuntary changes of the position of her hands, to my bewilderment.

Apart from the lecture days we were free to explore Paris. The great collections of paintings at the Louvre and elsewhere were anticipated pleasures; more novel were the street scenes, the life of the bistros, the craze for dressing children in Scottish tartan, and the French cinema where we discovered the art of Fernandel. This wonderful clown was unknown in England at that time. We sought out every film of his that we could find.

I also went to 12 rue de l'Odéon, the bookshop of Shakespeare and Company, publishers of James Joyce's *Ulysses*. The book was of course unobtainable in England. All except one copy of a printing of 500 copies had been seized and confiscated by the customs officers at Folkestone some years earlier, and individual copies continued to be prohibited imports. Knowing the readiness of my government to protect me from the moral corruption to which I exposed myself by buying a copy I made a brown-paper cover for the book and wrote on it a fictitious title which I judged to be boring enough to quench the curiosity of anyone who examined my baggage – 'An Analysis of the Epic Poem, from Homer to Joyce' by Johann Zult.

I had hoped to meet Joyce while I was in Paris and a meeting had indeed been arranged but he had to go urgently to Switzerland to see the eye specialist who cared for his dangerously failing eyesight. Instead I saw his amanuensis, Stuart Gilbert, who was going to give the lecture on Joyce in the series at the British Institute. Gilbert showed me the manuscript of *Finnegans Wake*, then in progress. It was supported on a lectern as Joyce liked to stand when he was modifying the texture of his prose. The arrangement seemed akin to the illumination of a mediaeval work, with verbal rather than graphic embellishments in the form of punning echoes of several languages, literary allusions, musical references and every device that a wide-ranging scholarship could bring to bear. I was particularly interested in a phrase which described the smoking of a pipe. I quote from memory but, I believe, accurately: 'with my GBD in my FACE and my solfanelli in my shelly-holders'. I happened to possess a GBD, which was a make of briar pipe, popular in those days. The letters GBD with FACE make up the octave of the tonic sol-fa, and 'solfanelli' is Italian for matches. And so on and on went the play of Joycean ingenuity.

I was more fortunate in meeting Jacques Maritain, in his home at Meudon. I knew him as a contributor to the *Criterion* and as a Thomist philosopher with a keen insight into the intellectual problems of the time. As we sat and talked in his tastefully plain, rather austere room I gained from him a deepening sense of that 'European mind' which was one of Eliot's constant objectives as an editor. British people are always susceptible to the urge to withdraw into their island mentality, and the lassitude after the 1914–18 war may have encouraged that. The ambiguity of Eliot's own position – not quite an American, not quite an Englishman – expressed itself naturally in cosmopolitan terms. One of the most powerful influences exerted by the *Criterion* was its responsiveness to the cultural forces in Europe.

Supported by my payment after the second lecture we decided to stay on in Paris until Christmas unless the money ran out before then. These were days of sheer delight, expressing themselves symbolically in a flashing electric sign which became for us a familiar sight. 'Chez Dupont', it proclaimed in bright red letters, 'Tout est bon.' It became our catch-phrase, our personal motto: *tout est bon.*

Arriving back in London we had just enough pennies for the tram fare to Clapham. The new year, 1935, looked full of promise. With the money from my *Criterion* article, published in the previous autumn, I had bought a portable typewriter of which I was immensely proud. It was a landmark, in its way, for it was the outward and visible sign of my professionalism as a writer. Who could tell what masterpieces might come clacking from those shining keys? I had had some poems published in the *Bookman* and I was contributing reviews regularly to *Time & Tide* and the *New English Weekly*. It seemed a propitious moment to say goodbye to our Clapham landlady and to move out of London to a place of our own.

We found a small cottage to rent – one room up and one down, with a lean-to scullery – in the Hertfordshire village of Radlett, and here we began a settled family life. Until the imminence of our first child made us look for something larger Barbara and I revelled in our possession of the tiny cottage and the independence it gave us. Instead of being confined to the upstairs rooms of the terraced house in Clapham we now had our own front door and our own garden. Tony and Ruth Barlow had also moved to Radlett, but to a flat, so our garden on summer afternoons brought the four of us together, lying on the lawn with a large freshly baked and rapidly disappearing cake between us. In retrospect it seems idyllic: perhaps it was.

The cottage was one of a pair, our neighbour being a countrywoman of great age and even greater energy who had her line of washing out in the garden at the crack of dawn. Her unquenchable cheerfulness was clouded only by what she regarded as the untimely death of 'Dad', with whom she had enjoyed a robust and unconventional relationship. Our landlady, by contrast, was a very refined and genteel lady who believed in fairies for the incontrovertible reason that she frequently saw them and spoke to them. Her admiring husband, usually to be found two paces behind her – as if as a mark of respect – often assured us that his wife 'always strikes the higher note'. And so she did.

Although Radlett was considered in those days to be 'country' it was also very convenient for London. I had only to bicycle to the Underground station at Edgware and if I arrived there early enough – before 7.30 a.m., I believe – I could buy at a reduced price what in those days was called a Workman's Ticket. My own work was finally loosening its ties with the family business as I found I could hope to survive as a freelance author. With her childhood background of the ups and downs of theatrical life Barbara was used to coping with times of shortage. Once a week we had our Sixpenny Day, when sixpence had to cover the cost of the day's food. It was no hardship. There's a lot to be said in favour of herrings.

Chapter Eleven

THE January edition of *Twentieth Century* in 1935 contained an announcement of its temporary suspension of publication. Subsequently it failed to reappear. Under the pressure of C.E.M. Joad's enthusiasm for a grand consortium of progressive groups the Promethean Society had merged with others who were expected to augment the journal's readership. Such hopes were disappointed. *Twentieth Century* had probably diffused its energies in too many directions; or perhaps it had fulfilled its proper mission. In 1931 it raised the one standard round which many of us could rally and it had that unique distinction for two years until the new generation of 'little reviews' began to appear. The original *Little Review* was of course an American enterprise launched by Margaret Anderson and Jane Heap, but the title is a good generic one and has been adopted in that sense. In Britain Geoffrey Grigson started *New Verse* in January 1933. *Cambridge Left* followed in the summer of that year, urging its readers to 'choose buttercups or hunger-marcher' and leaving little doubt as to which it recommended. Nineteen-thirty-four brought the *Left Review* and Roger Roughton presented *Contemporary Poetry and Prose* in 1936. The most direct challenge to *New Verse* came in 1937 from Julian Symons with his *Twentieth Century Verse*.

The list is far from exhaustive but sufficiently represents what was an important feature of the thirties. It was in the little reviews that reputations were very largely made and unmade, among ourselves. Undeniably we all hoped for wider recognition, for publication of volumes of our poems, acclamation of our novels, even some payment for our efforts. Meanwhile we read the latest *New Verse* or *Left Review* with all the close attention of a stockbroker noting the movements of share prices: Day Lewis up a couple of points, good half-yearly results expected from George Barker, Ruth Pitter dull.

One more of such publications requires to be mentioned here, though at the time I had not heard of it. This was *Purpose*, a quarterly with quite a substantial history but a much diminished impact. At the beginning of 1935 the suggestion was made that I should try to reanimate it. How this idea originated I do not know but I imagine it was part of the general rethinking of the Chandos Group, following the sudden death in the previous November of A.R. Orage. The convenor of the Chandos Group was W.T. Symons, who virtually owned and edited *Purpose* and had been closely associated with Orage in the great days of the *New Age* and more recently with Orage's *New English Weekly*.

I had become a frequent contributor to the *New English Weekly* and enjoyed a particular friendship with Philip Mairet, who was Orage's right-hand man and literary editor. It was Mairet who took command of the weekly after Orage's death and it was the stalwarts of the Chandos Group – Maurice Reckitt and V.A. Demant – who formed the paper's management committee with T.S. Eliot and Orage's widow, Jessie. At that time of sudden realignment I guess that Symons decided to overhaul *Purpose*, and it would probably be Mairet and Eliot who recommended me to him. In March I had a letter from Eliot which concluded:

> I shall be interested if you can do something with *Purpose*. I have known Symons, the Editor, for a long time, and he is an extremely nice fellow. I hope you will get something out of it. That is the main thing.

Before I had an opportunity to meet Symons there was a more immediate concern with David Archer's latest enterprise at the Parton Street bookshop. This was the publication of the third of his new poets. The second, George Barker, had had a success with his *Thirty Preliminary Poems* a year earlier. Now it was Dylan Thomas's *Eighteen Poems*, partly sponsored by the *Sunday Referee*, in whose columns Victor Neuberg had been the first to recognise Dylan's quality.

I had not met Dylan again since the tea-party at Janet Adam Smith's but I had seen more of his poems in the meantime and I was greatly excited by them. *Time & Tide* agreed that I should review the

Above: *Herbert Hawkins, my father (front row, left), was a passionate cyclist and a member of the local cycling club. My mother's brother, Sidney Shepherd, is third from the left in the front row.*

Left: *My great-grandfather Alexander Hawkins, founder of the family business.*

Below: *Myself, aged about eight.*

East Sheen Avenue.

Above: *My first childhood home was 103 East Sheen Avenue. Later we moved to Number 108.*

Stars of the 1920s music hall, (left) Little Tich and (below) Marie Lloyd.

Above: *A portrait taken when I was about twenty-six.* Left: *Barbara and I at our cottage in Radlett, Hertfordshire.*

Below: *Barbara, photographed a few months after we met.*

Left: *Charles Laughton as Angelo and Flora Robson as Isabella in Tyrone Guthrie's memorable 1933 production of* Measure for Measure.

Below: *Alan Herbert (A.P.H.) with his wife Gwen.*

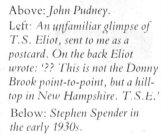

Above: *John Pudney.*

Left: *An unfamiliar glimpse of T.S. Eliot, sent to me as a postcard. On the back Eliot wrote: '?? This is not the Donny Brook point-to-point, but a hilltop in New Hampshire. T.S.E.'*

Below: *Stephen Spender in the early 1930s.*

Above: *Ezra Pound,
painted by Wyndham Lewis.*

Left: *Frieda Lawrence.*

DYLAN THOMAS
From the painting by Augustus John

Dylon to Desmond
August 1939

A characteristic card from Dylan Thomas – a copy of his portrait, inscribed and 'signed' with his upside-down photograph.

THE AUTHOR

DESMOND HAWKINS was educated at Bognor Regis and Cranleigh. He worked for a time in the family business, which provided excellent facilities for walking about London and writing poems in cafés. Deciding this must be bad for the family business he transferred his interests to writing, and his first contributions appeared in the Twentieth Century, New English Weekly and the Week-end Review. Many of his poems, reviews and articles have been accepted by The Listener, Spectator, New Statesman, Time and Tide, and several of the monthly reviews.

The back of the Penguin cover of Hawk among the Sparrows, *my first novel, published in 1939.*

book and I believe mine was the first signed notice to appear in the national press: it was certainly one of the most enthusiastic. Critics do not always want to recall every word they wrote fifty years ago but I am pleased to repeat this extract from my article:

> Mr. Auden is already a landmark. His own poetry stands clear above fashion. But the Audenesque convention is nearly ended; and I credit Dylan Thomas with being the first considerable poet to break through fashionable limitation and speak an unborrowed language, without excluding anything that has preceded him. Barker and others have promised this, but Dylan Thomas goes much further towards realization. This is not merely a book of unusual promise; it is more probably the sort of bomb that bursts not more than once in three years.

The date was 9 February 1935.

In the early spring of 1935 the editorial opportunity of *Purpose* encouraged me to start drawing together the group of potential contributors whom I hoped to introduce into it. There was an important legacy from the *Twentieth Century* of critics and essayists whose general intellectual stance I shared and with whom I had by this time formed close friendships – Hugh Gordon Porteus, Tony Barlow, George Pendle and Paul Beard. The two former were now, as I was, contributing to the *Criterion*. Among the poets I turned particularly for support to Randall Swingler, George Barker, John Pudney and Dylan Thomas. By May they were responding to my invitations. Barker wrote from Finchampstead, where he and Jessie were staying briefly:

> I am very glad to see that *Purpose* has actually got under way and send you about the only poem I have recently done apart from my very long one. I hope that you like it and if in the interval between now and your publication date I am able (I'm dry these days) to write anything of the sort that's useable I'll send it. What chances are there of my doing a briefish review – I have got to make an attempt at organising some critical ideas and can think of no better way of doing so.

In my reply I suggested that he should write an article on Ezra Pound, reviewing Pound's new volume of *The Cantos*. This is his answer:

I'm glad you like the poem; I like it a lot too, although it's a type of work with which I think I have finished. It seems so absurdly irrelevant to continue singing of personal things or even personal aspects.

But I write chiefly to ask if I can review Marianne Moore or Day Lewis or the book of William Empson's poems which I understand Chatto are about to publish. As for the article on Pound, *if* I am capable of doing this, I will. But I suffer much doubt of my critical faculty.

It must have been about a year since I had met Dylan Thomas and I imagine it was David Archer who put me in touch with him again. In mid-May Dylan wrote from Cheshire, where he was visiting:

Thank you so much for your letter. Of course I remember you well. And thank you for your criticism in Time and Tide. I've been so unwell during the last month or two that I haven't been able to write to you about it, but I do appreciate all the kind things you said. On the whole the literary weeklies have treated that book of mine in a very gentlemanly way, but, apart from your review and one other, there were no constructive comments. Those privately coded blocks of feeling, derived from personal, unpoetical, or even anti-poetical, complexes must certainly be done away with before I write any more – or, at least, before I write any better, and I must do something about my policeman rhythms.

I'm so glad to hear that you've got the opportunity of publishing uncommercial and 'tolerably specialised' criticism, and I'd be awfully pleased to do anything I could. I don't know whether I'm capable of even a 'tolerable' specialisation. Poetry, Jacobean and Metaphysical, and music, minus the more intri- cate technicalities, mysticism (honest), and psychology (abnormal for preference) are, for Purpose's purpose, about the only things I appreciate sufficiently. Perhaps I can do something for you on those lines?

I'm staying in Cheshire until the end of the week, and then returning to London for some days. Somebody told me you were living in the country, but, if you happen to be in town when I am, perhaps we could meet somewhere – 'somewhere' inevitably means a pub – and talk over things. If that's not possible, will you let me know before Monday?

And, of course, I'd be delighted to send you or, preferably to give you, some poems.

I arranged to meet Dylan when he returned to London from Cheshire though I am not sure if it was at a pub – which was to become our custom – or at Archer's bookshop, which would have been an obvious rendezvous. Times were changing there since the Romilly brothers ran away from their public school, Wellington, and started the magazine *Out of Bounds*. Archer, himself a Wellingtonian, was the publisher of this 'progressive journal of the public schools' which was dedicated to the destruction of the public-school system, as conventionally understood, and was instantly banned by almost every headmaster. Its editor, Esmond Romilly, had to live with the fact that he was Winston Churchill's nephew and therefore newsworthy. The bookshop acquired an added notoriety – or celebrity – and well-known visitors appeared more frequently. I recall one morning when Auden and T. E. Lawrence arrived almost simultaneously. Lawrence talked about an arm-test that interested him and I fancy he claimed to perform: the gripping of an army rifle by the muzzle and lifting it with an unbent arm to a horizontal position.

Others came and went, from curiosity or a desire to be 'in the swim', or simply because they were young and hopeful and needed the contact with kindred spirits. There was usually a fresh acquaintance to be made – new poets like Maurice Carpenter and Ruthven Todd, or such promising young novelists as Pamela Hansford Johnson and Rosalind Wade. By 1935, though, David Archer's own interests were moving more in the direction of social problems and away from literature as such.

The Parton Press edition of *Eighteen Poems* would be the obvious topic that Dylan and I discussed, together with the prospect of his contributing to *Purpose*. We very quickly found an easy basis for friendship and met frequently from then onwards whenever Dylan was in London during the next few years. The usual plan was to meet in the morning at opening time at one of the pubs in the Charlotte Street area and stay until closing time, after which we might move on to one of the many clubs which flourished outside the licensing laws. Our drink was beer, usually the popular mixture of mild and bitter, known jocularly as M & B or in the vernacular as 'an arf of arf-'n'-arf'. I never knew Dylan to drink anything other than beer in our long daytime sessions.

Sometimes John Pudney or 'Hugo' Porteus would join us but

usually we were on our own, with the possible addition of any congenial soul who happened to be drinking beside us and chipped into our conversation: Fluffy the chorus-girl, of whom more later, was one such. As for the conversation itself, what strikes me in retrospect is its variety. The topics mentioned in Dylan's letter are a good starting-point. Poetry 'Jacobean and Metaphysical' was an interest we shared. I later edited the volume of Donne's verse and prose in the Nelson classics series so we had a common enthusiasm to enjoy. 'Mysticism and abnormal psychology' were very much at the core of Dylan's outlook. He had a fund of stories about madness, lunatic asylums and strange symbolic possessions – usually funny stories, not solemn ones. He had a quickly volatile, chuckling, relishing sense of humour. He certainly loved the 'Gothic'. Beddoes must have been his sort of poet at this time though I can't say with certainty that we talked about him: I merely can't believe that we didn't.

Our own contemporaries were an inexhaustible topic – usually of derision, occasionally of grudging admiration, as is the way with competitive young men. If we had just acquired a fresh number of *New Verse* we sat in judgment on it to our own satisfaction, page by page, poem by poem. Eliot and Auden were virtually above criticism, but everyone else was fair game.

Dylan at this time was quite slim and there was none of the puffiness that his features developed later. He had an exceptionally fine complexion, a skin of milky purity and startlingly vivid eyes. In general there was a well-mothered, cherubic quality about him. I once described him as a 'deboshed choirboy' and I cannot improve on that. His lower lip had, in its fulness, an indulgent pouting quality – particularly when a cigarette hung, drooping, from it.

He could hardly have been more distinctly different from George Barker, with whom his name was often linked by critics in the same way that Auden's was linked with Spender's. Dylan and George were close in age and both had precocious talents which had not been polished at a university, but there the similarity ended. Barker was darkly handsome and liked to cultivate an elegant air of indolence. His voice was low-keyed and musical, his conversation among friends tended to be almost conspiratorial and shadowed. He loved the soft syllables of words as Swinburne loved them. In the gregarious life of London his impulse was to withdraw into a more private world, which he duly found in Dorset.

Dylan was not handsome. His attractiveness sprang from his ebullient vitality, which expressed itself in a seemingly unquenchable zest for whatever the minute-by-minute passage of the day had to offer. He had a natural bonhomie, an affectionateness, a sheer delight in warm human company, which I suppose lay at the root of his undoing later. Words to him were like flags and banners, to be seized and waved in tumultuous signallings. They were the raw stuff of great feats of eloquence, of oratory. His voice contained the nature of an actor. There was moreover something faintly strange and disturbing about his speech that I did not understand until much later, when I read Constantine Fitzgibbon's account of Dylan's childhood. Certain vowel sounds carried a preciously 'Kensington' overtone, about which I used to tease him. Being the 'Swansea Hamlet' was his own acknowledgment of it. I now realise that it was the legacy of those elocution lessons arranged by his father to iron out any 'Welshness' from Dylan's diction. When I hear a recording of one of his magnificent recitals of poetry I still detect the momentary over-fastidious colouring of a vowel for which those wicked old elocutionist practices were responsible.

During the summer of 1935 we decided to collaborate in what we spoke of as a book, but that was more truly an amusing game to play while we were drinking together. To give Dylan a source of income Geoffrey Grigson, who was then literary editor of the *Morning Post*, offered him the job of reviewing new thrillers and whodunnits – a not severely exacting task which earned him a few pounds. Consequently this sort of book became a topic of our conversation and we decided that the creation of such a literary work was not beyond our combined abilities. As candidate for the role of the corpse, without which no such book is complete, none could appeal to us more than the Poet Laureate. We dubbed him 'the King's Canary' and fell to considering which of our contemporaries might most convincingly be cast as the murderer. This offered immense scope for lampooning everyone in the literary world worth lampooning and even some who weren't.

The first step was to coin thinly disguised versions of their names so that, as examples, Middleton Murry and Christopher Isherwood became Widdleton Wurry and Christopher Wishicood. The full cast list, which survives, was undeniably scurrilous, probably actionable, and too often in the vein of what is called Fourth Form humour. It may not be dazzlingly witty to read but it was great fun to write. To settle down in the Marquis of Granby to a session on our *Murder of the King's Canary* was one of the undoubted pleasures of that summer. We lingered lovingly over the naming of participants and postponed the tedious business of writing the narrative of events. A plot capable of supporting about fifty suspects was not easy to come by.

A pseudonym to conceal our authorship was a clear necessity and Red Herring commended itself. I drafted a preliminary letter to the reader which, despite its roughness, may be worth exhuming for its atmosphere of the mid-thirties:

Dear Reader – Here begins my letter;
And so that you may know me better
I've signed my name and made my mark;
A pseudonym – It's just a lark –
This way I dodge the critics' rage.
'Red Herring' on my title-page
May leave them thinking, all their days,
That I'm some friend they ought to praise.
So there you are. You make your choice.
I may be Eliot or James Joyce
(And what a riot that would be,
The Dubliner or TSE).
Maybe I'm Pound or Raymond Mortimer
Or a secret devotee of Gautama;
Maybe I'm Roughton or Ruth Pitter,
Dylan Thomas (mine's a bitter),
Geoffrey Grigson or Keidrych Rhys,
Wystan Auden or MacNeice.
I might perhaps be Wynyard Browne
Or some such dashing man-about-town.
You take your pick, as I have said,
And make me – if you like – a Red:
Randall Swingler or David Daiches,
Or one of those who drops his aitches,
And therefore is esteemed by you
Authentically *Left Review*.
Your wildest choice will serve my end –
So long as you remain my friend.
                                    Red Herring

By September 1935 we had some kind of working plan. When Dylan went back to Wales he was to draft the first chapter. The customary pattern of his life seemed to require sorties to London which stimulated him and built up a necessary head of steam for the subsequent quiet spell at home when he concentrated on his writing. In London he had one or two guardian angels who cared for him in a more orderly way – Norman Cameron, for instance, himself a fine poet who merits more attention than he is given. Cameron would take Dylan home, sober him up and give him some peaceful surroundings in which to write. But when Dylan was on the rampage there was no stopping him; and the September visit was one such occasion, as I learned when he eventually wrote to me on 16 September:

> Are you annoyed at not hearing from me? The truth is that from the time I left you until the day before yesterday, when I arrived home, I've been on the blindest blind in the world and didn't know what day it was or what week or anything, lost most of my little property including many, to me, valuable papers, and, what is worse for me, my job on the Morning Post. I can only excuse myself by pretending that it was practice for the more alcoholic pages of our King's Canary.
>
> I don't remember whether you gave me the completed list of names of characters or not, and if you did I lost them. So, before I can begin my part, do send the full list along. I'll be able tomorrow, when my hand doesn't shake so much, to work on the opening pages but I can't do much without all the Chapfork Benders etc. So send 'em soon. We must – and the Lord knows it's my fault alone – get to work.
>
> What about the poems? Have you, as I thought you might, decided that the shorter one is better for your purpose?
>
> Write & tell me anyway. And I'm so sorry for the delay.
>
> P.S.
>
> Do you remember Fluffy, the
> chorus-girl with glasses?
> It was mostly her fault, the
> nice, nice bitch.

Fluffy was a chance acquaintance in the Marquis of Granby – a very attractive girl who was in a show at the Kingston Empire. She did indeed wear glasses, at any rate offstage, and confounded the popular rhyme by demonstrating that – where she was concerned – men *did* make passes at girls who wore glasses. She wanted Dylan and me to go out to Kingston to see her performance. I was unable to do so. Dylan apparently did go.

The loss of his job on the *Morning Post* calls to mind an earlier misfortune of the same sort, which was connected with Nina

Hamnett. Dylan and I seldom drank in the Fitzroy but we were there one day when Nina joined us and asked him if he had read her autobiography.

'Read it?' he replied. 'I certainly have. I had to review it for a Welsh paper and the editor was sued for libel, so I was sacked.'

'Oh were you one of them?' Nina said, 'I had a very clever lawyer who knew to a pound what editors would settle for out of court to avoid the expense of making a defence. And quite obscure papers too. That's where he was so clever. I believe he subscribed to a press-cuttings agency. I think he paid me more than the publishers did.'

I quite liked Nina but she was an acquired taste and she did not appeal to Eliot. When I organised an informal party of *Purpose* contributors to meet for a lunchtime drink occasionally his response to my invitation made one thing quite clear: he had an allergy.

> I shall drop you another line in a week or two to suggest lunch. I know the Marquis of Granby and its indifferent sherry quite well, and should be glad to drop in on your group there when it can be found, but not, if I may, when Nina Hamnett is to be there.

Just why he singled her out in that way is something of a puzzle. I doubt if I had mentioned her as there was little likelihood of her being there. The Marquis at lunchtime was not her scene and she was not a contributor to *Purpose*.

By this time, September 1935, I had established a good working relationship with the editor of *Purpose*, W.T. Symons, and its publisher, C.W. Daniel. They were men who belonged to an earlier generation of radical thought, taking their inspiration from Tolstoy. Daniel had originally started a publishing business to propagate Tolstoy's ideas and in 1909 he visited Tolstoy and stayed as a guest at Yasnaya Polyana. Subsequently Daniel launched a magazine called the *Crank* and cultivated his reputation as a crank who championed way-out opinions and minority causes. His militant pacifism landed him in gaol in 1916 and he was saved from a second imprisonment only when his friends subscribed to pay the fine imposed on him in 1918 for publishing a novel by a young unnamed woman dealing with homosexuality and conscientious objection to war: a publisher of courage whose list included D.H. Lawrence's play *Touch and Go* and the first translations into English of Ortega y Gasset and Kierkegaard.

Symons had first met Daniel in the days of the *Crank* and was similarly influenced by Tolstoyan ideals. The son of a marine insurance broker, Travers Symons had a conventional and reasonably affluent career as his natural inheritance, but he was unconventional in his sympathies and used his financial strength as a discerning patron of the reformist causes with which he identified himself. The Tolstoyan colony at Whiteways in Gloucestershire attracted him in 1905 and he spent five years there. He told me the colonists were so opposed to private property that they were reluctant to give their names to be included in the title-deeds. To celebrate the foundation of the colony they burned the deeds in a great bonfire, without foreseeing the difficulties which arose later when it became necessary to prove ownership of the land.

After a further five years, spent in India, he joined the ILP – the Independent Labour Party – but soon became absorbed in the Social Credit movement and the range of ideas that Orage was presenting in the *New Age*. When we came together in 1935 he was a dapper, sunny-natured man in his mid-fifties whose enthusiastic temperament fed on a store of hope that was by no means depleted by the disappointments accompanying his cherished causes. Though I did not share all his convictions I respected the spirit in which he held them.

The essence of our partnership was that he retained control of politico-economic policy, which meant in practice that he wrote the opening editorial pages from a Social Credit standpoint. The review section was my responsibility. The initiative for the middle articles passed increasingly to me but was always, rightly and properly, subject to his final approval. In that way, for all our difference in age and outlook, we settled down together. I was certainly not confined to literary subjects: one of my first actions was to invite an anthropologist, J.D. Unwin, to write for us.

I had first heard of Unwin when Tony Barlow showed me Unwin's thesis, *Sexual Regulations and Human Behaviour*. I was so impressed by it that I drew it to the attention of Eliot, who invited me to review it in the *Criterion*. In 1935 Unwin published what was destined to be his major work, *Sex and Culture*; in the summer of 1936, at the early age of thirty-nine, he died when a normally simple operation for appendicitis was complicated by his war wounds. It was a tragedy to be robbed of such a man at the height of his intellectual powers. Eliot had been closely following the development of Unwin's work. His interest was reflected in a letter he wrote to me after he had seen the second issue of *Purpose* (autumn 1935) with which I had been involved.

From the context of Eliot's letter it is clear that I was then anxious about the difficulty of earning a living as a writer and sought his advice and help. Proof-reading, which he mentioned, did not materialise but his other proposal had far-reaching consequences. This is what he wrote:

I am rather ashamed to have your second letter before I had answered your first, although it does indeed make the answer to the first considerably easier. I have meanwhile been thinking about it. All that I could do for the moment was to give your name as a possible proof reader to Mr. de la Mare, in whose department here such matters fall. Secondly I have thought of a small suggestion which I hope if you like it will fit in to the other work you will be doing. We used to have a fairly regular fiction chronicle which has fallen into desuetude. Orlo Williams, who used to write it, was at that time reviewing a good many novels elsewhere, and in a position not to miss much of any value. But he has now given up most of his reviewing and has completely lost interest in the criticism of fiction, which is what ought normally to happen to anyone after a few years. Now however little there may be worth recording I still think it would be worth while to have such a chronicle again twice a year. I say twice a year because I doubt whether there is material enough to justify a greater frequency. Would you care to undertake such a chronicle, at any rate for a year or two?

A certain number of novels come in to *The Criterion* as it is, heaven knows why, as almost none of them ever gets mentioned. I dare say you see others in other ways, and probably any novel that we ask for would be sent to us. I really do not want, however, a regular comb-out of the season's fiction, and I had rather risk overlooking something good than trying to cover the whole ground. What would be more suitable to *The Criterion* is occasional reflections on the state of the novel, with mention of any that were worth mentioning. Naturally you would have to guess at what were likely to be the books worth mentioning, or pick up the information by hearsay. It would be quite pointless to devote any specific attention to the great number of highly competent and insignificant novels that are written, so many of them by women. It is rather the exception that is interesting, and the book which would be neglected or condemned elsewhere. I'd like to know what you think about it.

In spite of the more cheerful tone of your second letter I shall continue to keep the problem in mind, and we will talk about it when we next meet.

I thought *Purpose* promising and Unwin good, and look forward to the January number.

Yours ever

T.S. Eliot

Chapter Twelve

By this time, autumn 1935, I had been writing book reviews and critical articles for about four years in an increasing variety of periodicals, with my interest divided more or less equally between poetry and fiction. The invitation to contribute a regular feature to the *Criterion* came as a welcome development for I rated its critical standards as the most rigorous in Britain, thanks largely to Eliot's own editorial influence. Moreover its Chronicles, as distinct from its individual book reviews, were intended to be wide-ranging surveys which gave to the chronicler the liberty and the space to choose a topic and elaborate it in suitable proportions. In the pinched and condensed journalism of today a 'canvas' of four thousand words must seem an epic invitation, but it was the normal scope of a chronicle in the *Criterion*. I was free to discuss fiction generally, or to comment in precise terms on some recent books, or to concentrate on the whole work of a single author – all of which I did at various times.

It was not a particularly strong period among novelists. On the whole it was in the short story that real talent more often appeared. Among those who worked in both media – for instance Elizabeth Bowen and Christopher Isherwood – the short story showed them at their best. The gaps left by the giants of an earlier epoch were not filled comparably. Hardy had died in 1928, Lawrence in 1930 and Joyce was embalming himself in *Finnegans Wake*. What survived, regrettably, was the censorious meddling which had conspired in an attempt to suppress Hardy's last novels, had banned or bowdlerised much of Lawrence and made sure that *Ulysses* shared its author's exile. For obvious reasons it was Paris and not London which now published the English prose works of Henry Miller and Lawrence Durrell; and in the spring of 1935 some prodnoses in Lancashire succeeded in a prosecution of James Hanley's novel *Boy*, which was all the more absurd as the book had been in circulation for several years. The National Council for Civil Liberties protested and I added my voice in the columns of *Time & Tide*:

> One fact that has not been mentioned is that *Boy* was widely attacked – notably by Mr. Hugh Walpole – when it first appeared. The Home Office could not (or most certainly should not) have been ignorant of this controversial debut; and one has always assumed that the book enjoyed therefore a tacit 'official' acceptance.
>
> The fact that certain Lancashire policemen want to protect local morons from learning what might happen to their run-away sons and brothers should not be permitted to end a Home Office toleration, which has lasted for three and a half years. I suggest that, if local censorships are to overthrow the apparent intentions of the national Home Office, they should enjoy only a local authority. As things are at present any one barbarian community in wildest England can silence an author from Land's End, as the saying is, to John o'Groats; regardless of the absence of any disapproval on the part of the Home Office.

Incidents of this kind were not isolated follies but part of the general stuffiness of the Establishment. There was therefore an almost retaliatory note in the enthusiasm which greeted the Group Theatre's season at the Westminster in the autumn. This began on 1 October 1935, with a double bill of Eliot's *Sweeney Agonistes* and Auden's *Dance of Death*, followed in January by *The Dog Beneath the Skin*, Auden's first collaboration with Isherwood. My second experience of the *Dance of Death* raised doubts about the professional standards of the production, but I rejoiced in the increasing momentum of verse-drama.

Towards the end of 1935, with Barbara becoming pregnant, it had to be admitted that our cottage was too small a place in which to rear a family. We therefore prepared to move to Stanford-le-Hope, a more dismal spot than its name suggested. It is part of the London straggle into Essex, a stopping-place on the Southend line. The principal feature of the environment was the huge circular tanks in which the oil companies stored their products. However, there was a house to let, with a proper kitchen and a second bedroom ready to be designated as a nursery, so we relinquished the pleasures that Brendon Cottage had given us and were more than compensated later by the birth of our first child, Mary Jane.

In November 1935 Dylan Thomas surfaced again, with a letter from his Swansea home announcing his imminent descent on London:

Can you come and have a drink next week? A morning drink if possible – say 12 o'clock in the Marquis on Tuesday or Wednesday morning? I'm up for about four days. We can discuss much belated Canary then. I've done a first bit but it's lousy, and I'm rewriting it. May have it ready. Hope so.

Now as to the poem for Purpose. Do for sweet Christ's sake use the one beginning Foster the Light, nor veil the cunt-shaped moon. The fact is: I was having a poem done in the coming Life & Letters, & had a letter from R. Herring today saying the poem had just been printed, owing to my abominable carelessness, in the Oxford Programme. As Life & Letters is just going to press, he wants another poem pronto. All I have are passages of that long thing I gave you beginning, Altarwise by owl light in the bleeding house. So do, do, Desmond, use the Foster rather than the Altar. (That is, of course, if you'd intended to use either.) After all, you see, L & L have paid me a fiver already for the poem they now can't print. What an existence. Excuse haste & violence.

Drop me a card, if you can, by Monday first post saying whether you're going to meet & – & when.

Yrs Dylan

Nice poem in S. Bookman. What shall we call him: Writhing Codd, Ruthven God?

The confusion over his poems was typical of the difficulties that sprang from his need to find an instant market for any of his work that was saleable. I had persuaded Symons that Purpose, unlike New English Weekly and most of the specialist journals, should pay its contributors. The scale was modest – half a guinea for a poem, if I remember rightly, increased later to a guinea – but at least it meant that I had something to offer.

The variations on the name of Ruthven Todd were part of the game we were playing with the ever-growing cast of our contemporaries to be included in the *Murder of the King's Canary*. The prospect of this remarkable collaboration continued to enliven our conversation but the narrative obstinately refused to start being written. In embryo it survived into the next year, on the evidence of a letter which Dylan dated 18 February 1936, though February must be a slip of the pen and should be January:

Dear Desmond,

I should have answered you such a long, long time ago that, in spite of my natural good manners, it's hardly worth apologising, is it? I am sorry, anyway, and I'm not dead – (I had my suspicions yesterday morning, though).

Thanks for Purpose; I liked the reviews and I'm so glad you said a few words about Cameron's poems – his book's been horribly neglected from what I can see from the periodicals that come into my Swansea retreat, ('retreat' it is, from the onslaught of my London enemies, from that ghoul of a Marquis – though here, admittedly, there's the very devil of a Mermaid). And I always like Porteous, don't you? (Though G.E.G. isn't all that good.)

Going to soak the Bookman for a guinea? I don't know if it'll like advanced young men now that Ruthven Todd's been given the push. He (Todd) is probably nice and is coming to London some time this month. I'm nice, too, but I won't be back until the middle of February – for a couple of weeks or more then, so let's meet. Let's meet in a pub like the Plough, or even somewhere in the East, but not in that bunch of Charlotte-street baNinas.

You did tell me – I mean, I didn't dream it, though thank God my dreams of that Papal paper are very rare – that you were going to do a fiction review for the Criterion, didn't you? That's fine. I must write a novel quickly for you to review it. (And the King's Canary shall *not* die. We'll have a shot at it, blast us we will.)

About poems: I don't know that I've got anything much good at the moment, but I probably will have by the time I see you. I'm working hard enough but so slowly, & a lot of my time for the last week or two has been spent in preparing a smug paper for the L.C.C. Institute of Education. You're not in a vast hurry for poems are you? I'll be in town not later than

February 17, and will send you a postcard, with dates for you
to pick from – as many as you like – a week before that.
                    Best wishes
                        Dylan
Remember me to Porteous if you see him. I'd like to meet him
again very much. Couldn't we arrange a mild, or a bitter, night
out all together?

The January issue of *Purpose* was the first to appear in the new style
that I had been discussing with Symons. The old-fashioned cover
was replaced with a new design by Hugh Gordon Porteus and there
were sixteen additional pages 'largely devoted to alert criticism of
current books and movements', to quote Symons's editorial comment, which added, 'We seek to overthrow idols only to build on the
places they cumber. It is our desire not merely to destroy what is
obsolete but to perceive and encourage what is timely.' In the four
issues during 1936 the contributors included George Barker, 'Tony'
Barlow, Porteus, Pudney, Swingler, Michael Roberts, J.D. Unwin,
James Hanley, Rayner Heppenstall and Dylan (with three of his
poems). For a first year it was a reasonably representative selection.
A further brief note from Dylan settled the date of his visit to
London as 10 February and he suggested meeting at the Plough on
any of the three following days. I have no detailed recollection of
meetings with him at this time, though it's a fair assumption that he
handed me the poem 'Find meat on bones that soon have none',
which appeared in the April issue of *Purpose*. It would probably have
been during this visit, or his next one in March, that he was having a
more than casual affair with a shop-assistant from one of the big
Oxford Street stores: her name was Betty and there was some talk of
the possibility that they might look for a cottage in the country,
perhaps in Essex near me, to set up house together. For Dylan it may
never have been more than a momentary fantasy but he might
already have begun to contemplate the idea of a relatively stable
relationship of the sort that he formed shortly afterwards with his
future wife, Caitlin. Regrettably it was taken all too seriously by
Betty. Mine became the avuncular shoulder on which she shed her
tears when Dylan dropped her.
The advice I gave her was inevitably disastrous. To rest any hope
on Dylan's pity was to admit defeat, I thought, but she might be able
to excite his jealousy: I urged her to make sure she had a boyfriend
with her when she next frequented the places where Dylan might see
her. As she told me afterwards, this strategy worked – up to a point.

Dylan joined her and her boyfriend over a drink but quickly became interested in her companion, to the exclusion of Betty. The young man was evidently fascinated by Dylan and the two men went off together leaving Betty alone. Worse was to follow. Before the night ended Dylan was feeling chilly so the young man gallantly took off his overcoat and lent it to Dylan. When Dylan caught the train back to Swansea he was still wearing the borrowed overcoat.

In April my first Fiction Chronicle appeared in the *Criterion* and Faber's offices on the corner of Russell Square became for me increasingly familiar. During the winter I had been subediting the memoirs of a London magistrate, Sir Chartres Biron, which Faber's wished to publish. They were an ill-written jumble of recollections, however, and needed a substantial revision: this was a straight-forward task which Eliot had arranged for me to do, a welcome supplement to my literary income. From time to time I called in to collect review copies, occasionally going up to see Eliot about some immediate matter before we went out to lunch. By degrees my original feeling of awe mellowed into an easier and more relaxed mood of friendship but there was always a measure of constraint proceeding from his reserved nature. I soon realised that he was a man whose relationships were secured in separate compartments, with the communicating doors between them normally locked and only opened after careful consideration. My place was in the *Criterion* part of his life. I had no idea where he lived or what friends he might have who were not authors of one sort or another. I once looked him up in the telephone directory when I had some urgent reason to speak to him out of his office hours, and I then found that he was not listed but that 'Mrs T.S. Eliot' was. This came as a surprise, though it was of course socially correct at that time for a wife to use her husband's initials and not her own. Little was known publicly of the circumstances of their separation. The day of the gossip-writer had scarcely dawned.

Thinking of Eliot's physical presence I recall the highly distinctive timbre of his voice, at once sonorous and dry. It had depth and roundness and volume, but also there was a crackling edge to it like the burning of dry twigs. His diction was crystal clear and faultless. The formality of his dress, the totally well-groomed appearance, seemed to reflect something more than a studied conventionality – it restrained the impulses of a dandy. There was always the danger that in a carefree moment he might be just that little bit too well dressed, too eager to blossom sartorially. The much cherished and tightly furled umbrella retained an aura of earlier days in a City bank.

In his features there was a tightening at the corners of the mouth which seemed to me to indicate the watchfulness and restraint of unusual self-discipline – a sort of clenching of the spirit. The measured tempo of his speech again suggested this strong element of self-control. Words were carefully weighed before utterance, with no sudden involuntary impromptus. Though his prevailing mood was undeniably serious, there was, however, a readiness to be amused and to laugh. I recall one episode in particular which, in its absurdity, caused us both a good deal of merriment.

It was an occasion when I had arrived early at Faber's to keep an appointment and I was chatting with the receptionist. I mentioned the piles of copies of the *Criterion* stacked up against a wall.

'Back numbers,' she said, 'they're going for salvage.'

'Really?' I said. 'You mean they're being destroyed?'

'Yes, the salvage men ought to be here by now to take them away.'

'Will anyone mind if I take one or two?' I asked.

'Bless you, no. They're waste paper. Help yourself.'

I began to look at the copies on top of the piles. Here was Volume Three, Number Nine, dated October 1924. I noted a short story by D.H. Lawrence – 'Jimmy and the Desperate Woman', in its first printed form presumably. I took it. Next, in October 1923, Eliot's essay 'The Function of Criticism'. That too I took. Finally, and most sensationally, I pulled out a copy of Volume One, Number One – the veritable first-born; and in it a long poem by Eliot. Yes, it was 'The Waste Land' making its first appearance. I gathered it with the other two volumes as the receptionist called to me 'Mr Eliot is ready now to see you. Please go up.'

After the usual preliminaries I showed Eliot the title page of 'The Waste Land' in its original form and asked him to sign it. He looked at it in some astonishment. How, he asked, had I managed to get hold of such a rarity? He himself had been trying to find one for a friend who was constantly badgering him to do so.

'You may be too late,' I said, 'but if we hurry down to the hall you might beat the salvage man to it.'

A search was made but there were few copies of the earliest dates and no more of the first one. The sense of pure farce was not to be denied and we went off laughing to walk through to Antoine's in Charlotte Street. At table Eliot's particular connoisseurship was in cheese. He liked to talk about cheese. Probably his only appearance in the correspondence columns of the *New Statesman* was in the form of a learned note on an American cheese. My much less sophisticated

*Inscribed for
Desmond Hawkins
by his friend T. S. Eliot*

THE WASTE LAND

By T. S. ELIOT

I. THE BURIAL OF THE DEAD

APRIL is the cruellest month, breeding
Lilacs out of the dead land, mixing
Memory and desire, stirring
Dull roots with spring rain.
Winter kept us warm, covering
Earth in forgetful snow, feeding
A little life with dried tubers.
Summer surprised us, coming over the Starnbergersee
With a shower of rain ; we stopped in the colonnade,
And went on in the sunlight, into the Hofgarten,
And drank coffee, and talked for an hour.
Bin gar keine Russin, stamm' aus Litauen, echt deutsch.
And when we were children, staying at the archduke's,
My cousin's, he took me out on a sled,
And I was frightened. He said, " Marie,
Marie, hold on tight." And down we went.
In the mountains, there you feel free.
I read, much of the night, and go south in the winter.

What are the roots that clutch, what branches grow
Out of this stony rubbish ? Son of man,
You cannot say, or guess, for you know only
A heap of broken images, where the sun beats,
And the dead tree gives no shelter, the cricket no relief,
And the dry stone no sound of water. Only

50

palate had just discovered Camembert and I ventured to praise it. 'Yes,' he said, 'at the right moment it is excellent, but it is impossible to have it at the right moment. Always it is too soon or too late.' He had a particular liking for Double Gloucester. Once he asked me to meet him for lunch at a club in St James's where the one outstanding merit of the place, in his view, was its Double Gloucester.

The tone of our lunchtime conversations remained essentially one of pupil and master. The difference in age was decisive; the man I saw was buttressed by success, almost omnipotent in his prestige, impregnably secure in my eyes. I failed to discern any of the deep stresses of his early married life, the anxious disappointments of his first attempts to earn a living – as I was trying to do – by book-reviewing and literary journalism. Perhaps it was those hidden qualities which prompted him to give me so much support and encouragement.

What I took to be a New England inheritance was a narrowly hierarchical sense of 'lesser breeds without the law'. To associate Eliot with any Nazi nonsense of racial purity would be preposterous but he gave some respect to the notion of cultural purity. I remember discussing William Saroyan with him at a time when I had just read Saroyan's first collection of short stories. I was impressed by them but Eliot dismissed Saroyan abruptly, with the comment, 'The only thing he ever says is "Please don't kick me, I'm only an Armenian." '

Occasions when I met Eliot in other contexts were few – the most notable being on Thursday afternoons at Gower Street in the salon of Lady Ottoline Morrell. How I first came to her attention escapes me. It may have been due to Frieda Lawrence or to John Pudney; or perhaps I had just appeared above the horizon when she was recruiting a new generation of authors. I recall an invitation to lunch – or more properly to luncheon – in the garden at Gower Street on a pleasant summer's day in the green shade of the plane trees. I felt I already knew her, from Lawrence's letters to her and his portrayal of Hermione in *Women in Love*. To describe her as a distinguished figure is perhaps to say no more than that I had already made up my mind that that is how I would see her. If so, she at least did not disappoint me. She was, as she once described herself, *ancien régime*. I retain an impression of colourful filmy muslins, a distinctive hair-style, a mesmeric tone of voice. Her face was as Lawrence described it, long and narrow. Her whole presence was so far from the commonplace that it touched the edges of eccentricity, which is perhaps what one looks for in an aristocrat. She had the ingrained assurance, the command of social initiatives, which gave flavour to her personality and made her easy to caricature or lampoon.

The great days of Garsington and the Bloomsbury set were past but 'the Ott' kept alive the tradition at her Thursday tea-parties. Hers was still a literary salon in the classic style, the twin magnets being the hostess herself and the wealth of talent among her guests. There might be a welcome opportunity to meet some of the Irish contingent – W.B. Yeats, James Stephens, George Russell – or the redoubtable Dame Ethel Smyth. Herbert Read I remember hanging back from conversation to save his voice because he had to give a lecture later. Once I fell in with Sturge Moore, an ancient ghostlike poet with a long white beard and the gentlest of manners: was it Housman who described him as 'a sheep in sheep's clothing'? He took me away with him after tea to pursue a long and inevitably depressing discussion of the 'new' poetry which had superseded all his cherished beliefs and made him obsolete. As I tried to explain to him the nature of my enthusiasm for Eliot and Pound and Auden he became increasingly baffled and mournful.

Most entertaining was a duet by James Stephens and George Russell, or A.E. as he was known. When they were in the mood they could rouse each other to a high pitch of eloquence in the Irish manner. Stephens was a grotesque little monkey-like figure while Russell was contrastingly mountainous. As they stood together in an animated disputation this physical disparity seemed to match their debating styles, Russell being weightily profound and oracular while Stephens was playfully witty.

I once sat beside Stephens at the tea-table when someone raised the question of whether physical beauty might not be a handicap rather than a blessing. Immediately he launched into an account of the tribulations that stemmed from his excessively handsome appearance, with outrageous stories of the Dublin police holding back great crowds of delirious admirers whenever he ventured out of doors. 'But that of course', he concluded, with a nice twist of mischief, 'was when I was young!'

On the same occasion Ethel Smyth was sitting nearly opposite Eliot and had been straining to hear him. She suffered from deafness, which she reckoned to counteract with an ear-trumpet in the form of a vast ram's horn. Even without the horn she was a memorable figure in her mannish shirt, collar and tie, with a trilby hat set rakishly on her head. At the moment when her attention was seized by Eliot he had made one of those undeniably commonplace remarks that even the greatest among us sometimes make, but unfortunately Dame Ethel misjudged it to be an utterance of quintessential wisdom. Lunging across with her ram's horn she asked him to repeat whatever he had said. Against the general hubbub he did so. 'What was that?' she shouted, looking startled. There was a sudden silence as she leaned over the table, projecting the great mouth of the trumpet towards Eliot's face. In firm, resonant but now clearly embarrassed tones, Eliot again repeated his words which somehow augmented their banality with each repetition.

'Oh,' she said, adding after a pause, 'really.' Like someone grappling with a mystery she sat back and lapsed into a thoughtful silence.

In this setting Ottoline inevitably overshadowed her husband, Philip, and he made it clear that he would not wish it to be otherwise. It was *her* show. A modest and unselfish man, he chose to keep in the background. Sometimes he stationed himself in an alcove, apart from the main arena, becoming a refuge for the shyer newcomer who found the roaring of the great lions too daunting. I think particularly kindly of his courteous and dignified conversation with Dilys Powell and me in such circumstances, on what was certainly my first visit and probably hers. Dilys had just returned from Greece, a modern incarnation of the Nut Brown Maid, darkly beautiful with her suntanned skin and jet hair.

Philip Morrell was by no means the nonentity that he was sometimes said to be. He had had political experience as a Liberal MP and he was an active student of political history, publishing a selected edition of Greville's diaries. What he lacked in wit and vivacity he made up in solid worth: that at any rate was Ottoline's attitude for she evidently drew strength from him and demanded respect for him. I find a characteristic reference to him in a letter she wrote to me in May 1936 after I had reviewed a biography of George III:

> We both admire so much your Review of George III in this week's 'New Statesman'. My husband seldom admires Reviews but he thinks this one excellent.
> Will you come to tea on Thursday next? It would be very nice to see you again.

A month later she was in Dorset and went to visit George Barker at Piddletrenthide. She told me in a letter that she found him much 'easier' than she expected, and 'obviously *very remarkable*'. Her readiness to cultivate a new generation of writers, to open her house and her heart to them, was endearing and impressive. Sadly, she had only two more years to live.

Admire her or mock her, she had great refinement of taste, a shrewd discernment of talent, and an engaging frankness about herself. Her epitaph could be written in her own words – 'too stupid to be in touch with pure intellectuals and too clearheaded to be in touch with the mediocre'.

Chapter Thirteen

THE spring number of *Purpose* in 1936 included Dylan Thomas's poem 'Find meat on bones that soon have none'. I admired it, then as now, but it contained an image which troubled me. This was 'a ram rose', which occurs twice. At the end of the first verse:

> Disturb no winding-sheets, my son,
> But when the ladies are cold as stone
> Then hang a ram rose over the hags.

And at the end of the third verse:

> A merry girl took me for man,
> I laid her down and told her sin,
> And put beside her a ram rose.

What, I wanted to know, was – among all the varieties of rose – a 'ram' one? It was evidently an important word to the poet, but what could his readers be expected to make of it? That kind of question was a recurring one in our conversations. I liked the dense textures and opacities of his verse but I also thought it was part of my usefulness as a critic to challenge his tendency to drift into privately coded obscurities which could become impenetrable. 'Ram rose' was a case in point and I wrote to him about it before I printed the poem. This was his reply:

It's funny about ram. Once I looked up an old dictionary and found it meant red, but now I can't find it in any dictionary at all. I wanted ram in the poem to mean red *and* male *and* horny *and* driving *and* all its usual meanings. Blast it, why doesn't it mean red? Do look up and see for me.

I'll be in town for about four or five days from the week-end of March 28 on. Monday's the 30th: what about our beer party Monday, Tuesday, or Wednesday? Do you think you could arrange it? I'll be going, on Thursday I believe, to Cornwall for the spring. (We moneyed poets. And do I get half a guinea for my ram-rose?)

I hope the Pope consents: I've never seen him human, only in his office telling me 'And what is more, surrealism is a dead horse.'

In that context 'the Pope' was T.S. Eliot. Whether he consented to join our beer party is beyond my recollection. Anyway, March came and went, and Dylan was soon writing cheerfully from Cornwall. The 'Canary' was still in his mind and my normal signature at that time, A. Desmond Hawkins, had been transformed by him and added to the cast list as 'B. Osmond Corkpins', which is how he now occasionally addressed me.

Sunday 11 April:

Dear Desmond, Address above. It's sunny all day here and rat to your nasty grey London. So sorry you couldn't make it last Monday; we might have got so pleasantly pissed and played darts again. See you when I come back in about seven weeks' time. Do send that ten bob on: I've finally let the M. Post down, and have nothing to live on now. Curse.

     Yours
      Dylan

Address isn't above, it's below: here:
Polgigga, Porthcurno, Penzance, Cornwall. That isn't three places, it really is my address.

25 April:

Dear Corkpins,

Did you get my letter? I've been expecting to hear from you. Don't the firm of Daniel send their contributors copies of their journals? Or do they just send them a bag of healthy nuts and a dirty postcard in Basic English? The Editor knows where to ram my rose. And Purpose owes me twenty pints.

Are there any Purpose books for me to review? My Morning Post is broken; so now I stand naked in Cornwall with no Conservative erection. Have you any books on Music or Magic you'd like to give me? Have you reviewed Harry Price? (He sounds like Purpose's cup of tea.) Would you like some ha ha dirt on Beverley Nichols's Gods and Public Anemones?

And do you remember talking to me about Time & Tide? Would it be wise for me to write to them for reviews, mentioning old Corkpins? Or could you do some back-stairs work? I used to sleep in Lady Rhondda's Valley. Really I do need some review work more than ever before. Has the Literary Review any books for me? And is it to print my story?

Do write and answer soon. I want books, books, books, any sort from anywhere. Books, books. (God, I'll have to learn to read. I wish you could review books by stars alone.)

Seen David Archer? Roger R. tells me that David's mother has sent him a riding-coat to go to Durham in, but that he hasn't arrived there yet; that people are coming quite openly with handcarts to remove all his books; that he says Gladstone used to call at his shop; (but nobody believes that, that's boasting).

If we ever – and we must – write the Canary, I've got some nice true stories for it about Havelick Pelvis. I met a woman down here who used to stay in his house a lot; she says that every morning of the first few weeks of her first visit he came into her bedroom with a cup of tea; when she'd finished it, he gave her another and asked her, 'Now do you want to make water?' Then he'd give her another cup of tea and ask her, 'Surely now you want to make water.' Then he'd give her another cup of tea and hold the chamber pot up invitingly and say, 'Now surely you must make water now.'

Don't forget: do write and tell me about reviews.

      Yours
      Dylan

The firm which published *Purpose* observed the usual practice of sending payments to contributors during the month following publication. With his chronic shortage of cash Dylan wanted a more immediate system. The *Literary Review* was a less stable periodical with which I was briefly associated as literary editor. It paid nobody and I doubt if it ran for more than a few issues. I cannot recall if it printed a story of Dylan's.

The reference to the Canary project is the last in his letters to me. As a topic of conversation we had exhausted its possibilities. To keep it alive we had to give it substance by starting to write it as a story; and this we failed to do. The simple truth is that we each had our own sort of writing to get on with and lacked the aptitude and the appetite for a murder-mystery in collaboration. It was one thing to invent comic names for our marionettes but quite another to elaborate a performance by them. The fun was in the invention, not the execution.

Dylan was more reluctant to let the idea die. He would occasionally return to it and acquire a fresh collaborator. In 1938 he enlisted Charles Fisher to work with him and, according to Constantine Fitzgibbon, an opening chapter was drafted by Fisher. Thereafter the project again languished until 1940 when Dylan was staying with John Davenport. The atmosphere was evidently conducive to a joint effort. Dylan once more conjured up the Canary and this time it took wing and flew. The parodies of individual candidates for the Laureateship – Eliot, Auden, Spender, Blunden, etc. – give the book an amusing start but the ensuing narrative is a heavy plod. The fictitious names were toned down from the original scurrility but, even so, the book was evidently regarded as unpublishable while the main characters were alive. When it was eventually published in 1976 it seemed tame and out of period.

While Dylan was in Cornwall in the early summer of 1936 I lost contact with him and heard no news of him from any mutual friends I was seeing in London. If I wrote to him in Cornwall or Swansea my letters went astray or were unanswered. In August I sent a letter to Swansea telling him the good news that I now had a daughter. I must also have mentioned Betty and her feelings towards him. I was of course unaware, then, of Caitlin's existence. He replied on 21 August:

Dear Desmond, I'm not dead or poxed – much – or paralysed or mute; just depressed as hell by this chronic, hellish lack of money; it's the most nagging depression, and is always with me; night and day in my little room high above the traffic's boom I think of it, of possessing it in great milky wads to spend on flashy clothes and cunt and gramophone records and white wine and doctors and white wine again and a very vague young Irish woman whom I love in a grand, real way but will have to lose because of money money money money.

I was in London three weeks' [*sic*] ago over the bankholiday,
behaving so normally that I'm still recovering; I knew it was
useless trying to get hold of you in holiday time; I stayed out of
the silly neighbourhood, in Chelsea with my Ireland. I may be
coming back in September.

No, no titles, (though I like Sunset over Nigeria, and you
can use that if you like, or Necrophilia in Mumbles).

Betty? Pff. She gives *me* a pain in the appendix. (And is it
only appendix?)

Remember me to your baby, I'll write it a dirty poem when
it's older.

Love, Dylan

This was my first intimation that Dylan was in love with anybody
'in a grand, real way', and he still did not reveal her name: simply she
was Irish. To my regret I never met Caitlin. After her marriage to
Dylan we made plans for them to come on a weekend visit to us in
Essex, but the plan fell apart as plans sometimes did.

The question of titles relates to two of his poems that I had
arranged to print in the forthcoming autumn issue of *Purpose*. I had
an editor's liking for a title, if only as a simpler way of identifying a
poem than by spelling out its first line. Dylan was opposed to titles,
however – not only for single poems but for books as well. His first
collection of poems had been entitled *Eighteen Poems* and now he was
insisting that his publishers, Dent's, should accept *Twenty-five Poems*
as the title for his new collection. He changed his attitude later but
was immovable in 1936. What might have been 'Sunset over
Nigeria' appeared in *Purpose* as 'Then was my neophyte'; and
'Necrophilia in Mumbles' was rejected as a title for 'Today, this
insect, and the world I breathe'.

Within a week a further letter urged me to arrange – somehow –
for immediate payment for these poems. He needed the fare to
London 'mainly to sit for a drawing for a frontispiece for a book'.
This book was to be a Welsh Journey or 'Celtic Totter' and a
publisher was on the point of commissioning it. Everything hung on
his ability to get to London without delay and he was therefore
writing what he called 'little belly-whine notes to all the few editors
(including Corkpins himself) who owe me pennies for stuff of mine
they've accepted but not yet printed'. Understandably this was an
appealing solution for any writer who lived from hand to mouth.
'Soon', he wrote, 'I'll really have to make a horrid little law of my

own that all poems by me, Rat Thomas, have to be paid for on acceptance, not on publication.'

That letter had a surprising sequel. A fortnight later, on 10 September, Dent's published *Twenty-five Poems*, containing both 'Sunset over Nigeria' and 'Necrophilia in Mumbles' – or their equivalent. Dylan acted promptly, to the extent of sending me a brief and hurried message:

> Dear D, Look: Dent has just brought out my book – unexpectedly. I didn't think it was coming out for weeks. It contains the two poems you've got to print in Purpose, I mean that you're going to print in Purpose. What does careful editor do about things like that, do you know?
>
> Love, Dylan

There wasn't much that 'careful editor' could do. *Purpose* was already printed. Its publication date was nominally 1 October but like all quarterlies it would be available earlier in the bookshops, probably by mid-September: so that, as near as made no difference, we had a dead-heat. It was not very satisfactory to either party but not very damaging either. What troubled me more was the evident confusion in Dylan's practice of double-selling his work, as in the earlier muddle with *Life and Letters*. I think I urged him now to go and see David Higham, whom I referred to rather grandly as 'my' literary agent although I had not yet published a book. I tended to give this advice to my friends at this time, as I certainly did to George Barker a few months later.

I must have met Higham with his partner, Laurence Pollinger, who handled the D.H. Lawrence estate: Frieda Lawrence introduced me to 'Polly' but it was Higham who was primarily concerned with discovering and encouraging new writers. As I was developing editorial contacts among my contemporaries Higham wished me to put him in touch with those I thought he could usefully represent. Dylan was an obvious case; I don't suppose I was the only one of his friends who urged him to let an agent sort out his publishing affairs.

His relations with his publishers, bedevilled inevitably by Dylan's wild behaviour, were further complicated by an almost farcical incompatibility of temperaments. The presiding mandarin in charge of Dent's New Poetry series was Richard Church, a timid, decent, worthy man who inspired in everyone a muted affection and a simultaneous desire to kick him. 'Mandarin' is hardly the right word, though, for one more like the virtuous apprentice whose little talents, by conscientious application, brought him at last to ride in the Lord Mayor's Coach.

For a time I lived near Richard Church in Essex and visited him occasionally. He was by then quite a successful novelist and quite a successful poet. The strain of it all seemed to weigh him down. Even his smile was a sad smile. We talked about gardening and he confessed to a great love of gardening. Nothing could give him greater pleasure than an hour or two in his lovely garden, just digging perhaps or pottering about. Alas it was never possible. He could hire a gardener for an hour for so much less than he could earn if he stayed indoors at his desk for an hour. So he stayed indoors. As he spoke he waved a gesture in the direction of a desk littered with papers and books. 'All this, you see,' he murmured, 'it has to be done.'

He was aware that he had at Dent's the only list of living poets that could compare, in numbers at any rate, with Eliot's at Faber's. The difference was one of age. In Church's 'stable' were W.J. Turner, Edwin Muir, Conrad Aiken, Frank Kendon, Gerald Bullett and Church himself – writers who were certainly not without talent but whose loyalties and affiliations seemed to belong mainly to the twenties and the Georgian succession. Norman Cameron and Hugh Sykes Davies added a newer note but the general context was one in which Dylan Thomas looked like the proverbial ugly duckling. His inclusion seems to have been a somewhat desperate and distasteful gamble by Church to offset the fact that Auden, Spender, MacNeice and Barker were comfortably settled under the Faber wing.

I am sure Church would have enjoyed and championed an historical 'roaring boy' in Elizabethan or Restoration terms but a real live one, who revelled in obscenities that he wanted Dent's to publish, was a different matter. In their professional relationship there could be no fruitful meeting of minds. Certainly Dylan's comments on Church were seldom infused with either respect or charity. When my copy of *Twenty-five Poems* reached me I asked Dylan to write something in it. He began to read aloud the blurb on the book-jacket in a parody of Church's manner:

This young Welsh poet has, during the last two years, attracted an unusual amount of attention with his Dionysiac verse. His name has appeared in several journals which take poetry seriously, and a small volume of his pieces issued by a bookseller immediately ran into two editions.

On the flyleaf opposite Dylan started to write what he described in a heading as a 'Proper blurb':

This young Welsh sod has, during the last two years, attracted no attention with his aphrodisiac verse. His name has appeared on the waiting-list of several lock hospitals, and a small volume of his pieces issued by a bookthief immediately ran into debt.

The printed blurb continued, with Dylan delightedly mocking its solemn tones:

It is obvious, therefore, that his work merits serious consideration, and should be offered to a wider public. He now appears in this series with a collection of poems carefully chosen to represent his distinctive personal voice. How that voice will develop remains to be seen, but meanwhile here is poetry that merits attention.

Dylan continued to write, following the pattern but hardly the mood of the original:

It is obvious, therefore, that his work merits no consideration, and should be offered to a smaller public. He now appears in this series with a collection of poems carefully chosen to represent his distinctive personal cock. How that cock will develop remains to be seen, but meanwhile here is poetry that merits the attention of snurges and clap-doctors.
                    Dylan September 1936

I reviewed *Twenty-five Poems* in the *Spectator*, conscious that Dylan was no longer a novelty waiting to be discovered – except by Edith Sitwell; and even the dear old parrot herself now brought up the rearguard so that we had to have a mournful celebration of the fact that there was no one left to discover him. The point I tried to make in my review was that it was no longer necessary – as it had been two years earlier – to mount a crusade to win a hearing for Dylan. It was more important to give the new collection the critical attention that brings a writer and his readers into tune with each other. I concentrated therefore on the nature of his poetry and the technical problems he was tackling. With that 'ram rose' in mind I commented incidentally that 'on the whole he has been less successful than before in subduing his material to a communicable form'. As this was construed by Fitzgibbon in his biography as my 'sitting on the fence' I add the conclusion of the paragraph:

> What is immediately memorable is the energetic, copious, vehement talent at work throughout. Of this there is no doubt. When in due course Mr. Thomas completes his excited discovery of new material and sets to work to refine and clarify it, he is likely to establish himself as a considerable figure outside the close atmosphere of fashion.

That still seems to me as unequivocal as any considered critical judgment should be. Dylan himself made a shrewd comment, quoted by his later biographer Paul Ferris, on his inability at this stage to get 'any real liberation, any diffusion or dilution or anything, into the churning bulk of the words'.

Later in the autumn of 1936 I made a move in a new direction which was to have greater consequences for me than I could have foreseen. It sprang from my continuing and deepening interest in radio. By now the days of cat's whiskers and crystals were long past and the BBC was the new powerful factor in mass communication. To its National Programme it had added, in 1927, the world's first alternative service – the Regional Programme, so named rather misleadingly since the London Region was its main contributor, together with the other regions. In modern parlance a Channel Two had been added to Channel One.

During the spring and summer I had been in desultory correspondence with the Talks Department about a programme that I wished to present on post-Georgian verse. No friend or acquaintance of mine had ever broadcast, so far as I knew, and the literary policy of the Talks Department was so unenlightened that I felt like a missionary volunteering to convert some remote heathen tribe. I was asked to submit my credentials to G.R. Barnes, whom I was to know later as television's first post-war Director, Sir George Barnes. The correspondence meandered on until November when Barnes told me that the BBC's current series of poetry readings, which would continue for some months, did not include 'modern poetry'. He raised a glimmer of hope, however: 'some time next year' perhaps.

It is a trivial incident in itself but worth mentioning in contrast with the BBC's challenging attitude musically. I first heard Bartok and Hindemith broadcast in the late twenties. In literature there was nothing comparable. As late as 1938 Herbert Read addressed an impassioned open letter to the newly appointed Director-General, appealing for a new initiative. My own opportunity came in 1940 when the Talks Department invited me to present its main winter series *The Writer in the Witness-box.*

Seen from without the BBC had an undeniably monolithic appearance in 1936. When a front door is closed, however, it is sometimes worth going round to the tradesmen's entrance. In addition to its two services for the Home audience the BBC had a fledgling third service, broadcast to the Empire. This was the embryo of today's World Service – programmes intended for English-speaking listeners overseas. By a happy chance John Pudney had recently been appointed as a producer in the Empire Service. Even happier was the fact that the Regional Programme had set aside a space on Friday afternoons when it gave listeners in Britain the opportunity to hear one of the Empire broadcasts, transmitted simultaneously. It was by this devious route that my family, friends and neighbours were able to read in *Radio Times* the following billing, on a Friday the 13th, which for me was not ill-omened:

A Nest of Singing Birds.
English Poets on English birds.

An anthology compiled by A. DESMOND HAWKINS
Reproductions of the songs of well-known English birds by
IMITO
The speakers include
LESLIE FRENCH
and
MARY O'FARRELL
Produced by JOHN PUDNEY
A programme broadcast each Friday to
listeners at home and in the Empire.

In retrospect it has a prophetic look about it. It brought together my two purest passions, for poetry and for birds, and it introduced me to what was to become eventually my professional career, broadcasting. Imito was a music-hall artiste whose presence emphasises the fact that recordings of bird-song, as we know them, were non-existent. The great pioneer of wild-life recordings, Ludwig Koch, had only just come to Britain – as an exile from Hitler's Germany. Today the sound library of the BBC's Natural History Unit has recordings available of at least a thousand different species of birds world-wide. Imito's was a dying trade, but in November 1936 I was grateful to him.

As I recall 1936 I find myself jotting down in a random way some of the events of that year which still give it a distinctive character. In January George V died. In May the Left Book Club was founded. In June Haile Selassie, driven from Abyssinia by the Italian army, had a popular welcome in London and went on to Geneva to address the League of Nations. Also in June the International Surrealist Exhibition opened in London. In July the Spanish Civil War began. Edward VIII abdicated in December. Put them together in their disproportion, great and small, and they reflect in a telling way the intellectual confusions and uncertainties that were transforming my post-war generation into one that might anticipate a second war.

When George V came to the throne I was two years old. When he died he was therefore the only King of England I had known, had heard and seen. He was simply 'the King' and in dying he somehow closed all my infant years, my schoolboy years, my adolescence. The old imperial England of Kipling and Elgar began to fade in the radio silence as the King's life ebbed away. The Great War was a sick memory which had achieved nothing and lingered now as a bitter legacy when German troops reoccupied the Rhineland in March. The high imperial destiny of European nations had become the merest parody in the posturing of Mussolini: in a striking reversal of roles it was the dignified figure of Haile Selassie, confronting the world assembly at Geneva, which embodied whatever we still meant by 'civilisation'. And in the background, as yet shadowy but sufficiently recognisable, were Gandhi and Nehru.

I see it now as a time of frustrated or misdirected idealism. I was one of the ten and a half million signatories in Britain of the Peace Ballot promoted by the League of Nations Union, and I joined the Peace Pledge Union. There was a widespread if ingenuous hope that war could be 'outlawed' and political justice achieved internationally by negotiation and consent: wildly utopian, no doubt, but these were to have been the fruits of the 1914–18 war.

The new King seemed to be in tune with this mood. My one clear recollection of him, years earlier as Prince of Wales, was as a pale young man, barely out of his teens, marching in a drab khaki uniform in Richmond Park in the early days of the war. It was his contemporaries who were decimated in those impressionable years. During the Depression his concern for the unemployed had seemed sincere and forceful. His general demeanour suggested new and less conventional attitudes. In the crisis that led to his abdication he became for many of us a rallying-point against the old reactionary Establishment. To dismiss the controversy as historically a storm in a teacup is to fail to comprehend the deeper inarticulate motions of social realignment. There was no legal impediment to the proposed marriage. It was a question of convention and ecclesiastical dogma. If no divorced person could enter the Royal Enclosure at Ascot – as was the rule then – could such a one be blessed by the Archbishop of Canterbury and ascend the throne? We were obliged to examine a whole range of social taboos – those unspoken and sometimes unadmitted rules that can be more potent and tenacious than codified ones. It is one of the functions of the monarchy in Britain to focus and give direction to forces aroused in this way. It moves when the majority is ready to move. In 1936 the majority was not ready.

Were we ready for surrealism? It is a strange question to ask in relation to 1936. A dozen years had passed since the publication of the *Manifesto of Surrealism*; the work of the surrealists was a normal part of the furniture in the world I entered as a literary beginner. The first copy of *transition* I bought was the issue of June 1930. I preserve and cherish it as a period exhibit, with its plates by Picasso, Klee and Miro and its contributions by Kay Boyle, Samuel Beckett, Harry Crosby and Tristan Tzara. *transition* may not have been exclusively surrealist in a purist sense but it justly made the editorial claim that it 'introduced into english [*sic*] the more valuable elements of *surréalisme*'.

The point of the 1936 exhibition in London, in retrospect, is that it was the last expression here of Parisian literary dominance. Surrealism was not peculiarly French but its international elements had accepted Paris as the headquarters of the movement, acknowledging the established European convention that, in matters of the arts, Paris was the final arbiter. This was patently so in respect of the graphic arts, but in literature too one had an uneasy sense that to be out of touch with Paris was to be provincial. The American view of Europe emphasised the city's already recognised status as the artistic capital and natural home of all that was truly avant-garde.

The spell was broken by the German occupation of the city four years later. Nowadays I don't detect much sign of British or American writers looking over their shoulders to Paris for inspiration or critical recognition. That part of the European tradition is atrophied. Its last full-scale display was in the Surrealist Exhibition in 1936 when already the English Channel seemed to be widening. What was happening on the European mainland was increasingly out of key with our daily life as we lived it. The polarisation of fascism and communism in an ultimate physical combat had no significant counterpart in Britain: the committed supporters of Oswald Mosley and Harry Pollitt had to be counted in hundreds, not millions.

The civil war in Spain, therefore, could arouse a disinterested idealism which had something in common with the cause-embracing volunteer spirit of Byron or Rupert Brooke. Those of my friends and acquaintances who went to fight in Spain did so in a comparable mood, seeing themselves as crusaders for liberty and peace. Paradoxically, for those with pacifist convictions, the preservation of peace had come to require a battlefield defeat of fascism. Four years later the idealism and the ideological substance had dwindled into a sombre negative struggle for our national survival. To oppose fascism in 1936 one did not have to embrace communism; but to overcome the armed forces of Germany after the blitzkrieg of 1940 one had eventually to make an alliance with the armed forces of Russia – and that was a different proposition. The initiative held by Europe since the Renaissance was doomed ultimately to pass to two vast military powers on its eastern and western flanks: and on these newly emerging superpowers the nations of Europe would in varying degrees become colonially dependent.

Later generations like to simplify the past, and it has seemed convenient to assume that the literary intelligentsia of the thirties was drawn into the Spanish Civil War by its unanimous hatred of fascism and its ingrained left-wing sympathies. There is the further suggestion that the aggressive nature of fascism confronted us with the stark choice of a small war immediately or a big war later. As a generalisation I suppose it does well enough, but it was hardly as simple as that. For what my testimony is worth I prefer to recall some of the men I knew, whose beliefs and actions sometimes reinforced and sometimes opposed my own. There was no harmonious concert of opinion. We were often confused, trying to reconcile irreconcilables and taking different paths from the same motives.

With very few exceptions the left-wing bias was undeniable. The success of the Left Book Club made that plain enough but it was certainly not the same as continental Marxism. It drew largely from a disoriented Liberalism which could find no viable 'left' in British politics: if John Simon was a Liberal and Ramsay MacDonald a socialist, then I was Father Christmas. Whatever ingredients were put into our radical concept we looked towards a revolution of some kind, even if we balked at the thought of violence. It is supremely the theme, for instance, of Auden's *The Orators*: and it was not simply to be a revolution in politics but in the broader moral organisation of society as well as, not least, in literature. The impetus which formed the Promethean Society in 1930 had been revolutionary in that sense. To link it with the actual revolution in Soviet Russia was a largely spontaneous and unconsidered response: there was at least a notional sharing of liberal principles – in sex and marriage and in women's rights, for instance – in the early stages of Soviet policy.

If I now recall the names of Randall Swingler, Stephen Spender, George Barker, John Pudney, George Orwell and Dylan Thomas as I knew them I can confidently attach to them, one and all, a 'left-wing' label. In that direction their sympathies lay undoubtedly. They were unanimous in wishing Franco ill. As friends together we had a great deal in common, or thought we had; yet how differently we responded to events in the last years of the decade.

Randall Swingler leaves a particularly strong impression on my mind. Physically he resembled a quieter, unemphatic Auden. A golden straw-thatch of hair and intensely blue eyes gave him a Scandinavian look. When I first knew him he and his wife Gerry lived at Milton-under-Wychwood. In this Cotswold setting Randall looked every inch a poet in the romantic English tradition. Great things were expected of him and he was soon in the lists of well-established publishers – Methuen issuing his poems, Chatto his first novel.

Gerry was a concert pianist who frequently broadcast duets with her twin sister, Mary Pepin. In the background of the marriage there was a vicarage childhood for one or perhaps both of them. To visit them at Milton was to make a firm connection with a very English cultural continuity. Partly it was the landscape, which I was meeting for the first time – the warm positive affirmation of Cotswold stone, the bright air stirring with the exuberance of downland, the ability to look over and across so much that was quintessentially English. Partly it was the quality of the rural cottage-home, the high endeavour and the gaiety, the dawning parenthood and the exulting ambitions that we shared. Of all my friends they had most conspicuously a steady tranquillity of spirit. I thought of Randall as a man wholly dedicated to the poetic role for which he seemed so well endowed.

By 1937 the Cotswold idyll was over. He and Gerry had moved into London. The change in the tone of his letters was disturbing:

The stride of my correspondence is painfully slow. This particular step has been hanging in the air for some two months now. I don't know what is the matter with me in that respect, but some constitutional weakness seems to prevent me finishing any letter I begin these days. However I am absolutely determined to finish this and to send it off.

Our life up here has been curiously torn and intensive. As you have probably guessed, I have felt the need to plunge back into political activity, with the pressure of war-fatalism and Spain and the general headlong destructivism about one all the time. You may perhaps deprecate this, but it has done me good, hardening and maturing many of my soft spots; and while it has meant that I have written practically nothing except a lot of criticism of one kind and another, it has left me very stripped of the clinging effects of what I have already written and eager to begin again. It has been a strange anxious wrestling winter.

With the welfare of his two infant children to consider Randall did not go to Spain, but his home became a sort of transit camp for members of the International Brigade passing through London. He and Gerry were drawn increasingly into the activities of Unity Theatre, which might perhaps be fairly described as the logical successor to the Group Theatre. The dramatic aims of Unity were explicitly 'proletarian' and propagandist. For Randall it was no great further step to join the editorial board of the *Daily Worker* and lose his identity in the anonymity of the Party – almost as if something monastic in his nature had found its personal solution.

John Pudney was essentially a clubbable man who could accommodate himself to the ways of the world with a humorous detachment. Politically a decent shade of pink he moved from the BBC to Fleet Street journalism, lost the fervency of his early poetry but found a new note in wartime as the poet–chronicler of the Royal Air Force. In the 1945 election he stood unsuccessfully as a Labour candidate.

Spender and Orwell went to Spain, Orwell as a combatant, Spender not. They stand out in retrospect as the two most impressive and ultimately influential of the politically motivated writers known to me. They entered the arena of bitter and vehement argument about the social responsibility of writers in a time of revolution and war, and in their different ways they found their own kind of unorthodox integrity – for which they were much abused by the conforming faithful. Of the two Spender had the subtler and more resourcefully critical intelligence, Orwell the more stubborn grip on principles. I guess Orwell spoke for them both when he finally denounced 'all the smelly little orthodoxies which are now contending for our souls'.

George Barker, in his remote Dorset village and subsequently in rural Sussex, stayed aloof from politics and the controversies of anti-fascist pacifists and pro-communist liberals. When the Spanish war ended in Franco's victory, however, his compassion was stirred by a photo of a slaughtered child and the news of many thousands of Republican refugees flooding into France. He wrote *Elegy on Spain*, a long poem designed for public recital and published anonymously by a Manchester bookshop in aid of the Refugee Rescue Fund. I saw him once more before he sailed to the United States, with Japan as his ultimate destination where he was to take up a lecturing appointment. Exile was his choice, as it was Auden's also.

The least political of poets was Dylan Thomas. He created his own ambience, and the wider atmosphere of the world around him seldom gained his attention. It is possibly significant that Orwell the Etonian and Oxbridge graduates like Spender and Swingler had innate conceptions of themselves as being – for good or ill – members of the ruling class and therefore obliged to formulate a style of leadership: in short, they had public responsibilities to which their private preoccupations had to be adjusted. Dylan and George Barker were exempt from such considerations.

Chapter Fourteen

DECISIONS that seem wise to those who make them must often appear to their friends as improvident or ill judged. Towards the end of 1936, with our baby only four months old, we decided to leave London and stake everything on my ability to survive as an author. It meant the end of my vestigial connection with the family business and a consequently more spartan style of life, but we were more impressed by the advantages. Barbara indeed felt even more emphatically than I did that we should have the courage of our convictions. Over the four previous years I had made a place for myself as a critic and reviewer, published a few poems and essays, and felt ready to embark on a novel. Reading and writing were now my natural activities and demanded all my attention.

There were other considerations, moreover. The tranquil obscurity of the countryside seemed a proper context for the novice founders of a family. The simple life was much in vogue in the thirties, with lingering Tolstoyan overtones. The part of Essex in which an author should find his congenial setting was certainly not on a housing estate in Stanford-le-Hope, but in the outer reaches of rural calm next to the borders of Suffolk and Cambridgeshire. Our hearts were uplifted at the very thought.

With the help of a friend and a mortgage we bought, for £300, a cottage at Radwinter, near Saffron Walden. In my mind it had a kinship with Brendon Cottage, our first real home at Radlett, and with Lawrence's cottage at Zennor. It stood in opposition to the suburban dormitories of Surrey and the cramped apartments of London, which the word 'home' had usually meant for me.

The Radwinter cottage had no name that I can recall. It had originally been a pair of Elizabethan one-up and one-down hovels with a staircase at each end of the building. The thatched roof had its eaves level with the bedroom floor: it was possible to stand erect in the middle but at the sides one had to crawl on hands and knees. The thick centre wall had been pierced downstairs to provide a passage from the living room to the kitchen. Lighting was by oil-lamps – a very pleasant source of light for reading. If we wanted more hot water than would fill a kettle we lit a fire under a copper. For cooking there was a black cast-iron range with a hob.

It all seems primitive by today's standards but it had qualities that I miss. The daily making of fire and making of light added moments of ritual and rhythm to the day's pattern, touching the elemental circumstances of human life. Kindling the first flame in the kitchen range in the cold breaking of morning light was a little occasion of triumph; and when the coals were burning well the opening of the front of the range sent a glow of warmth and colour and shadow-movement into the room. It is particularly the movement of shadows that I miss in modern living. We no longer have any responsive sense of true darkness and half-light and the different intensities of light that accompanied open hearths and hand-carried lamps.

The evening preparation of the oil-lamps was part of the syntax of life – a new paragraph in the day's events, a new chapter even. The immediate pool of light had a great purity of incandescence softening away into the surrounding shadows and the further darkness. Within the compass of the lamp was an island of civilisation, a well-lit table, books, dishes, cutlery: beyond were vague walls, darker corners and the black night pressing against the window. Within these shifting levels of definition the imagination could play freely.

Our next-door neighbour was a farm-worker who earned thirty-two shillings and sixpence a week: he was paid above the average rate because of his extra skills as carter and ploughman. Agriculture was the only employment in the district. The village had formed itself about a crossroads a few miles from its market-town Saffron Walden. The life of the village was closely knit, inbred, almost tribal in some ways. I remember the comment of a girl whose bride-groom-elect had in her eyes the great merit of being a cousin: 'I couldn't bear to marry a stranger,' she said.

Our neighbouring village, Hempstead, had a resident celebrity –

the 'royal' biographer, Hector Bolitho. He was the kind of popular best-seller that I regarded with envious disapproval. Books about the royal family were in great demand, particularly in the period of the Abdication, and Hector's friendship with the Dean of Windsor had given him opportunities that he quickly seized. He rightly took the view that success loses its point if you fail to enjoy it: he did not fail. The drawing up of his Rolls-Royce outside my cottage was the proper opening gambit, from which we made rapid progress.

He needed help with some research. The German authorities had released a substantial body of letters, written by Queen Victoria to the Prussian royal family, and Hector was commissioned to edit them for Yale University Press. To make the letters fully intelligible they needed to be set in the context of an historical narrative which clarified the topical references in the letters. He wanted me to dig out the historical material to match each letter; it was the sort of work that I could enjoy. An easy cycle ride took me each morning to Hector's house where I settled down to a day's work in his library.

The money Hector paid me for my research was certainly welcome as my average weekly earnings were insufficient to win any attention from the Inland Revenue. However, there were better times in prospect. By the end of 1937 I had delivered the text of my first book to the publishers, Nelson, for inclusion in their Nelson Classics. This was a selection of John Donne's verse and prose, with a substantial introduction – a modest enough achievement but one which gave me great satisfaction. 'At least', I wrote to George Barker, 'it means you can get "Death's Duell" intact for one and a tanner.'

During much of 1937 I lost touch with Dylan. His parents moved away from the familiar address in Cwmdonkin Drive, Swansea and Dylan himself went off again to Cornwall with Caitlin.

In the autumn he was back in Wales and wrote to me from the new home of his parents:

Dear Desmond,
I haven't seen you for a year, or perhaps more. Where are you living now and how are you? I'm coming to London at, I think, the beginning of next month. We must meet, there must be such a load of gossip for us both and stories, and intimate literary secrets. I've been in Cornwall all the summer, met Blakeston there who said you were turning up to stay outside Penzance. You didn't though, or did you? I'm beautifully married and how's your daughter? Let me know your town

days, I'm looking forward to a big beery lunch with you. If you want a poem or a dirty crack, you've come to the right shop.

Love,
Dylan

This was the first news I had of his marriage, which had taken place at Penzance in July. I still did not know who the bride was, and I was to remain ignorant of her name when he answered my enquiry. Judging from his reply I had told him that Barbara and I were anticipating the birth of our second child.

Dear Desmond, progenitive man of letters,

My wife is Irish and French, you haven't met her, she is two months younger than I am, has seas of golden hair, two blue eyes, two brown arms, two dancing legs, is untidy and vague and un-reclamatory. I am lost in love and poverty, and my work is shocking. I can let you have one longish and very good poem, unprinted, for an immediate guinea. It is this week's masterpiece, it took two months to write, and I want to drink it.

I'm a bumpkin, too, and my news is stale as New Verse. I haven't been in town since May, but I'm going up next week to try to write some quick advertisements for petrol and make enough money to buy my wife a ping-pong table. We competed, the week before last, in the Swansea Croquet Tournament, and only lost by one hoop.

If you want that poem, it's yours for a pound. I've come down one shilling, and it's forty lines.

Can you be in town Friday, Saturday, Sunday or Monday of next week?

Goodbye & good luck, cradle-filler
Dylan

Communication between us seems to have broken down and there was no meeting in London. When he wrote again, at the end of October, he and Caitlin were staying with her mother at Blashford, a village in the 'Augustus John' neighbourhood between Fordingbridge and Ringwood. I invited them to come on to us at Radwinter for a visit.

Dear Desmond,

No, my goodness, I had no letter from you. No-one can

have forwarded it from Wales. I am staying here near the New Forest, and am too broke to move. By crook I got from Wales, as I told you I would, but not to London. Here I feel planted for ever, or until next week. As soon as we're in London, I'll let you know. Thank you very much for the week-end invitation. I accept with pomp. The poem I have to revise. I thought it was perfectly correct – as to detail – before I read it again early one morning. Then I saw that the third verse, which deals with the faults and mistakes of death, had a brilliant and moving description of a suicide's grave as 'a chamber of errors'. I'm now working hard on the poem, and it should be complete in some days.

Lately, I've been receiving strange requests from magazines: first, for a kind of obituary notice, for New Verse, on Auden, or perhaps a tribute on his seventieth birthday; second, for a valuation (Symons's word) of Wyndham Lewis, for 20th Century Verse; third, for a description of my most recent trauma, with, if possible, ancestral symbols, for 'Transition'; & last for a contribution to a special number of Henry Miller's 'The Booster', completely devoted to 'The Womb'. Do you think this means, at last, that I'm a man of letters? The only contribution to give Mr. Miller, anyway, is a typewritten reply to the effect that I too am, passionately, devoted to the womb. And you, Mrs. Dyer. Looking forward to seeing you. Love, Dylan

Henry Miller was a relatively new figure at this time among writers of prose-fiction: 'novelist' is hardly the word for him. He was post-surrealist Paris, not really in the cosmopolitan style but more a native American writing from a foreign address. He was part of a new generation of American writers whom I was discovering for myself in 1936 and 1937. I had begun corresponding with Allen Tate and through him I had come to know the *Southern Review* and the group of poets and critics associated with it – notably Robert Penn Warren, R.P. Blackmur, John Crowe Ransom and Tate himself. Their critical work seemed to me particularly good and I invited them to form an alliance with *Purpose* by which we could select and reprint from each other. I made a similar alliance with Ransom and the *Kenyon Review* in 1940 but by then it was too late to be effective.

Another American group – of a very different ideological stripe from the southerners – was centred on New York and the *Partisan*

158

Review, to which I contributed a regular 'London Letter' until wartime conditions reduced my essential contacts and I suggested that George Orwell should replace me.

Some of this American interest was reflected in my correspondence with Eliot in 1937. Although Henry Miller's *Black Spring* was not available in Britain I reviewed it in my Fiction Chronicle. This was the third chronicle I had contributed to the *Criterion* and it seemed an occasion to take stock of what I was doing. I must have shown some anxiety: Eliot's reply was reassuring:

> We can talk about the chronicles when we meet, but meanwhile you have no cause to worry about them. I think this chronicle is much better than the first, partly no doubt because you have a more interesting lot of novels. In fact I think it is very good. I thought your comments on Cyril Connolly and Henry Miller extremely well balanced and just. As for who read such contributions besides myself, it is really no use for any contributor to the CRITERION to ask about readers. I don't know any more than you do, but I do think that after a lapse of time such a chronicle as this can show evidence of having made an impression on a surprising number and variety of people.
>
> Next week is getting pretty full, but I think lunch on Thursday would be possible if that day suited you.

Suit it evidently did. I wrote afterwards to George Barker 'I had lunch with Eliot on Thursday and he seemed very gay and much happier. I've never known him laugh so much.'

There was some talk of Eliot's coming down to Radwinter to visit us, and the idea seemed to appeal to him. In a letter at this time he wrote, 'I might be able to come down to you in August, and I should like to do so very much, but it is impossible to tell far ahead, as the summer always brings an incursion of American relatives and friends.'

Meanwhile I was devoting as much time as I could to the writing of a novel, with much encouragement from David Higham after he had read the outline with his professional agent's eye. A full-length book, however, represents a big investment of an author's energies for a return at some future time but with no immediate benefit. I had to earn a living week by week so it was literary journalism that often had priority. The truth is that my survival was in the hands of half a dozen editors. Fortunately for me there were some exceptional personalities among them. I learned a lot from them and I was buoyed up by their interest in my work. I think particularly, not only of T.S. Eliot, but of Joe Ackerley, Philip Mairet and George Stonier.

Ackerley was literary editor of the *Listener* when I knew him. Janet Adam Smith was responsible for the poems it published but the reviewing of books was Joe's province. He was a diffident, casual man to know in that context, saying little and seldom passing his personal opinion. I thought of him as one of those laconic sleuths in American fiction who seem reluctant to disturb the silence until some penetrating intervention demands to be made. There was no doubting the alert mind behind the mask of the relaxed indolent manner. He gave the impression of having exhausted or abandoned any personal ambitions he might once have had. The tonic quality of the man came from a dry realism, which was astringent and bracing in an impersonal way. Over several years we preserved the formal courtesies of editor and contributor: to do otherwise might have seemed to be an act of trespass.

Philip Mairet was quite different, an instinctively sharing spirit. He was of rather frail physique and softly spoken, with a slight impediment that somehow gave an added charm and elegance to his speech. As a young man he had been an actor at the Old Vic, which seemed a strange career for a man with a persistent stammer; but apparently his speech flowed easily and without interruption the moment he stepped on to the stage. He had a bookish manner, an air of lightly worn erudition. Intellectually he seemed to have browsed among the religio-philosophical fringes of the time without losing his balance. How he became associated with Orage I do not know but he was just what Orage needed as a supportive deputy in the running of the *New English Weekly*; and when Orage died it followed automatically that Philip succeeded him as editor.

When I first met him I had published nothing outside the *Twentieth Century*. He was the first full-time professional editor I visited. It was generally known that the *New English Weekly* gave opportunities to new writers, was indeed a kind of nursery slope for novices, so I sought its premises in a side passage off Chancery Lane. There were two permanent residents – Miss White, who ran the steady secretarial and administrative business of the office, and the literary editor, Mr Mairet. Orage came and went, in sudden bursts of excited activity. I seldom saw him.

George Stonier of the *New Statesman* belongs to a later period. Kingsley Martin, the general editor, seemed content to let Stonier run the literary section more or less as he pleased: this he did with the pleasantly wry humour that is enshrined in the title of his book, *Shaving through the Blitz*. It was his idea to organise the reviewing of new fiction on the basis of a troika consisting of Cyril Connolly, George Orwell and myself. Our styles were so different that we certainly made an interesting team.

Connolly's ultimate position was an aesthetic one. He looked for particular blends of taste and craftsmanship, with a sensitivity that savoured the individual brush-stroke. Orwell was quite the opposite, a puritan who saw language as a tool of surgical precision for cutting through conventional hypocrisies and revealing the social forces within personal acts. I stood somewhere between the two of them. I hated the later Wellsian view of the novel as a mere vehicle for an evangelistic 'message'. I believed novelists, like poets, should deepen and intensify our understanding of the human condition rather than expect to change it. Had I carried a banner I would have chosen to inscribe on it Ezra Pound's words – 'Great literature is simply language charged with meaning to the utmost possible degree.'

The indebtedness of my generation to Pound is not easy to calculate. What one breathes in from the atmosphere is usually too nearly anonymous for suitable acknowledgment. In the early thirties there was a fine dust of Pound on the furniture and it had a way of getting into the hair. I must concede that Ezra could also be a quarrelsome, explosive, intransigent bigot when he mounted a hobby-horse, but he happened upon us before our prejudices and personal interests had taken root. We loved his virtues and forgave his sins.

A particular incident in which I was involved with Pound concerns George Stonier. When the latest instalment of Pound's *Cantos* appeared in 1937 I invited Stonier to review the book in *Purpose* and make it the subject of a general reassessment of Pound's poetry. The result was an extensive, closely argued essay which, with a few reservations, was hostile in tone and plainly belittled Pound's work. The response from Eliot, when he read it, was not difficult to predict:

I wrote a letter to Ezra and then scrapped it, because with such a proud and touchy man as he, it is just as likely that a well-meant intervention may only incense him more. I now think it best to wait; and if you do get a roaring letter from him about Stonier, let me know at once, and I will then try to soothe him down. It is obviously much better that you should print a letter from me than one from Ezra – better for Ez I mean.

Discussion of the best way to answer Stonier and placate Pound continued ten days later in a further letter to me from Eliot:

Yes, I got quite to the end of your letter, and in fact I read it twice. I can see your point about a short article (I think it should be very short) instead of a letter to the Editor. It might be effective in making Ezra keep quiet, and if there is no response except a letter he may still think that a letter from himself is called for. I also think that it has additional advantages. I will meditate on that over the weekend, and in any case would be glad to know when you want copy for the next number.

Within a fortnight he had agreed to put his case against Stonier into an article:

I will try to let you have a nice little article about Stonier as soon as possible. I think it ought to be framed in such a way as to be rather a reproof to Stonier than a defence of Pound, because everybody seems to discount now what I say in praise of Pound's poetry.

He was as good as his word. A 'nice little article' entitled 'On a Recent Piece of Criticism' occupied five pages in the spring 1938 issue of *Purpose*. It exemplifies Eliot's concern for Pound's reputation and his personal loyalty to their friendship. As it is not well known I extract the following passages:

To me, it is occasion for distress that a reputable critic should dismiss in six pages of frivolity an author who, at the very least, has given thirty-odd years to the close study of his art, and who, at the very least, occupies a high place in the poetical history of a generation.

My indebtedness to Pound is of two kinds: first, in my literary criticism . . . and second, in his criticism of my poetry in our talk, and his indications of desirable territories to explore. This indebtedness extends from 1915 to 1922, after which period Mr. Pound left England, and our meetings became infrequent. My greatest debt was for his improvement of *The Waste Land*. But as for the poetry of 'the early Pound', there are only three or four original pieces that have made any deep impression upon me; and the Pound whom I find congenial is the author of *Mauberley*, *Propertius*, and the *Cantos*.

That Pound was Poe to my Baudelaire is simply nonsense: and what's more it's not so true of Baudelaire as all that.

The outcome was as peaceful as Eliot and I could wish. Stonier took Eliot's rejoinder in good part and made no further comment. Pound remained silent, although he was taking a general interest in my editorial policy in *Purpose* I had first approached him during the summer of 1937, possibly to contribute to the Symposium series that I was beginning to plan. His reply came from Siena and was handwritten, he explained, because he was 'away from typewriter'. He continued:

> My general state of feeling at moment is that the social credit *milieu* is all wet, a real contempt for literature and/or an utter ignorance of fact that any real writing ever existed, with a 'transcendental' section of s.c. as bad as Bloomsbury or the Times shiterary spoofliment.
>
> *General* abstract discussion is NOT a nice way of wasting time. Can you get an editorial formula which will distinguish between that and the constructive correlation which wd/be a legitimate desire??
>
> Also is yr. policy to *trust* your reader with available information or hide from it in fear it wd. damage his 'orthodoxy'?
>
> What circulation have you?
>
> Mentality of Mairet's public perhaps too soft to retain any nail I cd/ drive into it?
>
> > Yrs. willing to be corrected
> > E. Pound

The reference to 'Mairet's public' suggests that I had told him *Purpose*'s readers probably included a substantial proportion who also read *New English Weekly*, since both were committed to the Social Credit movement. Pound was an occasional contributor to *NEW*, often using the odd pen-name of 'Alf Venison'.

By the autumn he was back at his home in Rapallo and at the end of October he despatched two letters and a postcard to me within three days. The opening signal was benevolent:

> All right, I'll do something or other. Is the enc/ any use for your verse number/ possibly pseudonymous? In fact I think Mr. Venison may have done it. I don't suppose the ballad of Edward VIII can be printed in England YET??

It is probably impossible for me to do anything without trying to do too much/ BUT at this distance it may save time to ask a few questions without writing to find out whether you care to consider them.

Any help I can give in organization of collaborators? I don't mean trying to boss 'em or backseat driving the mag/ that must be done with ref/local conditions.

Lemme know contemplated SIZE of Purpose s:v:p:

This was characteristic of Pound as I came to know him – by turns rough and courteous, eager to bring together ideas and personalities, throwing out suggestions piecemeal – to be picked up or left lying. He was eager to make continental periodicals better known in Britain and to foster exchanges with them. He gave me lists of contributors to be sought out and books to be reviewed. And in forty-eight hours he had drafted the piece I originally invited from him:

I have written down a Consegna. Perhaps we might get off the mark NOW and save three months.

I think this ought to start discussion IF there is any discusser present.

It is also free from more specific personal attacks. I don't always manage that. Very hard if I think of some individual dung heap while composing.

Silence descended on Rapallo through the winter as I was not able to launch the Symposium series – for which Pound's *consegna* was intended – until the following spring, when I published my own preface 'to propose terms of reference and define the aims of the series'. In broad terms the intention was to look for correlations between contemporary literature and the politico-social preoccupation of the time. Pound was to make the opening contribution in the subsequent issue: proofs of his *consegna* therefore reached him in May and generated a weekly letter from him for the rest of the month, starting thus:

Dear Hawkins,

Herewith proofs and an, I think necessary, footnote bringing it up to date.

I am quite ready to go on with 'Purpose' either replying to the other parts of the symposium IF they interest me/or doing a more 'composed' and unified essay or taking up some other field of action.

I think my best collaborations have usually been when I was really cooperating in an editorial design. Yours isn't yet quite clear to me. And it don't exactly emerge from the copy of Purpose that I have here.

If you want to make a few hints, either re/unity of yr/next issue as planned/or of yr/general aim it might ameliorate my next outbreak.

Problem to ME is often WHY dont these highbrows unite/ why don't you amalgamate with X;Y;QZ. etc and concentrate what little intelligence is available so that one writes for at least the public of two unpopular reviews. Usually there ARE reasons for not amalgamating but the contributor is likely to see more clearly what belongs where; when he knows them. For example/what is there in TOWNSMAN that Purpose would not print?? What purpose is served by there being two printer's bills?? This is an INTERROGATIVE.

This was followed a week later by a long, discursive letter in which he sprang nimbly from one of his hobby-horses to another – commending Oswald Mosley's quarterly publication to me, praising Binyon's translation of Dante, reviling his enemies and championing some of the lower ranks in his private regiment, notably Basil Bunting and Louis Zukovsky. Here, with some curtailment, is Pound in characteristic form:

Dear Hawkins,
Taking yr. letter more or less in reverse and pell mell
   1.   I shd/ think I had said one hell of a lot about it/ – it being current verse, not mentioning the particular writers, but in my 'ABC of Reading' which the buggars [sic] dare not face.
   Same old local British fog/amateurishness, defeatism (intellectual defeatism).
   2.   I mentioned *Townsman* precisely because Duncan does NOT seem to have a lot [of] halfs and quarters whom he wants to ram down one's throat/
   and because he is ready to take up what I consider live lines.
   Bill Williams' 'Life on the Passaic River'.
   e:e: cummings 'EIMI' and 'Collected Poems'.
   Chris Hollis/ Claude Bowers/ W.E. Woodward/in history.
   Frobenius//

You might look at the British Union Quarterly/not that
there is any possibility of an amalgamation there/ In fact you
ought to be honourable opponents. NOT refusing to meet.

As to the other magazines you mention I agree. *Fig Tree*
afraid that mention of any heresy whatsoever will cause feeble
adherents to wander into bird life or whatever.

Murry is and always was baby shit.

and as for New and XX cent/verse, I still have to see any
intention on their part to face the KNOWN facts of history.

Do any English EVER read ANY foreign publications or even
learn anything save Berlitz phrase book in foreign tongues?

And of course old Wyndham L/ is still England's chief point of
interest, with Mons Eliot runting and rumbling in his sleep/
and getting off a real crack just when the pooplik thinks its his
final funeral and interment.

Ask Binyon for cantos of his Paradiso as they appear.

he is now naturally dead tired with the finishing of the
Purgatorio/ that will be out before you can use it. But it is our
bloomink DUTY to keep him going till he finishes the
Commedia.

If I have been a corner of yr/'world' you might start the idea
of England's loss/

Decades being 1917/Little Review New York
1927/Exile
1937 (or put it earlier, from 1912/Poetry
          1922/Paris publications
     1932 'Indice' Genova
1937 Broletto/
     the amount of stuff I have done in Italian.

Mistake to suppose the bastards have annihilated me merely
by excluding me from print in England during the reigns of
shit squire, murry etc///

I shd/ be glad to have you read my 'Revolution Betrayed' in
January Brit Union Quarterly of this year/ and let me know
what you make of it/ That would help me to find a focus for
further letters.

Yours etc EP.

A further letter followed a few days later, in the same vein. The
two topics he seemed most eager to pursue were the alleged British
indifference to anything published in a language other than English,
and the intellectual worthiness of fascism. These were not what I

wanted from him, but increasingly he seemed bent on creating for himself a hybrid persona combining equal parts of Nietzsche and Artemus Ward – at times menacingly oracular, at other times playing the hick philosopher from the mid-west in a parody of home-spun utterances by 'ole Ez'.

As is often the case with writers who are violent on paper Pound in person was very different from his epistolary self, as I learned when I spent a day with him in Kensington where he was staying for a brief visit with Ronald Duncan, whom I knew in those days as editor of the *Townsman* and very much a disciple of Pound's. His considerable success as a dramatist came later.

When I arrived at the Kensington flat Pound greeted me with the news that he had asked Oswald Mosley to join us for lunch because, he explained, it would be good for me to discover that the leader of Britain's fascists 'doesn't have horns and a tail'. It was an experience I would not have sought and in the event I was spared it. Ronnie Duncan went off for the day on his own business, Mosley did not appear, there was no provision for lunch in the flat and eventually Pound and I went out together in search of a meal.

Kensington High Street in the thirties catered mainly for middle class ladies on shopping expeditions, and their favoured eating-places were of the refined tea-shop kind. To one of these we went and sat at a table next to two women who were soon glancing with ill-concealed amazement at Pound. Men wearing beards were extremely rare in London and were considered 'bohemian' – an impression reinforced by Ezra's Byronic collar and corduroy jacket. I heard a stage whisper as one woman leaned towards the other and nodded meaningfully, 'You know who it is, Mabel?' Getting no reply she added triumphantly, 'Sir Henry Wood!'

There was a further sensation when he asked the waitress for fried bananas. This, he pointed out reasonably, was a familiar dish in America. In Kensington, however – even though they had bananas and a frying-pan – it was, in every sense of the words, not on.

After lunch we took a stroll in the vicinity, which for Pound was filled with nostalgic memories of a quarter of a century earlier. He spotted a chemist's shop that looked familiar: in we went to enquire if Mr So-and-so was still around. The assistant's expression was blank. The name meant nothing to him. We called at one or two other establishments where some dormant memory might have been rekindled by the mention of a bygone name or the recall of some half-forgotten landmark; but, alas, twenty-five years and the intervention of a war can sweep away many things that might with better luck have survived. Our stroll was a sad little pilgrimage to dismantled shrines and neglected altars. The Kensington of Ezra's salad days was already dim and dusty.

As we walked back to the flat we passed a beggar scraping a tuneless violin. 'Belongs to the same union as us' was Pound's comment as he dropped some coins into the man's cap. The wry modesty was genuine and part of the paradox that such apparent arrogance could accompany it. His brawling denunciations and meanly phrased vendettas were inextricably mingled with impulsive generosities and the decent humility of a scholar.

Back at the flat we spent the rest of the time in conversation about books and writers and the events of the hour. Pound stretched out in a large reclining chair with his feet on a stool, much as he looks in the Wyndham Lewis portrait. He had put on a sort of Edwardian smoking-jacket which gave him a curiously old-fashioned and gentle appearance. The revolutionary image that I had gained from his books and his letters to me was superseded by this new presence of a traditional bookman in the pre-war style, talking to me in an avuncular way about the writers of an earlier generation who had not in his opinion had the recognition they deserved. As a critic it was my duty, he urged, to fight against this neglect, to win a new audience for them. In his missionary enthusiasm I could hear echoes of the young impresario who championed Eliot, Joyce, Gaudier-Brzeska, Wyndham Lewis and their contemporaries in their obscurity twenty-five years earlier. Now he wrote down a list for me of those to whom full justice was yet to be done.

I could have put my shirt on Stephen Crane's name being included: *The Red Badge of Courage* was everyone's example of a neglected masterpiece. Ford Madox Ford and William Carlos Williams were no surprise either, nor was Cummings. G.S. Street was, though; I had not suspected that Pound's range extended so far. And for me the keenest pleasure was the presence of W.H. Hudson, to whose name Pound added the title of *The Purple Land*, with unerring perspicacity. Again I had not thought that his taste would encompass Hudson, forgetting perhaps that Pound's formative years were at the dawning of the present century. He must have known and probably endorsed Conrad's comment on Hudson's prose style – 'the fellow writes as the grass grows.' Anyway, there was Hudson on his list and I gladly accepted that particular charge from him as, in his own words, my 'bloomink DUTY'. When the fiftieth anniversary of Hudson's death passed largely unnoticed in 1972, I was at least able to broadcast a tribute to him in the BBC's Third Programme.

Inevitably I talked to Pound about Eliot. He was interested in my up-to-date account of the *Criterion* and its editor, while I wanted him to talk about their early days together. He made one comment that I believe I recall quite exactly, word for word: 'Had to marry him to a river-girl to keep him in Europe.' It was the phrase 'river-girl' that stuck in my memory. I could picture a débutante reclining on cushions in a punt at Boulter's Lock, but never before or since had I heard the expression 'river-girl' in conversation. I now know that it was fashionable slang of the period. Recently I came across an advertisement in an old periodical for Kate Collins's Sunburn Cream, described as 'indispensable to Golfers, Tennis-players, River Girls and Residents in the Tropics'.

Chapter Fifteen

DURING the winter of 1937/8 I again lost touch with Dylan Thomas. The weekend visit to Radwinter that he had accepted 'with pomp' languished and was postponed – partly, no doubt, because Barbara gave birth to our second child, Christopher, in late November. The poem that I expected from him for the January *Purpose* – a special issue devoted entirely to contemporary verse – did not materialise. In March I wrote to tell him we were about to move to Saffron Walden as the Radwinter cottage would be too small for our growing family. He replied on 16 March from Blashford where he and Caitlin were staying with her mother, as they had been when I last heard from him in October 1937. His letter, ornamented with bizarre drawings, was in a relaxed and happy mood:

> Dear Desmond,
>   It was very, very nice to hear from you, and very wicked of me not to have congratulated you on your safe delivery. I have just been reading a book by Dr. Carlos Wms, D.D., B.O., full of medical details, and I know what you must have suffered. In your sweet mirth, as T.E. Brown says in my favourite poem, God spied occasion for a birth; and who knows what little Hitler rocks dreamily at your feet. . . .
>   The poem that was meant for your stupendous number – there isn't, I suppose, a spare copy? – died, twisted in its mysteries and I am trying now to bury it in another poem which, when completed, I shall send to you along with a

photograph of Caitlin and myself breeding a Welsh Rimbaud on a bed of old purposes and new directions.

Answering your questions:

The Europa press belongs to George Reavey, that sandy, bandy, polite, lockjawed, French-lettered, i-dotted, Russian t'd, non-commital, B.A.'d, V.D.'d, mock-barmy, smarmy, chance-his-army tick of a piddling crook who lives in his own armpit. He diddled and swindled me, the awful man; I will get him to send you a review copy, *and* a photograph of his headquarters if he isn't sitting on them.

I am staying here charitably until next week when we go to London again with a pick and axe for the gold pavements. I am working busily on some new stories; I want to write a whole lot like that one you liked about Grandpa, stories of Swansea and me. I don't, by the way, think that that story is better than the one in the Faber book, or than others in my Europa mistake: these stories are more than 'free fantasy': they do mean a lot and are full of work.

Croquet is over; it's all shovehalfpenny & skittling squirearchy now; we've a rolling road here & an old inn and a wind on the heath. To heel, to hounds, to hell.

Do you ever see the little quarterly, 'Wales'? There's good writing in it. You might drop it a poem, care of me: it prints those English outsiders as well; and it pays nothing, on publication.

Shall we ever see you in London? Perhaps, later, when your moving's over, you'll invite us for a week-end? We are quite good, and hate babies.

Write soon; I'll send you a pretty poem. . . .

    Love,

      Dylan

The decision to leave Radwinter was a sad triumph of realism over the romantic imagination. With two infants to rear, and my bicycle as our only transport, the isolation from every service beyond the limited compass of the village shop was too severe a drawback; and we were soon going to need more house-space for Mary Jane and Christopher. A temporary palliative was to buy a car. For twelve pounds I acquired an open tourer made by Humber in the early twenties. In profile, from front to rear, it rose in tiers like a wedding-cake. Each part had been lovingly hand-made, but the weariness of accumulating years was undeniable. Before I could get it home to

Blashford
Ringwood
Hants.
March 16. 1938

Dear Desmond, It was very very nice to hear from you, and very wicked of me not to have congratulated you on your safe delivery. I have just been reading a book by Dr. Carlos Wms, D.D., B.O., full of medical details, and I know what y. must have suffered. In your sweet month, as T.E. Brown says in my favourite poem, God sped occasion for a birth; and who knows what little Hitler rocks dreamily at your feet as you, at your lettered desk, sit destroying a reputation with one critical hand and tossing all your Grigson-pips with the other.

The poem that was meant for your stupendous number — there isn't, I suppose, a spare copy? — died, twisted in its mysteries, and I am trying now to bury it in another poem which when completed, I shall send to you along with a photograph of Caitlin and myself breeding a Welsh Rimbaud on a bed of old purposes and new directions.

Answering your questions:
The Europa Press belongs to George Reavey, that sandy, bandy, polite lockjawer, French-lettered, i-dotted, Russian t'd, non-commital, B.A.'d, V.D.'d, mock-barmy, smarmy, chance-his-army tick of a

piddling crook who lives in his own armpit. he
diddled and swindled me, the awful man; & will
get him to send you a review copy, and a
photograph of his headquarters if he isn't sitting
on them.
I am staying here charitably until next week when
we go to London again with pick and axe for the
gold pavements. I am working busily on some new
stories. I want to write a whole lot like that one
you liked about Grandpa, stories of Swansea and
me. I don't, by the way, think that that story is
better than the one in the Faber book, or than others
in my Europa mistake: these stories are more than
"free fantasy": they do mean a lot, and are full of work.
    Croquet is over; it's all shovehalfpenny, &
skittling & squireachy now; we've a rolling road here &
an old inn and a wind on the heath. To heel, to
hounds, to hell.
Do you ever see the little quarterly, "Wales"? There's good
writing in it. You might drop it a poem, care of ...;
it prints these english outsiders as well; and it pays
nothing, on publication.
Shall we ever see you in London? Perhaps, later, when
your moving's over, you'll invite us for a week-end? We
are quite good, and hate babies.
Write soon; I'll send you a pretty poem; tell me about
your novel.
The art on these pages are sections of a large, &
utterly filthy, drawing which got a blob of ink in
the middle and is now lost to the peepers of
posterity. But there's plenty more dirt where of these
came from, and I am collecting together a whole album
of studies of
unnatural history.

Love,
Dylan

show to Barbara I had to stop at a garage for petrol and was not prepared for the garage-man's friendly comment: 'Considering making a change, sir, I expect? We've got some good second-hand ones, if you're interested.'

My initial pride in this venerable Humber never quite recovered from such an indignity, and there is no denying its imperfections. It preferred to remain stationary. To overcome its reluctance to move, its radiator had to be emptied and refilled with kettles of boiling water. When this strategy failed, as it frequently did, the last resort was to persuade a posse of neighbours to push it to a launching place over the crest of a hill.

On balance, then, we saw the wisdom of moving our brood to No. 18, West Road, Saffron Walden. This was quite a large Victorian semi-detached house, the owner of which – known as Auntie – lived in the other half. There was plenty of space for the children, a small study for me, and even enough rooms to accommodate two bank clerks as paying guests during the working week. The town was everything a market-town should be – mature architecture, good shops, a park, a cinema and that special feature of the nineteenth century, a Literary and Scientific Institute.

In retrospect the year 1938 seems to pulse with the menacing sound of a single word – Munich. But Neville Chamberlain's visit to Hitler belongs to the autumn of the year; ironically the earlier months were for me a buoyant and hopeful time. I was transformed from a literary critic to a fully fledged author when David Higham persuaded two publishers to commission books from me. In a letter on 4 February Eliot wrote to me, 'I am delighted to hear that you have placed your novel': this was *Hawk among the Sparrows* which Longman's had accepted on the basis of a synopsis and a first chapter. In July I wrote to George Barker, 'my novel came to a halt because I had no money for grocer, candlestick-maker etc. Now I've got a little and I've promised to finish it in a month. It should be out round Christmas.' It was in fact published just after Christmas, in January.

The other book owed something to my earlier friendship with Frieda Lawrence. As an impecunious student myself I knew the need for a single inexpensive volume to provide a first introduction to an author, in a widely representative selection. In the days before cheap paperbacks such series as Oxford's World Classics, Nelson's Classics and particularly Dent's Everyman Library meant a good deal to me as a reader and I had an ambition to contribute to them in terms of my own enthusiasms. Having added Donne to Nelson's Classics I was therefore delighted to have the opportunity to add a D.H. Lawrence selection to Everyman. With such a prolific and versatile writer it was important to display his range of achievement in verse, fiction, essay, travel-sketch and letters. Readers who found what they liked could then go on to Lawrence's individual books.

The general principle became something of a hobby-horse of mine. As a self-educator I felt acutely the need for much easier access to the whole body of our literature, too much of which was either out of print or too expensive. In an article in the *New English Weekly* a year earlier I had argued, against Sean O'Casey, that a National Theatre might be less valuable than a National Publisher, since – as I claimed – 'a book once printed is potentially a non-stop performance on a boundless tour.' Meanwhile I complained that there was no decent edition of John Skelton to be had and we were living on three dozen poets, with three hundred assorted anthology pieces from the rest.

It was a topic to which I returned from time to time among my friends, one of whom – William Johnstone – took a more than cursory interest in it. Johnstone was an artist whose abstract paintings attracted attention in the thirties. He was also a teacher with a particular interest in children's paintings, and his book *Creative Art in England* was an influential work in its time. When he became the Principal of the Camberwell School of Arts and Crafts he had a lively printing section which wanted material for the students to work on. He asked me to put together a collection of my published poems for this purpose and a slim volume entitled *Easter Garden* eventually appeared in a few dozen copies as the product of the printing students' efforts: as a collector's item it is extremely rare and, I regret to say, quite valueless.

It did, however, stimulate the thought that the activities of the students might have a more considered and continuing by-product in the form of reprints of neglected works that no publisher's commercial judgment would entertain. This appealed to me at once.

I turned first to Eliot, inevitably, inviting him to form an editorial committee with Michael Roberts and myself. He replied, 22 August 1938:

> I am quite willing to be a member of a *preliminary* committee in the company of Roberts and yourself, to examine the scheme and decide on the next steps. I don't think I could undertake to be a member of any permanent committee to deal with material and the machinery for printing and circulating it,

because I should not have the time, but I shall be very glad to help as much as I can at the beginning.

I drafted a prospectus of what I called Authors' Guild Editions. The general intention was to produce one book a year, edited by a member of the Guild without payment and produced by the London County Council printing school at Camberwell free of charge, on the understanding that the books were not offered for sale. Some copies would go to the Guild authors who prepared the texts, the rest to university and public libraries.

Eliot's response to my draft was to bring his own experience as a publisher to bear on it, with a battery of practical questions; but he did not dismiss it as unworkable and added a postscript which is worth quoting:

> Before any first list of books is settled upon, there are several people who have curious knowledge and might have useful suggestions: for instance, Ralph Hodgson or John Betjeman.

John Betjeman's curious knowledge reached me in the following January:

> TSE mentioned your scheme. A bloody good one. I should like to come in on it. I should like to see a reprint of Isaac Watt's poems (a complete or selected edition, possibly omitting some of his psalm paraphrases): Sir Samuel Ferguson: Rev. James Hurdis: Captn. William Kennish of the Isle of Man. I would undertake the last if the C'ttee thought him worth reprinting.
>
> I wish I had more free time. I have to write so much tripe for a living that the reviewing of good books is a slow process with me.
>
> Yours sincerely,
> John Betjeman

Our Authors' Guild project would clearly not have suffered from a lack of worthwhile subjects. The greater danger was that I was envisaging something more elaborate than the printing school would be able to sustain. An even greater defect was its timing, for which I could not be accountable. By the time the preliminary moves were completed the blight of impending war was already sapping energies appropriate only to peaceful conditions.

A more practical step in 1938 was to become literary editor of the

New English Weekly. I had always enjoyed the freedom and encouragement it gave me as a critic, and my experience with *Purpose* had given me confidence as an editor. A larger and more immediate outlet was attractive. The rough-and-tumble of weekly journalism adds the topical sharpness of debate that a quarterly must lack. I relished that, as I did the appetite of a weekly for a dependable flow of articles, poems and reviews. An editor must have the character of an impresario, finding a vicarious pleasure in the successes of his authors: I had been building up my own group of contributors to *Purpose* and wanted to publish their work on a more abundant scale. With Philip Mairet as general editor and Eliot on the management committee the *New English Weekly* was a congenial setting to work in.

I aimed to introduce more foreign contributors, particularly the Americans with whom I was already collaborating. I wrote to Allen Tate to enlist the support of himself and the *Southern Review* group, giving them this description:

> The paper was founded by Orage, as a successor to the New Age. It's always been a less professional and 'younger' paper than the other English weeklies, but still it has quite a fair reputation. Eliot, Pound, Dobree, Muir and Read have been occasional contributors, and I have brought in Michael Roberts, James Hanley, Elizabeth Bowen and one or two more – with most of the junior poets, Barker, Dylan Thomas, Julian Symons etc. All in all, I have a fairly strong list of contributors to call upon.

As to the readership, I described this to George Barker as 'quite a good audience, Eliot, Yeats, Duke of Windsor, Dylan, me, Uncle Tom Cobleigh etc'. I could have added that politically it had a commitment, as *Purpose* did also, to the Social Credit movement. It was to that extent on the right of centre, or at any rate not on the left. It is a paradox that the literary heroes of my generation were, in their different ways, on the right; and yet no coherent philosophy of the right emerged to oppose the strongly running tide of Marxist ideas and sympathies. Those I have in mind, in this context, are Lawrence, Yeats, Eliot, Pound, Wyndham Lewis and Joyce – to name the half-dozen writers who, in the late twenties and early thirties, had the strongest influence on the newly emerging generation. As writers they were greatly respected and almost immune to attack. By contrast Wells and Shaw were dismissed intellectually as 'old hat'; so was the whole ethos of the nineteenth-century Romantics. Lawrence was finding new religious values in his dark gods. Eliot proclaimed himself Classicist, Royalist and Anglo-Catholic. Joyce, in his sibylline ambiguities, was at least as likely to be Thomist as Marxist. Wyndham Lewis flirted with fascism, Pound embraced it in Mussolini's black-shirted version and Yeats supported General Eoin O'Duffy's Blueshirts in the Irish Republic. The need to choose a colour of shirt seemed to become paramount. Somewhat tardily the Social Crediters adopted a shirt of green – traditionally the colour of the ingenuous.

The justification of a political shirt is that it endorses and testifies to a heart beating with a positive emotional fervour for political action. In 1938 there was a heartfelt repugnance against the barbarism of totalitarian regimes in Europe, but there was not much positive fervour for any alternative. Communism might have been expected to gain from the loathing that Hitler's actions aroused, but there was a growing disenchantment with the sectarianism and intolerance of the hard left. In my own case the critical moment came in a long night of argument with Bill Warbey, better known in the post-war House of Commons as W.N. Warbey MP, on the extreme left of the Labour Party.

Bill and I had been friends since the earliest days of the Promethean Society. Another friend, Tony Barlow, was deeply engaged in a medical experiment in one of London's poorer suburbs: this was the Peckham Health Centre, a pioneer enterprise in community health-care, which significantly influenced the post-war concept of the welfare state. In any discussion of the radical social reforms we wished to see it was inevitable that the Peckham experiment would be mentioned and probably championed. Indeed Middleton Murry had gone so far as to say that acceptance of the Peckham principles must lead to a much broader social revolution. I assumed that Bill Warbey's support for Tony Barlow and his medical associates would be as enthusiastic as mine.

To my surprise and dismay I was wrong. As we explored the political implications of the Health Centre philosophy Bill's opposition to it stiffened. There was the matter of Communist Party policy to be considered. Like the magazine *Good Housekeeping* the Party had its jealously guarded Seal of Approval, which had not yet been awarded to Peckham. Even worse, the experiment was likely to be condemned as counter-revolutionary.

How could that be? If the general health and well-being of the working classes in Peckham were to take a turn for the better as the result of the doctors' efforts, what could be censured in that? On this question the ultimate position that Bill felt obliged to defend was devastating in its awful simplicity: a less discontented proletariat would be correspondingly less ready to come on to the streets and man the barricades. In short, any amelioration of the human condition would delay the apocalyptic moment of the 'Workers' Rising', which was Bill's equivalent of what the Second Coming is to a Christian.

Here then was the core of my personal dilemma in 1938, and worth citing now because I believe it was shared by many of my friends and was widespread among British intellectuals. If the liberal–humanist dynamic of the later nineteenth century was indeed exhausted where was the new revolutionary force we could adopt? The 'smelly little orthodoxies' that Orwell finally denounced were increasingly seen as variants of a central theme, whatever the colour of their shirt – the theme of a bureaucratic 'socialism', so called, which made the individual man or woman the total captive of the state and the party apparatus. Fascist or Marxist, it was in practice a philosophy of the faceless 'they' dominating the personal 'I'. We were all to become lumpenproletariat or saluting stormtroopers.

Those of us endowed with nonconformist impulses and Gladstonian blood-corpuscles made various minor forays in other directions. There was a new interest in the Church, which hitherto had seemed intellectually irrelevant: 'a lot of dead cod about a dead God' was Ezra Pound's inelegantly dismissive phrase, but there was an undeniable influence emanating from Eliot and Maritain. Moreover it was German churchmen who seemed to offer an effective opposition to Hitler. What was attractive in the Christian doctrine was its defence of individual identity and the right to make one's own moral decisions in those areas that the totalitarian state intended to usurp. Herein lay the prospect of a philosophy of the right that could have separated itself from the fascists and disowned them.

Social Credit also offered itself as an alternative to the totalitarian state but as a political force it must appear simplistic in retrospect. Major Douglas's financial panacea probably included some items of economic wisdom among its errors: the success of Roosevelt's New Deal and the gradual acceptance of welfare-state reflationary policies suggest as much. What the movement lacked was any recognition that the forces at large in Europe were emotional, quasi-religious and – if the word has meaning – *evil*.

In the summer of 1938 the *Spectator* ran a series of articles entitled 'What Should We Fight For?' contributed by writers aged under thirty, of whom I was one. The point I made then was that the personal answer and the national answer might be very different. My own inclinations were towards pacifism and the methods of passive resistance advocated by Gandhi, but the nature and existence of the British Empire made such policies unrealistic. 'We are a large landlord. We live well because the rents come in. We may have administered our property in accordance with the loftiest ideals but our title-deed was, and in the last resort still is, the sword.'

It was easy enough to envisage circumstances in which any British government would feel compelled to go to war; easy also to see that there were substantial alienations from such conventional policies. 'Men who feel a closer kinship with foreign political associates than with native political opponents, and men who have nothing that they value to defend, are unable to associate themselves with any "we" that might fight.'

These, it seems to me, were the elements of turbulent public debate in the weeks preceding Neville Chamberlain's visit to Berchtesgarden and the pathetic dream of 'peace in our time'. We were witnessing a European tragedy in which we had no direct stake and yet could hardly avoid being embroiled.

From Ezra in Rapallo came predictable comments on 'the goddam Czechs'. From Eliot came words of an altogether more ominous character:

> In the present state of public affairs – which has induced in myself a depression of spirits so different from any other experience of fifty years as to be a new emotion – I no longer feel the enthusiasm necessary to make a literary review what it should be.

I quote from his editorial statement announcing the closure of the *Criterion* in January 1939. It was Eliot's immediate reaction to Munich. Pound wrote to me, asking 'Have you any REAL news of reasons leading to Eliot's very SUDDEN chucking of the Criterion/// E showed no such intention when I saw him in London.' To all of us, I imagine, the decision came as a shock. I phoned Eliot immediately to plead with him to reconsider, but he was quite adamant. When I subsequently wrote to him he was evidently overburdened with the general response. His usual meticulous orderliness was awry; after some delay he sent two separate replies. In the first he made his position explicit enough:

I feel alternatively that (a) if the situation is hopeless, then the continuation of anything like the Criterion served no purpose except to disguise the hopelessness
(b) if the situation is not hopeless, then the termination of something that had gone on for 16 years, and survived into quite a different period from that for which it was originally designed, should clear the field for something younger and fresher and designed for the present time.

We must do what we can with what organs exist. I shan't forget my promise to the N.E.W. and to Purpose.

The second reply, written three weeks later, was altogether more relaxed and informal, with a sudden personal warmth breaking through:

I have your kind and gratifying letter in front of me, and it bears no evidence of my having answered it – when I don't keep a carbon, I mark letters with the date of my answer. Did I or didn't I? I have a dim recollection of having said certain things – or did I dream them? Anyway, if I didn't write, thank you now with all my heart; and if I did – well, then come and lunch with me on the first convenient occasion, and we will discuss Purpose and the N.E.W.
                    Yours always
                    T.S.E.

The shock of the Criterion's demise was accompanied by another startling event in the same month – the emigration of W.H. Auden to the United States. According to his companion on the voyage, Christopher Isherwood, the anti-fascist struggle did not mean anything to them any more. In the autobiographical Christopher and his Kind Isherwood presumes to speak for Auden as well as himself when he asserts, 'They had been playing parts, repeating slogans created for them by others.' In such circumstances the public criticism that followed was understandable, but I cannot accept this shallow view of Auden as a political zombie with a showbiz mentality. His earlier works, before the theatrical collaborations with Isherwood, were not a superficial shouting of ready-made slogans but a penetrating and often painfully formulated analysis of our generation's dilemma. His decision to leave a Europe that was bent on self-destruction sprang, I believe, from a disillusion that was in many ways akin to the sense of hopelessness that made Eliot close down the Criterion. Auden had discovered, as had others of his contemporaries, that when the chips were down he was at heart – in his own words – 'a selfish pink old liberal to the last'.

There was a third event in January 1939 which had a particular importance for me. My novel, *Hawk among the Sparrows*, was published. A separate American edition came from Knopf in New York, a Swedish translation appeared in Stockholm, and at a later date Penguin issued it in paperback. The publishers were persuaded by David Higham to scrap the existing contract and give me a fresh one which provided a regular monthly advance so that, without financial distractions, I could write a new novel in a year. This was an unusual arrangement and meant a great deal to a novelist with no assured income – the more so, with a wife and two children to support.

Looking through the faded press clippings and correspondence of that year I take pleasure now in one or two letters from fellow authors. V.S. Pritchett wrote, 'I've just finished reading your book and I'm as jealous as hell. It's first class.' And James Hanley's response was similar: 'When you make another writer jealous you can be sure you've done it.'

After a long silence Dylan Thomas became suddenly active as a correspondent in March. He was back in Blashford and wanting to do some reviewing:

> I'm very rude but please forgive me because I didn't mean to be. I've been away from this address, haven't been doing any work and letters have got muddled. I *did* receive your note about a poem, but I hadn't got one; I'd sent away the only one I had a few days before; I wish you'd been able to give me a little notice. But no blame on you about anything: it's I'm Uncle Dirty. And I tried to do something with that left-over lot of books, but it was so flimsy I couldn't make an entertaining article out of it. I'm wanting very much to review some more & punctually: give me the closing date. Thank you, Desmond, I hope you'll send them along soon. Has the N.E.W. reviewed 'Bitter Victory' by Louis Guilloux – the best modern novel I've read, I think anyway at the moment. No, perhaps not that, but very grand. Has your novel been reviewed in the N.E.W.? Or could I have it? I've seen some very pretty words about it. Best luck with it.
>
> Dent's are bringing out my new poems, plus ½ dozen stories, in the summer, under the name 'The Map of Love'. Do get hold of a review copy.

My son is almost as big as me, but not quite: you'd hardly recognise me, I've put on over 2 stone and am a small square giant now. Let me have the books soon. Apologies again. Give me the news.

Dylan

I must have replied immediately, promising to send a couple of novels for him to review, asking who published the one he admired so much and telling him that *Hawks among the Sparrows* had already been reviewed in the *New English Weekly*. He answered at once, only four days after his previous letter:

Dear Desmond,

Waiting for the two promised novels. 'Bitter Victory' by Louis Guilloux is published by Heinemann. If you can get me a copy – mine's a library one – I can promise you and the publishers to do a full, praising review.

I'm sorry your book's been reviewed already in the N.E.W. If you'll send me it, I can certainly do a notice of it in *Seven*, if nowhere else. But *Seven*, I'm afraid, is a quarterly & the Spring number's just come out.

When you see my new book, 16 poems & 7 stories, you'll be disappointed, perhaps, – or perhaps really my violence wasn't much good either – by the choice of stories. Blame that on dirty Church, not on me. I gave him a heap of stories to select from, & he didn't include one that had 'its moments of sensuality'. A few of the stories were written when I was five or six years younger, & are sure to look tame. That man's a pale beast.

What's your son's name?

Dylan

I had a review copy of my novel sent to him but don't know if he ever reviewed it in *Seven* or anywhere else. However, he read it instantly and wrote to me within a week:

This is only to tell you how much I liked the novel. Will it be too late to say things about it in the next *Seven*? I mean, will it do any good to the sales etc then? Anyway, I want the Opportunity of stating publicly my Appreciation and excitement. There were a few things I disagreed with – towards the middle, when you dealt with Ellen & Milly and their boys, you changed the style of writing too dramatically I thought, even though I liked what was going on very much – but mostly nothing but congratulations on one of the best first novels etc. How good to see & hear and feel, too, the real romance of the out-of-town middleclass; the half-finished buildings, the last bus home. Oh, I thought the vicar was not a success – the only one who wasn't completely useful to the book. But Mrs. S: You know such a lot about women, Mr. Hawkins, you *must* be a pansy.

   Claps & best wishes –
      Dylan

Chapter Sixteen

Dylan left Blashford at the beginning of April 1939, writing a month later from Laugharne. He was in low spirits and complained of asthma. Meanwhile I had been studying an advance copy of his *Map of Love* which I was to review in the *Spectator*. I thought the poems clearly superior to his previous collection. As I hoped, he had refined and clarified his techniques. His whole stance was more open towards the reader. I wrote in August to congratulate him and to comment in detail on what seemed to me the remaining problems. To my delight he wrote a no less detailed exegesis in reply. It is sometimes said that he was regrettably uncommunicative about his craft, but on this occasion he evidently enjoyed thinking aloud:

Dear Desmond,

Nice to hear. I've been back in Wales a good, in many ways, time now, since April. Too long not to know anything about you. Honestly, Tambimuttu had that buttu of a poem at the time I promised you one; and now of course I've nothing. I've got a short story, but it's longish, about the length of the straightforward stories I've been printing recently (if you saw them) in Life & Letters: perhaps 4000, or a bit under. No good? I'm trying to make my living out of straight stories now; I've got a contract too, & must finish a book of stories by Christmas. Auto-biographical stories, Provincial Autobiography, Portrait of the Artist as a Young Dog, or something like that.

Have you, as we boys are always asking each other, got far with your novel?

I'm very glad you're doing my book for the Spectator, and that you like it. There could have been a better selection of stories, I think, but Church was timid. I know that many of the poems are difficult, and will be called, though not by you, surrealist. (Aren't they, by the way, using 'surrealist' a bit more sparingly now?) I am trying hard to make them less Hide-and-Seek-Jekyll: (cf. your notes on mixed personality in the Spectator once). Few are stunt poems (cf. 'Fog has a bone' in my last lot). And the best are deeply emotional. That said, I agree that much of the poetry is impossibly difficult; I've asked, or rather told, words to do too much; it isn't theories that choke some of the wilder and worser lines, but sheer greed. I'll try to answer, in a discursive way, your questions and natural bewilderments. There isn't anyone living I wd rather write a review of me than you. (For that, which is very true, please substitute *magnificent* for every *interesting*.)

I. Or Nuts to You. Poem 13. 'Nut', yes, has many meanings, but here, in the same line as 'woods', I can't really see that it can have any but a woody meaning. The actual line is a very extravagant one, an overgrand declamatory cry after, in my opinion, the reasoned and quite quiet argument of the preceeding [*sic*] lines. The *sense* of the last two lines is: Well, to hell and to death with me, may my old blood go back to the bloody sea it came from if I accept this world only to bugger it up or return it. The oaktree came out of the acorn; the woods of my blood came out of the nut of the seas, the tide-concealing, blood-red kernel. A silly, far-fetched, if not, apparently, far-fetching shout – maybe – but, I think, balanced in the poem.

II. Here I can't get which poem you mean, so I'll take both First of all, the 3rd & 4th line of poem one (January 1939). Perhaps these lines should have been put in a pair of brackets, but I think that brackets often confuse things even more. The poem begins with a queer question about a bird and a horse: because one thing is made sweeter (qualify this word) through suffering what it doesn't understand, does that mean everything is sweeter through incomprehensible, or blind, suffering? (Later, the poem has a figure in it standing suffering on the tip of the new year and refusing, blindly, to look back at, if you like, the *lessons* of the past year to help him; and the case, which is really a case for a prayer, begins to make itself clear.) Then I, the putter of the question, turn momentarily aside from the question and, in a sort of burst of technical confidence, say that the bird and beast are merely convenient symbols that just *have* to suffer what my mood dictates, just *have* to be the objects my mood (wit or temper? but here 'mood' alone) has decided to make a meal upon & also the symbolic implements with which I cut the meal and objects up. Loose and obscure explanation; but writing freely like this is the best way, I believe, to get the stuff across, by writing around the difficulties & making notes on them.

III. The next things you wanted to discuss were stanzas three & four of the poem beginning 'I make this in A W.A.' (Work of Art, Workshop of Agony, Witbite of Agenwar). The stanzas are a catalogue of the contraries, the warring loyalties, the psychological discrepancies, all expressed in physical and/or extra-narrative terms, that go towards making up the 'character' of the woman, or 'beloved' would be wider and better, in whose absence, and in the fear of whose future unfaithful absences, I jealously made the poem. I didn't just say in one line that she was cold as ice and in the next line that she was hot as hell; in each line I made as many contraries as possible fight together, negate each other, if they could; keep their individualities & lose them in each other in an attempt to bring out a *positive* quality; I wanted a peace, admittedly only the armistice of a moment, to come out of the images on *her* warpath. Excuse me, but this note I wrote for a my-eye essay by H. Treece may as well come in now: 'I make one image, though "make" is not the word; I let, perhaps, an image be made emotionally in me & then apply to it what intellectual and critical forces I possess; let it breed another; let that image contradict the first, make, of the third image bred out of the other two together, a fourth contradictory image, and let them all, within my imposed formal limits, conflict.' A bit smug, and old stuff too, but it applies here. And the conflict is, of course, only to make peace. I want the lasting life of the poem to come out of the destroyers in each image. Old stuff again. Here, in this poem, the emotional question is: Can I see clearly, by cataloguing & instancing all I know of her, good and bad, black and white, kind & cruel, (in coloured images condensed to make, not a natural colour, but a militant peace and harmony of all colours), the emotional war caused by her absence, and thus decide for myself whether I fight, lie down and hope, forgive or kill? The question is naturally answered by the questions in the images and the images in the questions – if the vice-versa makes any different sense. Yes, the syntax of stanza 3 is difficult, perhaps 'wrong'. SHE makes for me a nettle's innocence and a soft pigeon's quilt; she makes, in the fucked, hard rocks a frail virgin shell; she makes a frank (i.e. imprisoned, and candid and open) and closed (contradiction again here, meaning virgin-shut to diving man, adding to the image, of course, digging out what is accidentally there on purpose) pearl; she makes shapes of sea-girls glint in the staved (diver-prised) & siren (certainly non-virgin) caverns; SHE IS a maiden in the shameful oak – :(here the shameful oak *is* obscure, a mixture of references, halfknown, halfforgotten, nostalgic romantic undigested and emotionally packed, to a naughty oracle, a serpent's tree, an unconventional maypole for conventional satyrate figures). The syntax *can* be allowed by a stretch or rack-stretches; the difficulty is the word Glint. Cut out 'Glint' and it's obvious; I'm not, as you know too well, afraid of a little startling difficulty. Sorry to be so conflicting and confusing; I hope this is the only method, though: this rambling and snatchy expansion.

IV. Poem 5. This is a very decorative poem, a poem, if you'll pardon me, on stained glass. There are many ornamental designs, but all, I hope utilitarian. And I really can't get down to explaining it; you just have to, or just don't have to, let the poem come to you bit by bit through the rather obvious poetry of it. It's not a really satisfactory poem, but I like it. The blue wall of spirits is the sky full of ghosts: the curving crowded world above a new child. It sounds as though it meant the side of a chemist's bowl of methylated spirits, & I *saw* that too and a child climbing up it. (There's a pretty fancy the stout young gentleman has. I'm 12 and a ½ stone now, by the way, a bull of a boy)

V. Poem 14. *On the angelic etna of the last whirring featherlands.* I wanted to get the look of this stanza right: a saint about to fall, *to be born*, heaven shifting visionarily under him as he stands poised, shifting changingly, the landscape moving to no laws but heaven's, that is: hills moving, streets flowing etc: the stained flats, the lowlying lands, that is, *and* the apartment houses all discoloured by the grief of his going, ruined forever by his departure (for heaven must fall with every falling saint): on the last wave of a flowing street before the cities flow to the edge of heaven where he stands about to fall, praising his making and unmaking & the dissolution of his father's house etc – (this, as the poem goes on to talk about, is his father-on-the-earth's veins, his mother's womb, *and* the peaceful place before birth): standing on an angelic (belonging to heaven's angels & heavenly itself) volcanic hill (everything is in disruption, eruption) on the last feathers of his fatherlands (and whirring is a noise of wings). All the heavenly business I use because it makes a famous & noble landscape from which to plunge this figure on to the bloody, war-barbed etc. earth. It's a poem written on the birth of my son. He was a saint for a poem's sake (hear the beast howl).

All very unsatisfactory. I wrote it down hurriedly for you: not so much as to try to elucidate things but to move them about, turn them different ways, stir them up. The rest is up to you.

Ah yes, *hyleg*. It's a freak word, I suppose, but one or two every now & then don't hurt; I think they help. It was what I wanted & I happened to know the word well. I dessay I could explain this selfishness at intolerable length, but I want you to have this scribble right away.

If you want the story – you *can* pay a bit? – let me know. If you give me a little time, I'll try to do a poem specially.

Dylan

If I can I'm going to be in London at the end of the month.

To such a splendid letter I certainly replied though I have no recollection of what I wrote, beyond a hope to meet him in London during the month. Dylan and I showed a nice appreciation of the probable requirements of posterity, in that he lost my letters to him, while I preserved his to me; but it makes a rather lopsided correspondence now. His next letter, in late August, enclosed a signed copy of Augustus John's highly romantic portrait of him – 'disguised as a contemporary of Shelley', as I wrote to tease him.

Dear Desmond,

A grand long letter, thank you. I'm looking forward to your review; hope my circuitous explanations helped.

Here is the young master's head, suitably signed.

I'm not at all sure that I can get to London this month; but I am due to be there on the 11th of Sept. to read poems in the Mercury Theatre, in connection with the Anglo-Welsh Dramatic Something. I'll be there then for a fortnight. Can I see you? I do want to.

He was not in London for the fortnight after 11 September and I can well believe the Anglo-Welsh Something was cancelled, in view of the declaration of war in the previous week. Our failure to meet then emphasises the growing rarity of meetings between us. Partly this was due to the fact that we lived at a distance from each other and from London, and had the new commitments of family life with infant children. The whole circle of friends who had met easily and casually at the Promethean Society and Archer's Bookshop and Mcg's Café had tended to lose that intimate coherence by 1939. Some still lived in London; some had gone abroad; others, as I myself, made brief visits to London to attend to professional business with editors and publishers and to enjoy such fleeting renewals of friendships as were possible; but there was an undeniable feeling of dispersal, of decline and frustration in our cherished endeavours, of a darkness descending. The closure of the *Criterion* was followed by other closures. A letter in October from Julian Symons, the editor of *Twentieth Century Verse*, catches the mood vividly:

I'm coming down to Finchingfield not this but next weekend, for Saturday and Sunday, and I hope we can meet then.

NEWS for you. *New Verse* and *Twentieth Century Verse*, are both, I think, dead. Grigson and I mourned through two or three lunches together fairly cheerfully, and talked about doing something but I don't see that we can. SEVEN I think intends to carry on, but I do not believe it will do so. The rise in cost of paper, about 15% now, will soon be prohibitive – really I think you may regard all verse magazines as dead if not buried. Ruthven Todd has written a thriller in a week, Roy Fuller is writing a thriller, I am writing a thriller – that is rather significant don't you think? – but of what? I think it means we are the LOST. Keidrych has got married to a fantastic but pleasant girl – Dylan drank 41 pints of beer on the wedding day and didn't get up for two days afterwards: local (Welsh) colour for the *Partisan Review*?

If you were in London you would be astonished by the disintegration of London literary guys, the state of moral disorder in the best of us, the hopeless BLANK that literary activity seems to present just now. Hence, I think, the thrillers

– that blank is the real literary gossip or perhaps something more than gossip.

The mood he described had been gathering and deepening through the spring and summer of 1939 as the prospect of war drew ever closer. The signals of what was to come may have been apparent for some time but my contemporaries had grown up in the belief that war was something that could be left out of account, was one of the human bogeys that would never quite invade real life. With the experience of 1914–18 fully digested what cause could now justify a second war and pardon a failure to negotiate?

The passing of Czecho-Slovakia carried with it the whole ethos of intellectual optimism – the progressive Wellsian conspiracy, the dawning May Day, the revolution painlessly directed from Bloomsbury armchairs. All that experimental theorising presupposed that the British Empire would lie in supine glory on the operating-table while the delectable surgery was performed by Fabian thinkers and planners and Audenesque healers. The possibility that the Empire might arrive by ambulance after a nasty smash-up in Europe had not been considered.

It is symptomatic that *New Verse* appeared in May as usual and *Twentieth Century Verse* brought out a double number for June and July, with neither giving any indication of possible closure. They both invited readers to take out annual subscriptions and *Twentieth Century Verse* announced a further double number for August/September, concentrating on drama. They are straws in the wind that blew them away during the summer months, for neither appeared again.

When it came the outbreak of war was quite unlike what had been expected. The immediate annihilation of entire cities by aerial attack did not happen. There was no great convulsive moment of high drama: instead we slipped unobtrusively into a new way of life that was most surprising in its dulness. In my quarterly letter to *Partisan Review* I described the day-to-day scene in Saffron Walden where I was living, during the first half of September. It was also published at home in the *Fortnightly* and it still evokes for me the distinctive atmosphere of those first days in wartime England:

That Sunday, it was fine and warm; as if defying us to believe the news on the radio. It was the usual Sunday of late summer, and there was no thunder to serve as an 'omen'. We were in the mood for omens, our ears already attuned to loud iron devastations; but there was none. The afternoon lay calm and warm and brilliant about the town and the usual people were walking up and down the High Street as they do on any Sunday when the weather is kind.

There is a turning of heads as military lorries go trundling past. Opposite the Methodist Chapel a party of soldiers is making a little square buttress of sand-bags round a harmless-looking gadget that might have been left there by a couple of absent-minded surveyors. A crowd leans on the railings, neighbour nudges neighbour, a voice every now and then whispers, 'Anti-aircraft gun.' The soldiers proceed with the erection of their little shrine by the wayside. They are young and conscious of the watching crowd. They move import-antly, like footballers.

Up the hill, outside the workmen's cottages, the children are beginning to reassert themselves. An old tennis-ball rolls along the gutter. In one doorway, a woman stands weeping, her mouth ugly with grief. Someone pats her on the shoulder. 'Her man's just now gone. They've called him up, d'you see?'

In the evening people paste brown-paper over the windows they can do without. The more Victorian sort of curtain is exhumed from old trunks in attics. The affluent, the ingenious, the prudent, have already provided blinds, squares of paste-board, wooden contraptions.

The air-raid warning comes like a school-bell at the begin-ning of a new term. New habits, a new discipline. We drink tea and decide to stay in bed next time until the danger is nearer. The children's indifference startles us into recollections of our own indifference, which astonished our parents twenty-odd years ago.

Germany is now knee-deep in pamphlets dropped from the air. Comic songs about Hitler have at last got past the radio censor, after years in the cupboard. People who take three lumps of sugar in their tea find it a little embarrassing to say so. There is no shortage of course, but the hostess thinks jealously of the reserve stock she has stored away.

New habits, a new discipline.

The London immigrants are settling down. The children have discovered the swings on the common, the broad lawns of the public gardens. Their immemorial games are played over again in unfamiliar streets, until the corner wall and the white door-step can be visualized by memory at night in bed. And Mary learns that Peggy is now at number 17 up the hill and not in the old address at Tottenham.

Three evacuated women stand chatting outside the Co-Op. Two of them are cross-eyed which gives their companion an unexpected distinction. They are comparing their own favourite methods of disposing of Hitler. One is prepared to cook him a complicated and reliably lethal dinner. The second votes for lead poisoning. 'That's it,' she says, 'red lead.' And she adds reflectively, 'Painful, that is.'

These ingenious and resourceful ladies would hardly have pleased Mr. Jarvis, whose invention is of a rustic crudity. No cooked dinners, however unwholesome, in Mr. Jarvis's plan; and no red lead either. Mr. Jarvis's mind does not turn aside to contemplate such refinements as that. His plan is simplicity at its simplest.

'The only solution I can see', said Mr. Jarvis, 'is to exterminate them all. Wipe them right out. Divide the country up among the other nations. A bit here, a bit there' – Mr. Jarvis's hands carved the air in liberal slices – 'and wipe Germany off the map.'

'But Mr. Jarvis', I said, 'it is a large nation! You can't massacre people by the million.'

'I know, it's very difficult.' Mr. Jarvis, like the Walrus, can shake his head very sorrowfully and sympathetically. 'Very difficult indeed. But what are you to do? Can you tell me that, Mr. H? This Prussian spirit can't be allowed to go on. We're too soft-hearted, that's our trouble. We should have finished them off last time. That's what a soldier said to me, after the Armistice.'

So far the soldiers have not said much this time. They are most vocal at the local cinema. Our first wartime film is one of Boris Karloff's Frankenstein horrors, and the young soldiers like to shout suitable jokes at the screen. But with all respect to Mr. Karloff, the high spot of the show is the news-reel, which is weeks old and therefore pre-war. It contains one supremely ludicrous line, three words making a grotesque echo from a past epoch.

'IF WAR COMES' says the news-reel, and the audience goes into a pandemonium of laughter and catcalls and cheers.

Outside the cinema it is completely dark. No light shows anywhere. No street-lamp, no lighted windows. The blackout is perfect. We grope our way into the house, decide not to switch on the hall-light.

New habits, a new discipline.

War has come, we say, no doubt about that. One no longer expects the dream to pass, the absurd nightmare to dissolve in laughter; as Karloff might laugh, washing away make-believe horrors. This is reality. Our senses begin to collect the evidence, these momentary scenes and fragments of conversation; and War spreads through the mind like a stain.

Chapter Seventeen

SAFFRON Walden had no equivalent to either Meg's Café or the Café Royal but there were fortunately some of my literary friends within cycling range. John Pudney and Crystal were in the vicinity of Dunmow, Alan Turpin lived at Great Sampford permanently and David Higham had a week-end cottage there; and, over the county border in Suffolk, Stephen Spender had a fine Elizabethan house at Lavenham.

Among those I have been calling the 'university poets' Spender was, in my estimation, second only to Auden. I read and reviewed each of his books as they appeared and I had no doubt they were important indicators of shifts and movements in the intellectual climate. I also enjoyed with him a desultory sort of friendship although our life-styles were very different and we met by chance more often than by design. At Lavenham, where he was very much on his own ground and correspondingly relaxed, he made one particular afternoon memorable for me by his entertaining account of some neighbouring children – teenagers – who had taken him completely into their confidence as an ally against the grown-up world. He had that sort of empathy in a remarkable degree and he exercised with a mischievous glee the finely shaded wit and perceptiveness of a young Fanny Burney or Jane Austen: without being in any way effeminate he had the same intuitive feminine quickness of touch that makes an exhilarating conversation.

With his acknowledged Jewish ancestry he might have sought to separate himself from a possible Nazi invasion by a wider stretch of water than the English Channel, but when he wrote to me a few weeks after the declaration of war it was from Blundell's School in Devon, enclosing a contribution to *Purpose*:

Dear Desmond,

I enclose my Notes, rather late I'm afraid, but I don't really suppose you'll be able ever to publish them. The war is more and more likely to hold everything up now, I'm afraid.

They are very rough, and written straight down, and in some places they should doubtless be more carefully considered; also they are inconclusive, because they are a sketch for the opening of a book which is a sort of parable about life in our time considered in terms of poetry in our times. I think it is a good idea, and I think I am on the right lines in writing it in this informal kind of way. Indeed, I ought to go much further and risk being even fantastic. The theological and academic atmosphere of dullness by which I am now surrounded makes me see how frightfully important it is to be oneself, and how much courage it requires, and how difficult it is within the English and American tradition.

I'm sure that if Eliot had to attend chapel here every morning he would know far more about the real gray workings of the English church than he does in London. The awful atmosphere of the readings from the lessons spreads grayness over everything, which affects the whole school.

   Yours,
      Stephen

His schoolmastering days were brief. By the end of the year he was back in London, having launched the first issue of *Horizon* in December. This monthly review, edited by Stephen jointly with Cyril Connolly, was a welcome innovation against the strongly running tide of closures. The future of *Purpose* was beginning to seem precarious but in the autumn issue Travers Symons gave a pledge to our readers that we would continue through 1940 in one form or another.

There was the more personal problem of individual survival. Dylan Thomas responded at first in an unexpectedly light-hearted way, writing to me on the day war was declared against Germany:

Yes, terrible, terrible. Being my hero, my chief concern, too, is to keep out of death's way. And no, I don't know what to do

Two Quarters   Two Shillings

PURPOSE

Editorial

In the Human Interest

Articles include

The Poetry of W. B. Yeats.
A Lecture
T. S. ELIOT

A Literary Transference
W. H. AUDEN

Some Notes on being a Poet
To-day
STEPHEN SPENDER

Poem
FREDRIC PROKOSCH

Reviews by
ELIZABETH BOWEN
EDWIN MUIR
HERBERT READ
T. S. ELIOT

General Editor:
W.T. SYMONS
Literary Editor:
A. Desmond HAWKINS

July
DECEMBER
1940

VOL. XII.   Nos. 3 & 4

either: declare myself a neutral state, or join as a small tank.

Hope you do my story, I want a pound badly. I liked your review very much, and thank you. I want to see Muir's review, too. Hope he agrees that the poems, as a whole, are better than any I've written. But a filthy time for a book. Only my Aunt Polly's bought one, I think.

And I want a pound quickly, too. No, sorry the short poem isn't finished yet. If it is, you must have it straight away.

My review of *The Map of Love* had appeared a week earlier in the *Spectator*: Edwin Muir's was in the October issue of *Purpose*.

By the middle of the month Dylan's mood had changed completely as he comprehended the crushing effect that the war would have on the pattern of life he had designed for himself at Laugharne. In the meantime I had written to Humbert Wolfe, who was both a poet of the older generation and also a senior official in the Ministry of Labour and National Service. I hoped he would understand the predicament of younger poets – I mentioned Dylan and George Barker by name – who had little to offer as warriors but much as writers if they could continue writing. There was the further problem for some of us who might become total or partial 'objectors' on grounds of conscience. Wolfe's reply was courteous and helpful: the exchange of letters did more credit to him than to me.

Dylan also had written to Wolfe, as he now told me:

So you've been trying to pull strings too, have you, you old racketeer? You should be ashamed: go on and fight for culture like a fool: don't attempt to get anything out of the fucking war. I wrote to Mr. Humbert Wolfe, and what does he do but send me a copy of a letter he wrote to you. So you were there first; alright then, I shan't tell you the famous man *I'm* writing to. (If he sends me a copy of a letter to you, we may as well send out circulars signed with both our names.) But do you think there's any possibility at all of wheedling oneself – whining, under protest – into any governmental job? I wrote to Norman Cameron who told me that every literate or semi-literate party-goer in London is stampeding the Ministry of Labour, willing to do anything from licking stamps & bums to writing recruiting literature or broadcasting appeals for warm bodies to become cold. The question of conscience *can*, apparently, be ignored, even among our honourable intelligentsia. And what work would there be, even if we did manage to fawn in, in the

Government? Principle prevents us, I hope, from propaganding; I personally know nothing of any foreign language except a very little about the sanitary-towel of the gardener's wife & a few Welsh dirty words. I can't decipher anything, not even poems.

What I'm doing is writing urgent & bad-tempered letters to everybody who has ever said publicly that I am a better poet than Alfred Noyes, & telling them that, unless someone does something soon, there'll be one better-than-Alfred-poet less, that the Armed Forces are not conducive to the creation of contemplative verse, and that all my few sources of income are drying up as quickly as blood on the Western Front. Though it will probably leave my correspondents unmoved, there is nothing else that I can think of to do. The Army Medical Corps is presumably admirable, but I don't want to help – even in the most inefficient way – to patch poor buggers up to send them out again into quick insanity and bullets. Have you any suggestions? I know you must be trying, too, all that you can think of. (The literary Left, I suppose, is having a loud whack at the Nazi nightmare; or can it do its work better in safety? Auden is in America, isn't he? And the very best place, too, for a militant communist at this time.) Come & stay here, completely out of harm's way, & help compose letters to the Big Boys. It's speed that counts now; jobs must be obtained, or exemption promised, before conscription & military – 'What would you do if you saw a soldier raping John Lehmann?' – tribunals. And what – as a matter of interest – did you reply to Wolfe?

Love,
Dylan

Speed was not quite so important as Dylan believed. Conscription, in the first instance, applied to men aged twenty to twenty-two. Dylan was within weeks of his twenty-sixth birthday – and I, incidentally, was a further six years his senior. There was time enough to come to a well-considered decision. Despite that, the mood of the moment was undoubtedly precipitate and almost melodramatic as a confusion of motives pulled violently this way and that. Between a selfish cowardice and the normal instinct for self-preservation it is not easy to draw an unwavering line: young men do not seek death without a cause. For the pacifist there was the problem of, in effect, condoning the evils of Nazi Germany. For the writer, for the artist in any medium, there was the classic problem of the Ivory Tower in its most severe form: was it possible to insulate one's self from a great national cataclysm and yet remain in the midst of it? The paradox that every artist must come to grips with is one that Dylan and I knew well in the words of one of our favourite poets, John Donne – 'No man is an Island, entire of itself; every man is a piece of the Continent, a part of the main.' Yet equally there are times when some – in good conscience – must go underground, into hiding or exile, if not into blunt resistance, accepting the personal isolation.

Conscription raised a fresh issue – particularly in Wales, traditionally the strongest centre of resistance to compulsion. Earlier in the year the government had given a pledge against the use of conscription but had swiftly reversed its policy under pressure from the French. It was this virtual enslavement by the state – an innovation of the present century – which strengthened our sense of alienation, and yet at the same time gave an inevitability to the drift into mass-destruction. Perversely the easy way out might be to go with the tide into the old comradeship of our fathers' war, and its futility. When Dylan wrote to me on 24 September it was with considerations of this sort in his mind:

I've filled up that questionnaire from David Higham. A lot of good will come from that. My only special qualification I put as reading poems aloud. Not 'If' to the troops, either. I've no wish to propagandise, nor to do anything but my own work. I'm Mr. Humanity and can't kill or be killed (with my approval). Like you, I shall wait, register as an objector, and see. Chapel Wales is down on conscription alright, but my objection can't be on chapel-religious grounds, and I'd have little support. What have we got to fight for or against? To prevent Fascism coming here? It's come? To stop shit by throwing it? To protect our incomes, bank balances, property, national reputations? I feel sick. All this flogged hate again. We must go on with our out-of-war life. It's a temptation, in the pubs, on Saturday nights, in the billiard saloon, to want to allow myself to get that fuggy, happy, homosexual feeling, and eat, sleep, get drunk, march, suffer, joke, kill & die among men, comrades, brothers, you're my pal, I'm with you son, back to back, only die once, short life, women and children, here's a photograph of my wife, over the bloody, down the bloody, here's to the bloody, shit and blood. But the temptation's not too strong, and the sanity of the imagination is. I'd like you very much to send me your collected advice; there must be lots of tips. Thank you for your letter. Write soon.

As I had been a member of the Peace Pledge Union for some time I assume I advised Dylan to get in touch with the nearest branch of the PPU; and I passed on to him anything I had learned about the pitfalls in registering as a pacifist. He wrote to me again in mid-October:

Thank you for the tribunal talk. I'll be wary.

I wrote to the Welsh secretary of the Peace Pledge Union. He said that membership of the PPU would be an advantage, as tribunals are often impressed by the fact that one is associated with people of similar opinions. But it wouldn't be of much help to say one joined the PPU in October, 1939. Anyway I'd prefer to be alone. You know, don't you, that a written statement will have to be sent in first, & then read aloud by the objector. If I write a statement soon, in preparation, I'll send you a copy for criticism etc. And you do the same. This Welsh secretary man says that he does not think it advisable – unless one is quite inarticulate – to be represented by a lawyer. I'm getting in touch with a barrister I know, just in case, & will tell you if he tells me anything interesting. I'm trying hard to think of respected gentry to get testimonials from. I know one defrocked bard.

This Welshman also says that, in his opinion, a few testimonials as to my literary capabilities, invaluableness and/ or etc would be of great assistance too – as well as testimonials as to my sincerity & hate of killing. Any very respectable literary testimonialist that you can think of? *Do tell me a few people*.

I'm afraid I couldn't with honesty *plead* as a Christian, although I think I am one.

Yes, please, I should like to do some reviews of novels. Any chance of getting some of the novels about Wales that are coming out now – in particular – 'How Green Was My Valley' by Richard Llewelyn (Michael Joseph). I could do a snappy article. But any novels will do.

Wales will do that little story of mine. Sorry about *Purpose*.
Dylan

Oh, I forgot. I'm thinking of compiling for *Life & Letters* a thing called 'Objection to War'. Objections, not generalised but whole-heartedly practical, of various people, mostly writers. *Not* a Pacifist, pro-Russian, Mosleyite or literary peace-front, but the individual non-party non-political objections of people like you & me. I think, at this time, when many people who appeared trustworthy are turning out as penny heroes, guttersnipes, rattlesnakes, mass-minded fools or just lazy buggers, it would be valuable. Will you write your Objections – to war, to this war, to any war – briefly. Will Barker write too? I'm getting in touch with him. *Life & Letters* will give the Objection a few pages. Write soon.

I do not know what response he had from other writers to his anti-war symposium. He made no further reference to it in his subsequent letters to me, which were mainly about the novels I had sent him to review for the *New English Weekly*. On 2 November he wrote:

In your last letter, which I had Friday, you said the novels from New English would probably have reached me by that time. Not a sign of them – though what sign they are supposed to make I don't know. Will you see what's happened? I want a fortnight to do them in – & *from* the date they arrive.

By the way, do you know what periodicals there are nowadays which print longish stories? I've got a good one, & want some crinkly for it.

Dylan

Rayner Heppenstall tells me his novel 'The Blaze of Noon' is due out now. I don't know the publishers. Do you think I could have it for review?

The parcel of novels arrived safely and he sent me his review of them with an undated letter. The pages of the review were not numbered, he explained, in case I wanted to 'chop it about'. He thought it might be too long and perhaps his autobiographical introduction should be cut. 'I'll get better,' he added, 'when I get more into novel-reading – I'm out of practice.' He again asked for Rayner Heppenstall's novel. I had already given a review copy of this to Elizabeth Bowen for her article on recent fiction in the next issue of *Purpose* but I may have got hold of a separate copy for the NEW and sent that to Dylan with other books. I heard no more from him until the end of January, by which time he was not at Laugharne but back at Blashford with Caitlin's mother and apologising for the lateness of the review. This had not materialised; in its stead he sent a short story.

During the autumn of 1939 I had moved with my family from Saffron Walden to one of the neighbouring villages, Great Sampford. Alan Turpin, who lived alone there, invited us to occupy the spare rooms in his house and make a combined household with him. He had the generous idea that the place could be a refuge for Barbara and the children when he or I, or both of us, were called up. It was his intention to join the Friends' Ambulance Unit. Meanwhile during that first winter of the war he and I spent the daytime working on our novels, coming together in the evening to read our latest pieces aloud, with Barbara as instant critic. It could not last. However, I did at least complete my new novel, *Lighter than Day*, and deliver it to Longman's.

Attached to Alan's house was a small orchard, where he kept half-a-dozen geese, and a kitchen-garden which supplied the vegetables for a huge stock-pot that was kept going for a week before it was cleaned out and refilled. We became much taken with the idea of a partial self-sufficiency, to offset a dwindling income. In the spring, with two local friends, we rented a place with enough land to develop as a smallholding, with goats and poultry to supply our needs and earn some extra money. I became fascinated with the breeding of ducks and geese particularly, and I liked the new balanced lifestyle – daytime hours working out-of-doors, and writing in the evenings and at night. Rural life, especially village life, became increasingly attractive as its rather phlegmatic stability offset the nervous, febrile quality of London.

The problem with livestock was to get any kind of adequate feedstuff. Rationing was severe and ingenuity was needed to discover sources of scraps or waste that could be rendered palatable to animals. This was a problem I shared with George Orwell, who also ventured into poultry-farming. When he finally gave up he wrote to me, 'Hope you haven't had to put down too many hens. I got rid of the 20 or so I had left. It's bloody to think they are still feeding race-horses.' It was typical of him to see the survival of race-horses as a sternly moral question rather than an economic one. As the British don't eat horses, and horses don't lay eggs, the beasts could only be symbols of a pleasure-seeking privileged class. The puritan in Orwell would not consider the preservation of a minimal breeding stock as the seed-corn of the bloodstock industry which, once lost, could not be replaced.

My editorial experience with *Purpose* and the *New English Weekly* made me eager to undertake something on a more ambitious scale and free from a mandatory association with a narrowly political doctrine such as Social Credit. The closure of the *Criterion* and my growing involvement in prose rather than poetry stimulated me to produce a twice-yearly volume, equivalent in size to a full-length book and devoted entirely to imaginative fiction, documentary and criticism. The prime intention would be to divert attention from poetry to prose. *Centaur* was my proposed title and I invited Elizabeth Bowen, V.S. Pritchett and James Hanley to form an editorial board with me. In my judgment Elizabeth was the highly fastidious representative of the classic English novel, V.S.P. was the contemporary master of the short story and James Hanley's authentically working-class characters were a necessary antidote to the fashionable cult of a so-called 'proletarian' literature. As a trio they covered the full octave of what I was aiming at. Fred Warburg, a new force in publishing, was keen to undertake the venture and at first seemed able to raise the necessary financial backing. Elizabeth and I sat through hopeful lunchtime discussions, but one obstacle succeeded another and the negotiations dragged on. The hard truth was that wartime uncertainties discouraged the taking of risks. It requires more than ordinary optimism to invest in a future that nobody can predict.

Sadly, therefore, *Centaur* never got off the drawing-board. A less hazardous prospect followed when the literary editor of the *Spectator*, Derek Verschoyle, departed to join his regiment: he was, I believe, a reservist Guards officer. I had been a frequent contributor of his, and he said he wanted me to take over the job until he returned. This seemed to me a useful task to tackle and I discussed its implications with Eliot. On 6 May 1940, he wrote an encouraging letter:

> I think it would probably be a good thing if you would tackle the SPECTATOR for a time. It is not as if you were having to give up another job in order to take it. You are therefore, I assume, perfectly free to chuck it up if you find the environment uncongenial. I don't know Wilson Harris personally, but if the occasion presents itself I should be delighted to write to him in your favour. I should think that the SPECTATOR would be much more to your liking than any other of the prosperous reviews, and you would certainly be several hundred per cent superior to —— as a literary Editor.

Wilson Harris was the managing director of the *Spectator*, with a decisive voice in the matter.

In the same letter Eliot answered my request for his signature on a sort of round-robin that I was preparing to help Dylan Thomas if he came before a tribunal as a conscientious objector. Dylan's age-group must have been called up at this time. Rather surprisingly no letter survives from him to me to throw any light on his circumstances in the spring of 1940 but Eliot's letter makes it clear that I was canvassing support in the form of a collective testimonial:

> As for Dylan Thomas, I should certainly sign a letter testifying to his gifts and accomplishments as a poet and a prose writer, and could also say that I had not the slightest reason to doubt the genuineness of his convictions, but as I have never talked to him on the subject (I think it is really several years since I have seen him), or seen them expressed in print, and indeed had never heard them before you wrote, I don't see how I could say more than that. It all depends on how you word the letter.

I cannot recall if such a letter was ever written, signed and delivered. In any case, it was not needed. Dylan was classified as medically unfit. So, at a much later date, was I – which lends a certain irony to the *Spectator*'s decision not to consider the appointment of any man of military age but to ensure a measure of permanence and stability by selecting a woman. They made a good choice, but she did not stay very long.

This was a disappointment but it was accompanied by a yet more grievous decision. Travers Symons could no longer find the means to sustain the publication of *Purpose*. Eliot's reception of the news was sympathetic as always, and as always practical:

> Dear Desmond,
>
> I am grieved and disappointed over the Spectator. I have not heard who has got it. I am also grieved, though not surprised to learn that Symons must give up Purpose. I wish that I could hold out any hope that we could take it on, but I feel quite sure that Fabers would never consider such a thing at the present time. Have you drawn up any statement of running expenses, as the paper has been run heretofore? That would be useful. I should certainly tackle Tom Burns, if I were you: he's about as enterprising as any publisher. I don't know where one could turn for private support; because the sort of people who would

be most interested are those who will be doing what they can to keep the N.E.W. going. I don't think that one could have any expectation of making it sell like *Horizon*: it is too good. *Horizon* is just good enough and not too good, to attract the people who would previously have supported magazines like the Mercury and Life & Letters; and it does not impose the strain of too hard or too unfamiliar thought. There is of course something anachronistic about it. But I think that if *Purpose could* be kept going it might develop into something much more important, and something much more appropriate to the next decade.

The date on the letter – 28 May 1940 – adds its own comment. The German blitzkrieg was at its height following the invasion of Belgium and Holland, which effectively outflanked the Maginot Line. Within weeks France had capitulated, signing an armistice on 22 June. As the British evacuation from the European mainland proceeded, a dull and ominous haze of smoke clouded and obscured the skies of south-east England. Even in north Essex this daytime gloom persisted for days and brought an unmistakable message. There were rumours of imminent German landings. Our co-tenants departed suddenly to the healthier climate of the Lake District. The nearby RAF base at Debden became a target for German bombing attacks and we found a new use for a grand piano as an air-raid shelter: its stalwart legs seemed best able to support the weight of a collapsing roof, so underneath it we all crawled. On some nights I went out as an unarmed volunteer to share the patrol duties of the village's Home Guard. The only shot fired by our unit was directed at a tempting and finally irresistible rabbit in the moonlight.

There was clearly no hope of finding a new backer for *Purpose*. The *New English Weekly* was also in difficulties and Symons's home became its final headquarters. It was typical of him to want the closure of *Purpose* to be done in good and honourable style. We had taken subscriptions for 1940 and had so far published the winter and spring issues. To meet the outstanding obligation he planned a double-size summer number as our farewell publication; and it was to be more of a bang than a whimper. There were substantial articles by Eliot, Auden and Spender, plus a section of book-reviews by Elizabeth Bowen, Eliot again, Edwin Muir and Herbert Read. For two shillings – or ten of today's pence – it was not a bad buy.

Among the novels reviewed by Elizabeth Bowen was my own, *Lighter than Day*. I took the title from a passage of Emily

Dickinson's. It was appropriate to the final scene in the novel but later events gave it a larger significance, for which I repeat it here:

> I could hear buildings falling, and oil exploding, and people walking and talking gaily, and cannon soft as velvet from parishes that did not know that we were burning up.
> And so much lighter than day was it, that I saw a caterpillar measure a leaf far down in the orchard; and Vinnie kept saying bravely, 'It's only the fourth of July.'

For me, prophetic words. In the great fires that followed the bombing of the area known as St Paul's Churchyard many publishers and booksellers, who concentrated there, were destroyed. Longman's, in Paternoster Row, were among the casualties. The entire stock of my novels, with many others, went up in flames and perished. It was the end of an epoch, so far as I was concerned. I worked fitfully on a fresh novel but the world to which it belonged had ceased to exist and I abandoned it.

What occupied me principally in the autumn of 1940 was something quite new to me – broadcasting. I had written scripts for the BBC, with John Pudney's encouragement, but I had never spoken into a microphone. Now I was invited to present a weekly series of twelve programmes in which writers of different kinds – journalists, poets, short-story writers, critics, novelists, etc. – talked to me about their work. With the producer, Christopher Salmon, I worked out an impressive list of speakers – Tom Driberg (alias 'William Hickey' of the *Daily Express*), Sir Hugh Walpole, Walter de la Mare, Stephen Spender, V.S. Pritchett, T.S. Eliot, Cyril Connolly and George Orwell among them – and each Friday night at 7.40 p.m. we broadcast from an underground studio in Broadcasting House. A signal in the studio of a particularly unwelcome sort meant that the watchers on the roof had blown their whistles to indicate that enemy bombers were uncomfortably close. This was usually accompanied by the closure or power-reduction of various BBC transmitters, to confuse German navigators who used BBC transmissions as aids in direction-finding. Those listening at home came to know that an abrupt drop in volume meant that London was under attack.

When it was not safe or feasible to leave Broadcasting House at night one might sleep on the floor in the big Orchestral Studio. Mattresses stretched from wall to wall and an odd miscellany of people, each carrying a rug, picked their way among those already sleeping and chose a spot to doss down. I spent only a part of each week in London: if I had a phone call at home from the programme secretary advising me to buy a bottle of honey and glycerine on my way to Portland Place I knew that the production-office had been wrecked by a bomb-blast. I liked to sip the honey and glycerine before a broadcast, to soften my throat. The bottle was kept in the office. I think I bought three replacement bottles before the series ended.

The London that had given me so much in the thirties was dying. Nowhere was this more evident than in the Langham Hotel, that epitome of solid upper-class stability. Situated across the street from Broadcasting House and All Souls, Langham Place, the Langham had a long and enviable tradition as the home-from-home for families of gentlemen visiting London. As the bombing intensified the resident guests became fewer and the impeccable service slightly peccable at first, deteriorating gradually as the damage increased and staff were harder to recruit. The hotel's bar – known as the Bolivar and approached by a side entrance – took on an informal role as a BBC Club, an identity made formal and official later. The occasion of the Friday broadcasts usually entailed an hour or two relaxing and chatting in the lounge of the Langham, which had fine large windows and glass lights overhead. More often now the glass was underfoot and there were sudden dramatic interruptions. I remember sitting there with Tom Driberg when a man pushed through the street door shouting 'Aerial torpedoes! Aerial torpedoes! That's what they're using now – aerial torpedoes!' Others crowded in after him. In that ambience it still seemed an uncouth way to behave; but for the poor old Langham Hotel it was the equivalent of *The Last Days of Pompeii*.

The nightly bombing produced new social customs and habits. The warning sirens usually sounded at about the same time each evening, so it was prudent to be in or near one's overnight lodging beforehand. On one occasion the sirens wailed earlier than usual, when I was having a solitary drink in a pub far from my intended bolt-hole. The publican closed his doors and shepherded his few customers down into the cellars. There we stayed through the night, going upstairs during a lull to stand in the street and look up at the sky. We were an oddly assorted group and as the hours passed I began to sketch a poem, describing the scene and the mood we shared. The poem, 'Night Raid', has appeared in several anthologies but I have never put it into a book of my own: I do so now, as a

companion-piece to that other scene on Armistice Day 1918, with
which this book began.

> The sleepers humped down on the benches,
> The daft boy was playing rummy with anyone he could get,
> And the dancing girl said, 'What I say is,
> If there's a bomb made for YOU,
> You're going to get it.'
> Someone muttered, 'The bees are coming again.'
> Someone whispered beside me in the darkness,
> 'They're coming up from the east.'
> Way off the guns muttered distantly.

> This was in the small hours, at the ebb.
> And the dancing girl clicked her teeth like castanets
> And said, 'I don't mind life, believe me.
> I like it. If there's any more to come,
> I can take it and be glad of it.'
> She was shivering and laughing and throwing her head back.
> On the pavement men looked up thoughtfully,
> Making plausible conjectures. The night sky
> Throbbed under the cool bandage of the searchlights.

Postscript

WHEN I began this personal story on Armistice Day 1918 I intended to close it on the bombing of London in 1940 which effectively ended the era of peacetime so far as I was concerned. The years between the wars carried me from the fears and anxieties of early boyhood to that pitch of confidence that a man enjoys when he feels he has found his vocation and set up his own family life. More generally it is the coming-of-age during that period, of the writers of my generation within the literary world of London, that I have sought to describe.

The second war dispersed, transformed and destroyed so much which I had taken for granted that it is the natural place to halt at. But of course life is not lived in neat historical compartments, and the broad tide of life does not halt. At worst there are loose ends to be tidied up. At best there are fresh impulses already taking form.

For the individual a time of war is a lottery too vast for the imagination to span. To some it brings intolerable suffering, to some a simple five-letter word – death – to others a wrenching and dislocation of their deepest aims and purposes: others again find an unforeseen fulfilment in it, a touch of heroism, an unsuspected potential. To weigh up a personal profit and loss in such circumstances would be tasteless and ridiculous. All that requires my comment, from hindsight, is the difference between the pre-war world of literature and its post-war equivalent. What I realise now, though it did not occur to me at the time, is that what my friends and I thought of as *our* revolution was being overtaken by a different sort of revolution that wartime conditions greatly accelerated.

A simple anecdote will illustrate the point. In the summer of 1940 the BBC's Air Correspondent, Charles Gardner, went to Dover to cover the Battle of Britain and recorded what was then known as a 'running commentary' on the dogfights overhead between British and German fighter pilots. That broadcast aroused a considerable outcry of protest against the treatment of an event in which brave men were risking and indeed losing their lives 'as if it were a cricket-match or a horse-race'. Had Gardner's description appeared in print next day in a newspaper there would have been no such protest. It was the immediacy of radio that was unfamiliar and disturbing.

Ten years earlier ambitious young authors would have seen their opportunities in three media – verse, fiction and some form of literary criticism or *belles lettres*. Hard-back volumes of their printed words would be the fruit of their labours. Any other enterprise would be a novelty in the pioneering atmosphere of the mid-thirties. There was the embryonic film-documentary tended by John Grierson. There were the first essays in radio drama by the BBC and a more sustained avant-garde drama in the Group Theatre but these were all marginal digressions from the central preoccupation with words in print, words in books, words in weekly periodicals and monthlies and quarterlies and annuals, words in the traditional forms that we had inherited.

The first effect of the war was to erode those traditional forms, to restrict the supply of paper, to divert the financial resources and to absorb the manpower. At the same time the new media – and particularly radio – began a rapid expansion. In previous wars the conflicting nations had broken off all contact. In 1916 the *Daily Mail* was not read in Munich, nor the *Berliner Tageblatt* in Cheltenham, but in 1940 the voice of 'Lord Haw-Haw' broadcasting from Hamburg was as familiar in Britain as any native comedian's, just as the BBC's broadcasts were widely heard on the European mainland, in Germany itself and in the German-occupied countries also.

Nor was it only in the realm of unabashed propaganda that the new medium of broadcasting had a revolutionary impact. It could do much to surmount the mental and emotional barriers which, in the previous war, had so markedly come between the civilians at home and the armed services overseas. Both groups now took part in, and listened to, the same broadcasts of the day's events. To speak of them as being on the same wavelength was literally and happily true.

I have already described the beginnings of my own love-affair with the 'wireless'. In 1940 the BBC greatly expanded its broadcasts to North America, with the consequence that the head of its documentary or 'Features' department, Laurence Gilliam, invited a number of authors to write scripts for him. I was one of them, along with Louis MacNeice, Stephen Potter, Edward Sackville-West and others. My particular assignment, shared with MacNeice, was a weekly series *The Stones Cry Out* in which we gave a documentary treatment to a famous London landmark destroyed by German bombing.

I also became involved with the BBC's Far Eastern Service, where I found myself working with George Orwell and William Empson. To replace my vanished role as literary editor of *Purpose* and the *New English Weekly* I now invited Eliot and Dylan Thomas to read their poetry into a microphone instead of giving it to me to print. And instead of writing a Fiction Chronicle for the *Criterion* I accepted Empson's invitation to broadcast to China, where there was most improbably alleged to be an audience for my views on the novels of Ivy Compton-Burnett.

What was happing to us all was that we were making the first moves towards the multi-media world that we know today, with its instant coverage, its eyewitness testimony, its documentary verisimilitude. If I set down Then and Now side by side, and examine them, the most striking difference is that today's talents are diffused so much more widely. There are still, thank goodness, poets and novelists among us but we are increasingly a nation of visual rather than verbal appetites. The passing of over sixty years has not diminished the force of what must have seemed a rather bizarre prophecy when Thomas Hardy made it – 'Perhaps the cinematograph will take the place of fiction, and novels will die out, leaving only poetry.' His old-fashioned word 'cinematograph' transposes easily enough into motion-picture, movie, telly, video cassette.

If I fail to see literary giants in the eighties of the same stature as those who impressed me in the thirties the failure may be my misfortune, and no more than that. I suspect, however, that the close and narrow concentration on intensely shared objectives was a vital part of the alchemy that produced *Ulysses*, *The Rainbow*, 'Hugh Selwyn Mauberley' and *The Waste Land*. To reach the full height of achievement great creative talents need a passionate and critically informed commitment in the audience to lift a performance into something memorable.

I look back to that pre-war world with gratitude for its high seriousness and its fun. That it should disintegrate in destructive violence was the special tragedy that I share with my contemporaries, but perhaps I was luckier than I realised. The incendiaries and explosives raining down on London, which destroyed my novels, deflected me into the new medium of radio documentaries – from *Lighter than Day* to *The Stones Cry Out*. The world I had grown up in was lost; but a new world lay ahead.

Index

217

Picture Acknowledgments

Pages 1, 3, 4 below, 5 above and below left, 6 below, 7 and 8 are from the author's and other private collections. Page 2: Central Reference Library and Information Services, Richmond. Pages 2 below left and 4 above: The Raymond Mander and Joe Mitchenson Theatre Collection. Page 2 below right: Popperfoto. Page 5 below right: Humphrey Spender. Page 6 above: Tate Gallery, London.